CONNECTING

Books by Lee Gutkind

*Surviving Crisis: Twenty Prominent Authors Write
About Events That Shaped Their Lives*

An Unspoken Art: Profiles of Veterinary Life

*The Art of Creative Nonfiction:
The Literature of Reality*

Creative Nonfiction: How to Live It and Write It

*Stuck in Time: The Tragedy of
Childhood Mental Illness*

One Children's Place: Inside a Children's Hospital

*Many Sleepless Nights: The World of
Organ Transplantation*

Our Roots Grow Deeper Than We Know

The People of Penn's Woods West

God's Helicopter (a novel)

*Best Seat in Baseball, But You Have to Stand:
The Game as Umpires See It*

*Bike Fever: An Examination of the
Motorcycle Subculture*

CONNECTING

TWENTY PROMINENT AUTHORS WRITE ABOUT RELATIONSHIPS THAT SHAPE OUR LIVES

EDITED BY LEE GUTKIND

Jeremy P. Tarcher/Putnam
a member of Penguin Putnam Inc.
New York

Most Tarcher/Putnam books are available at special quantity discounts for bulk purchases for sales promotions, premiums, fund-raising, and educational needs. Special books or book excerpts also can be created to fit specific needs. For details, write or telephone Putnam Special Markets, 200 Madison Avenue, New York, NY 10016; (212) 951-8891.

Jeremy P. Tarcher/Putnam
a member of
Penguin Putnam Inc.
200 Madison Avenue
New York, NY 10016
www.penguinputnam.com

Library of Congress Cataloging-in-Publication Data
   Connecting : twenty prominent authors write about relationships that shape
our lives / edited by Lee Gutkind.
      p.   cm.—(Creative nonfiction reader series)
   ISBN 0-87477-904-9 (acid-free paper)
   1. Authors, American—20th century—Biography.   2. Authors, American—20th
century—Family relationships.   3. American prose literature—20th century.   4. Life
change events—United States.   5. Friendship—United States.   6. Family—United
States.   7. Autobiographies.   I. Gutkind, Lee.   II. Series.
   PS135.F36   1998   97-22756 CIP
   810.9'0054—dc21
   [B]

Book design by Ralph Fowler
Cover design by Jim Warner
Cover photo © by Photonica

Printed in the United States of America
1   2   3   4   5   6   7   8   9   10

ACKNOWLEDGMENTS

I wish to thank the editorial board of the journal *Creative Nonfiction*, Lea Simonds, Laurie Graham and Patricia Park, managing editor Leslie Boltax Aizenman, assistant editor Jessica Rohrbach, Putnam/Tarcher editor-in-chief Irene Prokop, and The Juliet Lea Hillman Simonds Foundation for ongoing support.

CONTENTS

INTRODUCTION: FROM FICTION AND POETRY—TO NONFICTION: AN EVOLUTION

Lee Gutkind

I had known Marc all of my life—thirteen years; we lived in the same neighborhood, and my mother and his mother and their friends played poker together each Thursday night, rotating from house to house. When "the girls," as they called themselves, came to our apartment to play, I usually stayed in my bedroom or sat in the hallway, listening to them talking and laughing, their plastic poker chips clicking on the kitchen table—which is how I first heard Marc's mother, Doris, discuss doctors' reports relating to Marc's leukemia and recount his dim prospects for survival.

From that point on, I did everything I could to intervene and make Marc's final years happy. I am not certain I understood exactly what I was doing: I had never known anyone my age who was dying or who had died. But the concept of death—the finality of it—both intrigued and frightened me. If Marc was dead, I reasoned, my own demise could be close behind.

In my obsession to save or extend Marc's life, I devoted hours and days to interacting with him after school and on weekends. But despite my efforts, he was losing weight and strength—clearly withering and dying. My rescue fantasy soon became an obsession.

I made up games to play with Marc, and I imagined wild adventures that we experienced together. We were two lone soldiers fighting the invasion of Pittsburgh by Chinese communist soldiers. We communicated with each other every night on make-believe walkie-talkies. We dated beautiful women, drank beer, and partied at our fraternity house. Eventually, as a last-ditch effort, I entered into a long but futile dialog with God, who swooped down from out of the sky in a military helicopter, repeatedly beseeching him to commute Marc's death sentence. But to no avail. Marc died, as everyone expected.

Years later, I wrote a book about Marc—an honest and accurate account of the fun and sadness we shared, true and imagined. After circulating this memoir to a number of publishers who rejected it, while asking if I had ever written any fiction, I couldn't help but get the hint. I made the decision to call it a novel (I changed names and locales) and eventually found a publisher. Had I not switched genres, *God's Helicopter* would probably not have been published for many years. Today, however, the literary world has different and certainly more eclectic interests than fiction alone, as evidenced by the remarkable emergence of creative nonfiction, which is how *God's Helicopter* might be labeled if it were published today.

The current interest in "creative" or "literary" nonfiction was actually initiated three decades ago, around the time I began writing *God's Helicopter,* primarily by Tom Wolfe *(The Right Stuff),* Gay Talese *(Honor Thy Father),* and others who adapted the literary techniques of fiction writers (scenes, dialogue, description, point of view) to the most dramatic real-life stories. But back then, few scholars or critics championed their cause, while colleagues (editors and other reporters) were mostly jealous and annoyed by the attention (and money) they were receiving. "New journalism," the term Wolfe and Talese used to describe this genre, soon became cultural history, along with bell-bottoms, the Beatles, and acid trips.

More recently, poets Diane Ackerman *(A Natural History of the Senses)* and Mary Karr *(The Liars' Club)* and fiction writers like Tobias Wolff *(This Boy's Life),* John Edgar Wideman *(Brothers and Keepers),* and Cynthia Ozick *(Fame and Folly)* have gained international recognition for their experimentation with and embrace of creative nonfiction. In fact, more than half of the writers in this reader have had careers and lives as poets or fiction writers before they crossed genres and achieved excellence in nonfiction. This is not surprising when you think about it. Most poets affirm that their poems are not only true but accurate, and most fiction writers admit that their stories are mostly based on real life, albeit somewhat scrambled and reimagined. My book, *God's Helicopter*, was neither scrambled nor re-imagined to any great extent, but it came at a time when stories about friends and family were much more acceptable in another genre.

That time has changed. All the essays in this reader are family oriented, mostly centering around the the impact and legacy of parents and friends. But in the final analysis, of course, family, friends, and story are what literature—and life—are all about. And the best stories, which originate in the heart and are the truest, both literally and metaphorically, are rooted in the earliest memories of our lives, when families (parents, siblings, grandparents) and friends are the predominant shaping forces—influences that invariably last a lifetime.

JOYCE CAROL OATES

Most writers rely on narratives to compel readers into an essay, but in "They All Just Went Away," Joyce Carol Oates does so with the power of her prose and the keenness of her detailed observations. She sets the scene, an abandoned neighborhood and an empty disintegrating house. Daringly, she stops time to share information about landscape architecture and modern art. When the reader is sufficiently integrated into the quiet culture of Millersport, New York, Oates introduces her characters and allows her story to begin.

THEY ALL JUST WENT AWAY

I must have been a lonely child. Until the age of twelve or thirteen, my most intense, happiest hours were spent tramping desolate fields, woods, and creek banks near my family's farmhouse in Millersport, New York. No one knew where I went. My father, working most of the day at Harrison's, a division of General Motors in Lockport, and at other times preoccupied, would not have asked; if my mother asked, I might have answered in a way that would deflect curiosity. I was an articulate, verbal child. Yet I could not have explained what drew me to the abandoned houses, barns, silos, corncribs. A hike of miles through fields of spiky grass, across outcroppings of shale as steeply angled as stairs, was a lark if the reward was an empty house.

Some of these houses had been inhabited as "homes" fairly recently—they had not yet reverted to the wild. Others, abandoned during the Depression, had long since begun to rot and collapse, engulfed by vegetation (trumpet vine, wisteria, rose of Sharon, willow) that elsewhere, on our property, for instance, were kept neatly trimmed. I was drawn to both kinds of houses, though the more recently inhabited were more forbidding and therefore more inviting.

To push open a door into such silence: the absolute emptiness of a house whose occupants have departed. Often, the crack of broken glass underfoot. A startled buzzing of flies, hornets. The slithering, ticklish sensation of a garter snake crawling across floorboards.

Left behind, as if in haste, were remnants of a lost household. A broken toy on the floor, a baby's bottle. A rain-soaked sofa, looking as if it had been gutted with a hunter's skilled knife. Strips of wallpaper like shredded skin. Smashed crockery, piles of tin cans; soda, beer, whiskey bottles. An icebox, its door yawning open. Once, on a counter, a dirt-stiffened rag that, unfolded like precious cloth, revealed itself to be a woman's cheaply glamorous "see-through" blouse, threaded with glitter-strips of gold.

This was a long time ago, yet it is more vivid to me than anything now.

This was when I was too young to think the house is the mother's body; you have been expelled and are forbidden now to reënter.

Always, I was prepared to see a face at a high, empty window. A woman's hand uplifted in greeting, or in warning. *Hello! Come in! Stay away! Run! Who are you?* A movement in the corner of my eye: the blurred motion of a person passing through a doorway, or glimpsed through a window. There might be a single shriek of laughter from a barn—piercing as a bird's cry. Murmurous, teasing voices confused with wind rippling through tall, coarse, gone-to-seed grass. Voices that, when you pause to listen, fade immediately and are gone.

The sky in such places of abandonment was always of the hue and brightness of tin, as if the melancholy rural poverty of tin roofs reflected upward.

A house: a structural arrangement of space, geometrically laid out to provide what are called rooms, these divided from one another by verticals and horizontals called walls, ceilings, floors. The house contains the home but is not identical with it. The house anticipates the home and will very likely survive it, reverting again simply to house when home (that is, life) departs. For only where there is life can there be home.

I have never found the visual equivalent of these abandoned farmhouses of upstate New York, of northern Erie County, in the area of the long, meandering Tonawanda Creek and the Barge Canal. You think most immediately of the canvases of Edward Hopper: those dreamily stylized visions of a lost America, houses never depicted as homes, and human beings, if you look closer, never depicted as other than mannequins. For Hopper is not a realist but a surrealist. His dreams are of the ordinary, as if, even in imagination, the artist were trapped in an unyielding daylight consciousness. There seems almost a kind of rage, a revenge against such restraints, in Hopper's studied, endlessly repeated *simplicity*. By contrast, Charles Burchfield, with his numerous oils and watercolors—frequently of upstate New York landscapes, houses, and farms—rendered the real as visionary and luminous, suffused with a Blakean rapture and a kind of radical simplicity, too. Then there are the shimmering New England barns, fields, and skies of our contemporary Wolf Kahn—images evoked by memory, almost on the verge of dissolution. But the "real"—what assaults the eye before the eye begins its work of selection—is never on the verge of dissolution, still less of appropriation. The real is raw, jarring, unexpected, sometimes trashy, sometimes luminous. Above all, the real is arbitrary. For to be a realist (in art or in life) is to acknowledge that all things might be other than they are. That there is no design, no intention, no aesthetic or moral or teleological imprimatur but, rather, the equivalent of Darwin's great vision of a blind, purposeless, ceaseless evolutionary process that yields no "products"—only temporary strategies against extinction.

Yet, being human, we think, To what purpose these broken-off things, if not to be gathered up, at last, in a single ecstatic vision?

There is a strange and profound and unknowable reality to these abandoned houses where jealously guarded, even prized possessions have become mere trash: windowpanes long ago smashed, and the spaces where they had been festooned with cobwebs, and cobwebs brushing against your face, catching in your hair like caresses. The peculiar, dank smell of wood rot and mildew, in one of the houses I most recall that had partly burned down, the smell of smoke and scorch, in early summer pervading even the lyric smell of honeysuckle—these haunting smells, never, at the time of experiencing, given specific sources, names.

Where a house has been abandoned—unworthy of being sold to new tenants, very likely seized by the county for default on taxes and the property held in escrow—you can be sure there has been a sad story. There have been devastated lives. Lives to be spoken of pityingly. How they went wrong. Why did she marry him, why did she stay with him? Just desperate people. Ignorant. Poor white trash. Runs in the family. A wrong turn.

. . .

Shall I say for the record that ours was a happy, close-knit, and unextraordinary family for our time, place, and economic status? Yet what was vividly real in the solid-built old farmhouse that contained my home (my family consisted of my father, mother, younger brother, grandfather, and grandmother, who owned the property—a slow-failing farm whose principal crop had become Bartlett pears by the time I was a girl) was of far less significance to me than what was real elsewhere. A gone-to-seed landscape had an authority that seemed to me incontestable: the powerful authority of silence in houses for which the human voice had vanished. For the abandoned house contained the future of any house—the lilac tree pushing through the rotted veranda, hornets' nests beneath eaves, windows smashed by vandals, human excrement left to dry on a parlor floor once scrubbed on hands and knees.

The abandoned, the devastated, was the profound experience, whereas involvement in family life—the fever, the bliss, the abrasions, the infinite distractions of human love—was so clearly temporary. Like a television screen upon which antic images (at this time, in the fifties, minimally varying gradations of gray) appear fleetingly and are gone.

I have seemed to suggest that the abandoned houses were all distant from our house, but in fact the one that had been partly gutted by fire—which I will call the Weidel house—was perhaps a half mile away. If you drove, turning right off Transit Road, which was our road, onto the old Creek Road, it would have been a distance of a mile or more, but if you crossed through our back potato field and through the marshy woods which no one seemed to own, it was a quick walk.

The Weidels' dog, Slossie, a mixed breed with a stumpy, energetic tail and a sweet disposition, sand-colored, rheumy-eyed, as hungry for affection as for the scraps we sometimes fed her, trotted over frequently to play with my brother and me. Though, strictly speaking, Slossie was not wanted at our house. None of the Weidels were wanted.

The "Weidel house," it would be called for years. The "Weidel property." As if the very land—which the family had not owned in any case, but only rented, partly with county-welfare support—

were somehow imprinted with that name, a man's identity. Or infamy.

For tales were told of the father who drank, beat and terrorized his family, "did things to" his daughters, and finally set the house on fire and fled and was arrested, disappearing forever from the proper, decent life of our community. There was no romance in Mr. Weidel, whom my father knew only slightly and despised as a drinker, and as a wife- and child-beater. Mr. Weidel was a railway worker in Lockport, or perhaps an ex-railway worker, for he seemed to work only sporadically, though he always wore a railwayman's cap. He and his elder sons were hunters, owning a shotgun among them, and one or two deer rifles. His face was broad, fair, vein-swollen, with a look of flushed, alcoholic reproach. He was tall and heavyset, with graying black whiskers that sprouted like quills. His eyes had a way of swerving in their sockets, seeking you out when you could not slip away quickly enough. *H'lo there, little Joyce! Joycie! Joycie Oates, h'lo!* He wore rubber boots that flapped, unbuckled, about his feet.

Mrs. Weidel was a faded-pretty, apologetic woman with a body that seemed to have become bloated, as with a perpetual pregnancy. Her bosom had sunk to her waist. Her legs were encased, sausagelike, in flesh-colored support hose. *How can that woman live with him? That pig.* There was disdain, disgust, in this frequent refrain. *Why doesn't she leave him? Did you see that black eye? Did you hear them the other night? Take the girls away, at least.* It was thought that she could, for Mrs. Weidel was the only one in the family who seemed to work at all regularly. She was hired for seasonal canning in a tomato factory in lower Lockport and may have done housecleaning in the city.

A shifting household of relatives and rumored "boarders" lived in the Weidel house. There were six Weidel children, four sons and two daughters. Ruth was a year older than I, and Dorothy two years younger. There was an older brother of Mr. Weidel's, who walked with a cane and was said to be an ex-convict, from Attica. The eldest Weidel son, Roy, owned a motorcycle, and friends of his often visited, fellow-bikers. There were loud parties, frequent disputes, and tales of Mr. Weidel's chasing his wife with a butcher knife, a claw hammer, the shotgun, threatening to "blow her head off." Mrs. Weidel and the younger children fled outdoors in terror and hid in the hayloft. Sheriff's deputies drove out to the house, but no charges were ever pressed against Mr. Weidel. Until the fire, which was so public that it couldn't be denied.

There was the summer day—I was eleven years old—that Mr. Weidel shot Slossie. We heard the poor creature yelping and whimpering for what seemed like hours. When my father came home from work, he went to speak to Mr. Weidel, though my mother begged him not to. By this time, the dog had dragged herself beneath the Weidels' house to die. Mr. Weidel was furious at the intrusion, drunk, defensive—Slossie was his goddam dog, he said, she'd been getting in the way, she was "old." But my father convinced him to put the poor dog out of her misery. So Mr. Weidel made one of his sons drag Slossie out from beneath the house, and he straddled her and shot her a second time, and a third, at close range. My father, who'd never hunted, who'd never owned a gun, backed off, a hand over his eyes.

Afterward, my father would say of that day that walking away from that drunken son of a bitch with a rifle in his hands was about the hardest thing he'd ever done. He'd expected a shot between his shoulders.

The fire was the following year, around Thanksgiving.

After the Weidels were gone from Millersport and the house stood empty, I discovered Slossie's grave. I'm sure it was Slossie's grave. It was beyond the dog hutch, in the weedy back yard, a sunken patch of earth measuring about three feet by four with one of Mrs. Weidel's big whitewashed rocks at the head.

Morning glories grew in clusters on the posts of the front porch. Mrs. Weidel had planted hollyhocks, sunflowers, and trumpet vine in the yard. Tough, weedlike flowers that would survive for years.

It had been said of Ruth and her sister Dorothy that they were "slow." Yet Ruth was never slow to fly into a rage when she was teased by neighborhood boys or by her older brothers. She waved her fists and stammered obscenities, words that stung like hail. Her face darkened with blood, and her full, thick lips quivered with a strange sort of pleasure. How you loved to see Ruth Weidel fly into one of her rages; it was like holding a lighted match to flammable material.

The Weidel house was like any other run-down wood-frame house, said by my grandfather to have been "thrown up" in the nineteen-twenties. It had no cellar, only a concrete-block foundation—an emptiness that gradually filled with debris. It had an upstairs with several small bedrooms. There was no attic. No insulation. Steep, almost vertical stairs. The previous tenant had started to construct a front porch of raw planks, never completed or painted. (Though Mrs. Weidel added "touches" to the porch—chairs, a woven-rush rug, geraniums in flowerpots.) The roof of the house was made of sheets of tin, scarred and scabbed like skin, and the front was covered in simulated-brick asphalt siding pieced together from lumberyard scraps. All year round, a number of the windows were covered in transparent duct tape and never opened. From a distance, the house was the fading dun color of a deer's winter coat.

Our house had an attic and a cellar and a deep well and a solid cement foundation. My father did all the carpentry on our house, most of the shingling, the painting, the masonry. I would not know until I was an adult that he'd come from what's called a "broken home" himself—what an image, luridly visual, of a house literally broken, split in two, its secrets spilled out onto the ground for all to see, like entrails.

My mother, unlike Mrs. Weidel, had time to houseclean. It was a continuous task, a mother's responsibility. My mother planted vegetables, strawberries, beds of flowers. Petunias and pansies and zinnias. Crimson peonies that flowered for my birthday, in mid-June.

I remember the night of the fire vividly, as if it had been a festive affair to which I'd been invited.

There was the sound of a siren on the Creek Road. There were shouts, and an astonishing burst of flame in the night, in the direction of the Weidel house. The air was moist, and reflected and magnified the fire, surrounding it like a nimbus. My grandparents would claim there had never been such excitement in Millersport, and perhaps that was true. My father dressed hurriedly and went to help the firefighters, and my mother and the rest of us watched from upstairs windows. The fire began at about 1 A.M., and it would be past 4 A.M. before my seven-year-old brother and I got back to bed.

Yet what was so exciting an event was, in fact, an ending, with nothing to follow. Immediately afterward, the Weidels disappeared from Millersport and from our lives. It was said that Mr. Weidel fled "as a fugitive" but was captured and arrested the next day, in Buffalo. The family was broken up, scattered, the younger children placed in foster homes. That quickly, the Weidels were gone.

For a long time, the smell of wood smoke, scorch, pervaded the air of Millersport, the fresh, damp smell of earth sullied by its presence. Neighbors complained that the Weidel house should be razed at the county's expense, bulldozed over, and the property sold. But nothing was done, for years. Who knows why? When I went away to college, the old falling-down house was still there.

How swiftly, in a single season, a human habitation can turn wild. The bumpy cinder driveway over which the eldest Weidel son had ridden his motorcycle was soon stippled with tall weeds.

What had happened to Roy Weidel? It was said he'd joined the Navy. No, he had a police record and could not have joined the Navy. He'd disappeared. Asked by the police to give a sworn statement about the night of his father's "arson," he'd panicked and fled.

Signs were posted—"NO TRESPASSING," "THIS PROPERTY CONDEMNED BY ERIE CO."—and they, too, over a period of months, became shabby and faded. My parents warned me never to wander onto the Weidel property. There was a well with a loose-fitting cover, among other dangers. As if *I* would fall into a well! I smiled to think how little my parents knew me. How little anyone knew me.

Have I said that my father never struck his children, as Mr. Weidel struck his? And did worse things to them, to the girls sometimes, it was whispered. Yes, and Mrs. Weidel, who seemed so soft and apologetic and sad, she, too, had beaten the younger children when she'd been drinking. County social workers came around to question neighbors, and spread the story of what they learned along the way.

In fact, I may have been disciplined, spanked, a few times. Like most children, I don't remember. I remember Mr. Weidel spanking his children until they screamed (though I wasn't a witness, was I?), but I don't remember being spanked by my parents, and in any case, if I was, it was no more than I deserved.

I'd seen Mr. Weidel urinating once at the roadside. The loose-flying skein of the kerosene he'd flung around the house before setting the fire must have resembled the stream of his urine, transparent and glittering. But they laughed, saying Mr. Weidel had been too drunk, or too careless, to have done an adequate job of sprinkling kerosene through the downstairs of the house. Wasn't it like him, such a slovenly job. Only part of the house had burned, a wall of the kitchen and an adjoining woodshed.

Had Mr. Weidel wanted to burn his family alive in their beds? Mrs. Weidel testified, no, they'd all been awake, they'd run out into the yard before the fire began. They'd never been in any danger, she swore. But Mr. Weidel was indicted on several counts of attempted murder, along with other charges.

For so many years the Weidel house remained standing. There was something defiant about it, like someone who has been mortally wounded but will not die. In the weedy front yard, Mrs. Weidel's display of whitewashed rocks and plaster-of-Paris gnomes and the clay pedestal with the shiny blue glass ball disappeared from view within a year or so. Brambles grew everywhere. I forced myself to taste a small bitter red berry but spat it out, it made my mouth pucker so.

What did it mean that Erie County had "condemned" the Weidel property? The downstairs windows were carelessly boarded over, and both the front and rear doors were unlocked, collapsing on their hinges. Broken glass underfoot and a sickish stench of burn, mildew, decay. Yet there were "touches"—on what remained of a kitchen wall, a Holstein calendar from a local feed store, a child's crayon drawing. Upstairs, children's clothes, socks and old shoes heaped on the floor. I recognized with a thrill of repugnance an old red sweater of Ruth's, angora-fuzzy. There were broken Christmas-tree ornaments, a naked pink plastic doll. Toppled bedsprings, filthy mattresses streaked with yellow and rust-colored stains. The mattresses looked as if they'd been gutted, their stuffing strewn about. The most terrible punishment, I thought, would be to be forced to lie down on such a mattress.

I thought of Mrs. Weidel, her swollen, blackened eyes, her bruised face. Shouts and sirens in the night, the sheriff's patrol car. But no charges filed. The social worker told my mother how Mrs. Weidel had screamed at the county people, insisting her husband hadn't done anything wrong and shouldn't go to jail. The names she'd called them! Unrepeatable.

She was the wife of that man, they'd had babies together. The law had no right to interfere. The law had nothing to do with them.

.   .   .

As a woman and as a writer, I have long wondered at the well-springs of female masochism. Or what, in despair of a more subtle, less reductive phrase, we can call the congeries of predilections toward self-hurt, self-erasure, self-repudiation in women. These predilections are presumably "learned"—"acquired"—but perhaps also imprinted in our genes, of biological necessity, neurophysiological fate, predilections that predate culture. Indeed, may shape culture. Do not say, "Yes, but these are isolated, peripheral examples. These are marginal Americans, uneducated. They tell us nothing about ourselves." They tell us everything about ourselves, and even the telling, the exposure, is a kind of cutting, an inscription in the flesh.

Yet what could possibly be the evolutionary advantage of self-hurt in the female? Abnegation in the face of another's cruelty? Acquiescence to another's will? This loathsome secret that women do not care to speak of, or even acknowledge.

Two or three years later, in high school, twelve miles away in a consolidated district school to which, as a sophomore, I went by school bus, Ruth Weidel appeared. She was living now with relatives in Lockport. She looked, at sixteen, like a woman in her twenties; big-breasted, with full, strong thighs and burnished-brown hair inexpertly bleached. Ruth's homeroom was "special education," but she took some classes with the rest of us. If she recognized me, in our home-economics class, she was careful to give no sign.

There was a tacit understanding that "something had happened" to Ruth Weidel, and her teachers treated her guardedly. Ruth was special, the way a handicapped person is special. She was withdrawn, quiet; if still prone to violent outbursts of rage, she might have been on medication to control it. Her eyes, like her father's, seemed always about to swerve in their sockets. Her face was round, fleshy, like a pudding, her nose oily-pored. Yet she wore lipstick, she was "glamorous"—almost. In gym class, Ruth's large breasts straining against her T-shirt and the shining rippled muscles and fatty flesh of her thighs were amazing to us; we were so much thinner and less female, so much younger.

I believed that I should protect Ruth Weidel, so I told none of the other students about her family. Even to Ruth, for a long time I pretended not to know who she was. I can't explain how Ruth could have possibly believed me, yet this seems to have been so.

Quite purposefully, I befriended Ruth. I thought her face would lose its sallow hardness if she could be made to smile, and so it became a kind of challenge to me to induce Ruth Weidel to smile. She was lonely and miserable at school, and flattered by my attention. For so few "normal" girls sought out "special-ed" girls. At first she may have been suspicious, but by degrees she became trusting. I thought of Slossie: trust shows in the eyes.

I sat with Ruth at lunch in the school cafeteria and eventually I asked her about the house on the old Creek Road, and she lied bluntly, to my face, insisting that an uncle of hers had owned that house. She'd only visited a few times. She and her family. I asked, "How did the fire start?" and Ruth said, slowly, each word sucked like a pebble in the mouth, "Lightning. Lightning hit it. One night in a storm." I asked, "Are you living with your mother now, Ruth?" and Ruth shrugged, and made a face, and said, "She's O.K. I see her sometimes." I asked about Dorothy. I asked where Mrs. Weidel was. I said that my mother had always liked her mother, and missed her when she went away. But Ruth seemed not to hear. Her gaze had drifted. I said, "Why did you all move away?" Ruth did not reply, though I could hear her breathing hard. "Why did you abandon your house? It could have been fixed. It's still there. Your mom's hollyhocks are still there. You should come out and see it sometime. You could visit me." Ruth shrugged, and laughed. She gave me a sidelong glance, almost flirtatiously. It was startling to see how good-looking she could be, how sullen-sexy; to know how men would stare at her who would never so much as glance at a girl like me. Ruth said slowly, as if she'd come to a final, adamant conclusion to a problem that had long vexed her, "They all just went away."

Another time, after lunch with Ruth, I left a plastic change purse with a few coins in it on the ledge in one of the girls' lavatories, where Ruth was washing her hands. I don't recall whether I left it on purpose or not. But when I returned, after waiting for Ruth to leave the lavatory, the change purse was gone.

Once or twice, I invited Ruth Weidel to come home with me on the school bus some afternoon, to Millersport, to have supper with my family and stay the night. I must not have truly believed she might accept, for my mother would have been horrified and would have forced me to rescind the invitation. Ruth had hesitated, as if she wanted to say yes, wanted very badly to say yes, but finally she said, "No. I guess I better not."

RICHARD FORD

Richard Ford begins "Accommodations" as if he is in the middle of a long story and someone has asked a provocative question that he begins to answer—by repeating the question: "And what was it like to live there?" This is an effective device to compel a reader into an essay, but even more effective is the way that Ford deflects the question and paints a portrait that vividly represents all the memories the question evokes concerning his residence as a young boy in a traveler's hotel. In the end, as if to frame his portrait, he asks another question that, in fact, represents the theme or focus of the essay: "How permanent is real life?" This he answers directly with a definitive statement and one final question for readers and writers alike: "Everything counts, after all. What else do you need to know?"

ACCOMMODATIONS

And what was it like to live there? From my childhood, this memory: I am in bed. It is one o'clock in the morning. I am eleven years old, and in a room inside my grandfather's hotel—the room connecting to his. I am awake, listening. This is what I hear. Someplace, through walls, an argument is going on. A man and a woman are arguing. I hear some dishes rattle and then break. The words "You don't care. No, you don't" spoken by a woman. How far away this goes on I can't tell. Rooms away is all. I heard a door open into the hall, and a voice that's louder—the man's—say, "Better you than me in this is what I know. You bet." I hear keys jingling, a door close softly, then footsteps over the carpeted hallway. And then a smell of sweet perfume in my room, an orchid smell, all around me where I'm alone and in the dark, lying still. I hear an elevator grate drawn back. A second woman's voice farther away, talking softly, then the door closes, and it's quiet again inside. I hear a bus hiss at the station across the city street. A car horn blows. Somewhere outside someone begins to laugh, the laughter coming up off the empty pavement and into the night. Then no more noises. The perfume drifts through my room, stays in the air. I hear my grandfather turn in his sleep and sigh. Then sleep comes back.

This was the fifties, and my grandfather ran the hotel where we lived—in Little Rock, a town neither exactly south nor exactly west, just as it still is. To live in a hotel promotes a cool two-mindedness: one is both steady and in a sea that passes with tides. Accommodation is what's wanted, a replenished idea of permanence and transience; familiarity overcoming the continual irregularity in things.

The hotel was named the Marion, and it was not a small place. Little Rock was a mealy, low-rise town on a slow river, and the hotel was the toniest, plushest place in it. And still it was blowsy, a hotel for conventioneers and pols, salesmen and late-night party givers. There was a curving marble fish pond in the lobby; a tranquil, banistered mezzanine with escritoires and soft lights; a jet marble front desk; long, green leather couches, green carpets, bellboys with green twill uniforms and short memories. It was a columned brownstone with a porte-cochère, built in the twenties, with seven stories, three hundred rooms. Ladies from the Delta stayed in on shopping trips. The Optimists and the Rotarians met. Assignations between state officials went on upstairs. Senator McClellan kept a room. Visiting famous people stayed, and my grandfather kept their pictures on his office wall—Rex Allen the cowboy, Jack Dempsey the boxing champion, June Allyson and Dick Powell, Harry Truman (whose photograph I have, still), Ricky Nelson, Chill Wills. Salesmen rented sample rooms, suicides took singles. There were hospitality suites, honeymoon suites, a Presidential, a Miss America, Murphy beds, silver service, Irish napkins. There was a bakery, a print shop, an upholsterer, ten rooms (the Rendezvous, the Continental) for intimate parties, six more for large, and a ballroom with a Hammond organ for banquets. There was a beer bar in the lower lobby, a two-chair barbershop, a cigar stand, a florist, a travel agent, a news agent, a garage where you parked for nothing while you stayed. There was a drummer's rate, a serviceman's rate, a monthly rate, a day rate, even an hourly rate if you knew my grandfather. Everything happened there, at all hours. Privacy had a high value. To live in a hotel as a boy knowing nothing was to see what adults did to each other and themselves when only adults were present.

My grandfather, Ben Shelley, was a man of strong appetites— food, but other things, too. The usual things. He was a fatty who played winter golf in pleated gabardines, shot pool and quail. He qualified as a sport, a Shriner, a wide, public man, a toddling character in a blue suit with change in his pockets and a money clip. To me, he was the exotic brought to common earth, and I loved him. "The latchstring is always on the outside" was his motto, and he winked at you when he said that, smiled between his thick amorous lips, as though his words meant something else, which they may have. I could think different of him now, see him through new eyes, revise history, take a narrower, latter-day view. But why?

He had been a boxer—a featherweight, a club fighter; worked dining cars on the Rock Island as far as Tucumcari, waited tables in El Reno, been a caterer's assistant at the famous Muehlebach in Kansas City. That was the way up in the hotel business, and such work was his by nature. Service. That word meant something it doesn't mean now.

What his skills were, his acumen, his genius that got him down to Little Rock and into a good job in 1947, I don't know. Loyalty and firmness, I imagine. Discretion, certainly. A lack of frankness. Gratitude. Still good qualities. People liked him, liked staying there—which were similar experiences. Everyone approached him smiling, as if he knew something private about them, which he undoubtedly did. They were in his house when they were in his hotel, and he spoke to them at close range, in cagey whispers, his big stomach touching them. He held their arm, cradled their elbow, spoke while he seemed to look away, smiling. He knew the joke, that was his business, exactly. Nothing in the private sector deserves privacy but sex. And that was in the air about him and the whole place. A hotel is for that as much as—maybe more than—anything. And he knew it mattered less what you did than whether someone knew about it.

Normal life, I know now, is life that can be explained in one sentence. No questions needed. And that, I lacked. "You live right here in the hotel?" is what I heard. Afterwards, a smile. These were Southerners, guests I met briefly. They wanted their own straight line on the eccentric, which is what I was to them; wanted always to compare and contrast lives to their own. It is the Southerner's favorite habit. My story, though, took too long to get into, and I wouldn't: my father was sick; he traveled for a living; my mother drove him; I was from another city, not here; these were my grandparents; I liked it here. It was only that complicated, but I left it alone. Accommodating your own small eccentricity to yourself is enough. And even that moves you toward remoteness, toward affection for half-truths, makes you conspiratorial, a secret-keeper.

Certain things *were* acknowledged lacking. Neighbors. There were none of those. Only employees, guests, "the Permanents" (old bachelors, old shopkeepers, old married couples in cheap rooms with no better homes to hold on to), lobby lizards—older men with baffling nicknames like Spider, Goldie, Ish—men who lived out in town but showed up each day. These were all. No one was my age ever. There was no neighborhood of other houses, no normal views out windows, no normal quiets or light. We were downtown, detached from normal residential lives. Town—the real city, the coarse town mix—started just outside the lobby door: a liquor store, two cheap movies, a pool room, a less-good hotel with whores, the bus depot. Everything was immediate. No delays. At night, out my window from floor six, I could see the town signs with black sky behind, a green beacon farther off, could hear the Trailways heave in and out. I saw sailors, single women, older black couples standing down on the pavement stretching, taking their look around at a strange city, using the phone on the wall, the bathroom, staring across Markham Street at the hotel where they weren't staying the night. Then getting on the bus again for St. Louis or Texas or Memphis. Then gone. Was it lonely for me? No. Never. It is not bad or lonely to see that life goes on at all times, with you or without you. Home is finally a variable concept.

Travelers—our guests—were people I did not know. They appeared with bags, wives, and kids—their cars outside. They looked around the lobby, glanced into the fish pond, sniffed the air, checked in, *became* guests, walked toward the elevators and disappeared. I almost never noticed them again, did not even imagine them—their days, their houses in other states, their fatigues, where they'd already been that day, where they lunched, whether they'd argued or why, where they might go next. I resisted them. It might have seemed a conversation would take too long, go nowhere. I did not really like traveling, I think now. Traveling and hotels reflected things different at heart.

And, of course, we lived *in,* in an apartment with four rooms where we did not own the furniture but where we liked it—room and board the highly valued parts of our deal. We ate where we pleased—in the big kitchen downstairs or in the dining room— The Green Room—in our apartment. We ordered room service. Laundry was free. A lot was free. My grandfather kept bird dogs in the basement. We had TV early, our car had a good spot in the garage and got washed every day. The sheets were always clean. We saw few visitors. Complete freedom within limits. But if my grandfather lost his job—always the backstage scare story—we lost it all. How fast we could be "put on the street" for some vague infraction observed by the captious owner was a topic much reviewed by my grandmother, who had been poor, though not by my grandfather, who had been poor, too, but couldn't imagine it anymore, and who too much loved his work. Employment was undemocratic then. It lacked the redress we take for granted now—the doctrine of fairness. Hotels were thought to run best as sufferance, with things in limbo. And every morning in the dark before work, my grandfather would sit in a chair in his underwear, just before lacing his shoes, and pray out loud for his job, thank God for loyal employees, for his good boss, and for the trust he felt he had, pray for the future. I could hear this from my bed in the next room. It seemed prudent to me, as it still does.

Whatever his duties—and they were not so clear-cut to me—he was up at six to do them, gone down the elevator in his loose blue suit to "put in an appearance." Mostly his job was simply that. Being there and only there. A presence and conserver to his employees, a welcoming man to guests. He "toured the house," saw that operations were operating. That is how a hotel was run. He signed checks. He hired people, fired them. He ate *in* to prove his food was good, lived in for the same reason. His prosperity (in conspicuous evidence, always) promised others the same. In this he was not an *hôtelier,* not an innkeeper, he was a hotelman. He would not have been happy to manage something else—a store or a row of trailers. He did not look forward to advancement, only to more of the same. Time has gone when men inhabited their jobs in that way, when occupation signaled that.

And what did I do? Little. I was there, too. I lived *inside* and did not think of outside. I took few duties. I stood, I watched things pass by me. I rode the elevators, I chatted up bellboys and waiters and room clerks. I slouched around, watched lights light up on the PBX, saw operations operating over and over. I fed the fish. I was prized for my manners, for my height, for the fact that my father was sick and I was here—bravely and indefinitely. I was thought to be interested in hotel work and said that I was. I was curious, un-perplexed, un-self-centered, as useless as any boy who sees the surface of life close and reclose over facts that are often not easily simplifiable. We can become familiar with a great many things.

. . .

To make regular life seem regular need not always be to bleach the strong colors out. But just for a time it can help. When you look for what's unique and also true of life, you're lucky to find less than you imagined.

How permanent is real life? That's the question, isn't it? The one we both want and don't quite want to hear told. Queasy, melancholic, obvious answers are there. In the hotel there was no center to things, nor was I one. It was the floating life, days erasing other days almost completely, as should be. The place was a hollow place, like any home, in which things went on, a setting where situations developed and ended. And I simply stood alongside that for a while in my young life—neither behind the scenes nor in front. What I saw then—and I saw more than I can say, more than I remember—matters less than what I thought about it. And what I thought about it was this: this is the actual life now, not a stopover, a diversion, or an oddment in time, but the permanent life, the one that will provide history, memory, the one I'll be responsible for in the long run. Everything counts, after all. What else do you need to know?

JOHN MCPHEE

In "Rising from the Plains," John McPhee, a longtime *New Yorker* staff writer, works with history and narrative in a number of distinctively different ways. Most obvious are the episodic excerpts from the partially unpublished journal of Ethel Waxham, a slim young Ph.D. from Wellesley College, who arrived in Wyoming in 1905 to teach at a remote one-room schoolhouse. In addition to presenting Waxham's voice directly, McPhee summarizes and supplements her story with a narrative of evocative drama and detail culled from a myriad of other sources—from library research to interviews with friends and family.

RISING FROM THE PLAINS

On October 20, 1905, the two-horse stage left Rawlins soon after dawn. Eggs were packed under the seats, also grapes and oysters. There were so many boxes and mailbags that they were piled up beside the driver. On the waybill, the passengers were given exactly the same status as the oysters and the grapes. The young woman from Wellesley, running her eye down the list of merchandise, encountered her own name: Miss Ethel Waxham.

The passenger compartment had a canvas roof, and canvas curtains at the front and sides.

The driver, Bill Collins, a young fellow with a four days beard, untied the bow-knot of the reins around the wheel, and swung up on the seat, where he ensconced himself with one leg over the mail bags as high as his head and one arm over the back of his seat, putting up the curtain between. "Kind o' lonesome out here," he gave as his excuse.

There were two passengers. The other's name was Alice Amoss Welty, and she was the postmistress of Dubois, two hundred miles northwest. Her post office was unique, in that it was farther from a railroad than any other in the United States; but this did not inconvenience the style of Mrs. Welty. Not for her some false-fronted dress shop with a name like Tinnie Mercantile. She bought her clothes by mail from B. Altman & Co., Manhattan. Mrs. Welty was of upper middle age, and—"bless her white hairs"—her gossip range appeared to cover every living soul within thirty thousand square miles, an interesting handful of people. The remark about the white hairs—like the description of Bill Collins and the estimated radius of Mrs. Welty's gossip—is from the unpublished journal of Ethel Waxham.

The stage moved through town past houses built of railroad ties, past sheepfolds, and was soon in the dust of open country, rounding a couple of hills before assuming a northwesterly course. The hills above were the modest high points in a landscape that lacked exceptional relief. Here in the middle of the Rocky Mountains were no mountains worthy of the name.

Mountains were far away ahead of us, a range rising from the plains and sinking down again into them. Almost all the first day they were in sight.

As Wyoming ranges go, these distant summits were unprepossessing ridges, with altitudes of nine and ten thousand feet. In one sentence, though, Miss Waxham had intuitively written their geologic history, for they had indeed come out of the plains, and into the plains had in various ways returned.

The stage rolled onto Separation Flats—altitude seven thousand feet—still pursuing the chimeric mountains.

Lost Soldier was another sixteen miles and thus would take three hours.

We rattled into the place at last, and were glad to get in to the fire to warm ourselves while the driver changed the load from one coach to another. With every change of drivers the coach is changed, making each man responsible for repairs on his own coach. The Kirks keep Lost Soldier. Mrs. Kirk is a short stocky figureless woman with untidy hair. She furnished me with an old soldier's overcoat to wear during the night to come. . . . Before long, we were started again, with Peggy Dougherty for driver. He is tall and grizzled. They say that when he goes to dances they make him take the spike out of the bottom of his wooden leg.

There were four horses now—"a wicked little team"—and immediately they kicked over the traces, tried to run away, became tangled like sled dogs twisting in harness, and set Peggy Dougherty to swearing.

Ye gods, how he could swear.

[Ethel Waxham's first destination was a place called Red Bluff Ranch, owned by a family named Mills, where she would live while she taught school.]

Miss Waxham's school was a log cabin on Twin Creek near the mouth of Skull Gulch, a mile from the Mills ranch. Students came from much greater distances, even through deep snow. Many mornings, ink was frozen in the inkwells, and the day began with ink-thawing, followed by reading, spelling, chemistry, and civil government. Sometimes snow blew through the walls, forming drifts in the schoolroom. Water was carried from the creek— drawn from a hole that was chopped in the ice. If the creek was frozen to the bottom, the students melted snow. Their school was fourteen by sixteen feet—smaller than a bathroom at Wellesley. The door was perforated with bullet holes from "some passerby's six-shooter." Over the ceiling poles were old gunnysacks and over-alls, to prevent the sod roof from shedding sediment on the students. Often, however, the air sparkled with descending dust, struck by sunlight coming in through the windows, which were all in the south wall. There was a table and chair for Miss Waxham, and eight desks for her pupils. Miss Waxham's job was to deliver a hundred per cent of the formal education available in District Eleven, Fremont County, Wyoming.

> The first fifteen minutes or half hour are given to reading "Uncle Tom's Cabin" or "Kidnapped," while we all sit about the stove to keep warm. Usually in the middle of a reading the sound of a horse galloping down the frozen road distracts the attention of the boys, until a few moments later six-foot George opens the door, a sack of oats in one hand, his lunch tied up in a dish rag in the other. Cold from his five-mile ride, he sits down on the floor by the stove, unbuck-les his spurs, pulls off his leather chaps, drops his hat, unwinds two or three red handkerchiefs from about his neck and ears, takes off one or two coats, according to the temperature, unbuttons his vest and straightens his leather cuffs. At last he is ready for business.
>
> Sandford is the largest scholar, six feet, big, slow in the school room, careful of every move of his big hands and feet. His voice is subdued and full of awe as he calls me "ma'am." Outside while we play chickens he is another person—there is room for his bigness. Next largest of the boys is Otto Schlicting, thin and dark, a strange combi-

*nation of shrewdness and stupidity. His problems always prove,
whether they are right or not! He is a boaster, too, tries to make a big
impression. But there is something very attractive about him. I was
showing his little sister how to add and subtract by making little lines
and adding or crossing off others. Later I found on the back of Otto's
papers hundreds and hundreds of little lines—trying to add that way
as far as a hundred evidently. He is nearly fifteen and studying division. . . . Arithmetic is the family failing. "How many eights in
ninety-six?" I ask him. He thinks for a long time. Finally he says—
with such a winsome smile that I wish with all my heart it were
true—"Two." "What feeds the cells in your body?" I ask him. He
thinks. He says, "I guess it's vinegar." He has no idea of form. His
maps of North America on the board are all like turnips.*

Students' ages ranged through one and two digits, and their intelligence even more widely. When Miss Waxham called upon
Emmons Schlicting, asking, "Where does digestion take place?,"
Emmons answered, "In the Erie Canal." She developed a special
interest in George Ehler, whose life at home was troubled.

*He is only thirteen, but taller than Sandford, and fair and handsome.
I should like to get him away from his family—kidnap him. To think
that it was he who tried to kill his father! His face is good as can be.*

At lunchtime, over beans, everyone traded the news of the
country, news of whatever might have stirred in seven thousand
square miles: a buffalo wolf trapped by Old Hanley; missing horses
and cattle, brand by brand; the sheepherder most recently lost in a
storm. If you went up Skull Gulch, behind the school, and
climbed to the high ground beyond, you could see seventy, eighty,
a hundred miles. You "could see the faint outlines of Crowheart
Butte, against the Wind River Range." There was a Wyoming-
history lesson in the naming of Crowheart Butte, which rises a
thousand feet above the surrounding landscape and is capped with
flat sandstone. To this day, there are tepee rings on Crowheart
Butte. One of the more arresting sights in remote parts of the West
are rings of stones that once resisted the wind and now recall what
blew away. The Crows liked the hunting country in the area of the
butte, and so did the Shoshonis. The two tribes fought, and lost a
lot of blood, over this ground. Eventually, the chief of the Shosho-

nis said, in effect, to the chief of the Crows: this is pointless; I will fight you, one against one; the hunting ground goes to the winner. The chief of the Shoshonis was the great Washakie, whose name rests in six places on the map of Wyoming, including a mountain range and a county. Washakie was at least fifty, but fit. The Crow would have been wise to demur. Washakie destroyed him in the hand-to-hand combat, then cut out his heart and ate it.

Despite her relative disadvantages as a newcomer, an outlander, and an educational ingénue, Miss Waxham was a quick study. Insight was her long suit, and in no time she understood Wyoming. For example, an entry in her journal says of George Ehler's father, "He came to the country with one mare. The first summer, she had six colts! She must have had calves, too, by the way the Ehlers' cattle increased." These remarks were dated October 22, 1905—the day after her stagecoach arrived. In months that followed, she sketched her neighbors (the word applied over many tens of miles). "By the door was Mrs. Frink, about 18, with Frink junior, a large husky baby. Ida Franklin, Mrs. Frink's sister and almost her double, was beside her, frivolous even in her silence." There was the story of Dirty Bill Collins, who had died as a result of taking a bath. And she fondly recorded Mrs. Mills' description of the libertine Guy Signor: "He has a cabbage heart with a leaf for every girl." She noted that the nearest barber had learned his trade shearing sheep, and a blacksmith doubled as dentist. Old Pelon, a French Canadian, impressed her, because he had refused to ask for money from the government after Indians killed his brother. "Him better dead," said Old Pelon. Old Pelon was fond of the masculine objective pronoun. Miss Waxham wrote, "Pelon used to have a wife, whom he spoke of always as 'him.'" Miss Waxham herself became a character in this tableau. People sometimes called her the White-Haired Kid.

"There's many a person I should be glad to meet," read an early entry in her journal. She wanted to meet Indian Dick, who had been raised by Indians and had no idea who he was—probably the orphan of emigrants the Indians killed. She wanted to meet "the woman called Sour Dough; Three Fingered Bill, or Suffering Jim; Sam Omera, Reub Roe. . . ." (Reub Roe held up wagons and stagecoaches looking for members of the Royal Family.) Meanwhile, there was one flockmaster and itinerant cowboy who seemed more than pleased to meet her.

In the first reference to him in her journal she calls him "Mr. Love—Johnny Love." His place was sixty miles away, and he had a good many sheep and cattle to look after, but somehow he managed to be right there when the new young schoolmarm arrived. In the days, weeks, and months that followed, he showed a pronounced tendency to reappear. He came, generally, in the dead of night, unexpected. Quietly he slipped into the corral, fed and watered his horse, slept in the bunkhouse, and was there at the table for breakfast in the morning—this dark-haired, blue-eyed, handsome man with a woolly Midlothian accent.

> *Mr. Love is a Scotchman about thirty-five years old. At first sight he made me think of a hired man, as he lounged stiffly on the couch, in overalls, his feet covered with enormous red and black striped stockings that reached to his knees, and were edged with blue around the top. He seemed to wear them instead of house shoes. His face was kindly, with shrewd blue twinkling eyes. A moustache grew over his mouth, like willows bending over a brook. But his voice was most peculiar and characteristic. . . . A little Scotch dialect, a little slow drawl, a little nasal quality, a bit of falsetto once in a while, and a tone as if he were speaking out of doors. There is a kind of twinkle in his voice as well as his eyes, and he is full of quaint turns of speech, and unusual expressions.*

Mr. Love travelled eleven hours on these journeys, each way. He did not suffer from the tedium, in part because he frequently rode in a little buggy and, after telling his horses his destination, would lie on the seat and sleep. He may have been from Edinburgh, but he had adapted to the range as much as anyone from anywhere. He had slept out, in one stretch, under no shelter for seven years. On horseback, he was fit for his best horses: he had stamina for long distances at sustained high speed. When he used a gun, he hit what he was shooting at. In 1897, he had begun homesteading on Muskrat Creek, quite near the geographical center of Wyoming, and he had since proved up. One way and another, he had acquired a number of thousands of acres, but acreage was not what mattered most in a country of dry and open range. Water rights mattered most, and the area over which John Love controlled the water amounted to a thousand square miles—about one per cent of Wyoming. He had come into the country walking, in 1891, and now, in 1905, he had many horses, a couple of hundred cattle, and several thousand sheep. Miss Waxham, in her journal, called him a "muttonaire."

He was a mirthful Scot—in abiding contrast to the more prevalent kind. He was a wicked mimic, a connoisseur of the absurd. If he seemed to know everyone in the high country, he knew even better the conditions it imposed. After one of her conversations with him, Miss Waxham wrote in her journal:

It is a cruel country as well as beautiful. Men seem here only on sufferance. After every severe storm we hear of people's being lost. Yesterday it was a sheep camp mover who was lost in the Red Desert. People had hunted for him for a week, and found no trace. Mr. Love—Johnny Love—told of a man who had just been lost up in his country, around the Muskrat. "Stranger?" asked Mr. Mills. "No; born and brought up here." "Old man?" "No; in the prime of life. Left Lost Cabin sober, too."

Mr. Love had been born near Portage, Wisconsin, on the farm of his uncle the environmentalist John Muir. The baby's mother died that day. His father, a Scottish physician who was also a professional photographer and lecturer on world travel, ended his travels and took his family home. The infant had three older sisters to look after him in Scotland. The doctor died when John was twelve. The sisters emigrated to Broken Bow, Nebraska, where in the eighteen-seventies and eighties they all proved up on homesteads. When John was in his middle teens, he joined them there, in time to experience the Blizzard of '88—a full week of blowing snow, with visibility so short that guide ropes led from house to barn.

He was expelled from the University of Nebraska for erecting a sign in a dean's flower bed, so he went to work as a cowboy, and soon began to think about moving farther west. When he had saved enough money, he bought matching black horses and a buggy, and set out for Wyoming. On his first night there, scarcely over the border, his horses drank from a poison spring and died. What he did next is probably the most encapsulating moment in his story. In Nebraska were three homes he could return to. He left the buggy beside the dead horses, abandoned almost every possession he had in the world, and walked on into Wyoming. He walked about two hundred miles. At Split Rock, on the Oregon Trail—near Crooks Gap, near Independence Rock—he signed on as a cowboy with the 71 Ranch. The year was 1891, and the State of Wyoming was ten months old.

Through the eighteen-nineties, there are various hiatuses in the résumé of John Love, but as cowboy and homesteader he very evidently prospered, and he also formed durable friendships—with Chief Washakie, for example, and with the stagecoach driver Peggy Dougherty, and with Robert LeRoy Parker and Harry Longabaugh (Butch Cassidy and the Sundance Kid). There came a day when Love could not contain his developed curiosity in the presence of the aging chief. He asked him what truth there was in the story of Crowheart Butte. Had Washakie really eaten his enemy's heart? The chief said, "Well, Johnny, when you're young and full of life you do strange things."

Robert LeRoy Parker was an occasional visitor at Love's homestead on Muskrat Creek, which was halfway between Hole-in-the-Wall and the Sweetwater River—that is, between Parker's hideout and his woman. Love's descendants sometimes stare bemusedly at a photograph discovered a few years ago in a cabin in Jackson Hole that had belonged to a member of the Wild Bunch. The photograph, made in the middle eighteen-nineties, shows eighteen men with Parker, who is wearing a dark business suit, a tie and a starchy white collar, a bowler hat. Two of the bunch are identified only by question marks. One of these is a jaunty man of middle height and strong frame, his hat at a rakish angle—a man with a kindly face, twinkling shrewd eyes, and a mustache growing over his mouth like willows bending over a brook. It may be doubtful whether John Love would have joined such a group, but when you are young and full of life you do strange things.

At Red Bluff Ranch, Mrs. Mills once twitted Mr. Love for being Scottish when other Scots were around and American in the presence of Americans. For a split second, Mr. Love thought this over before he said, "That leaves me eligible for the Presidency." Out of Mr. Love's buggy came a constant supply of delicacies and exotic gifts—including candy, nuts, apples—which he came by who knows where and liberally distributed to all. Miss Waxham began to look upon him as "a veritable Santa Claus"; and, predictably, at Christmastime Santa appeared.

> *And the next day was Christmas. . . . Just before supper the joyful cry went up that Mr. Love was coming, and actually in time for dinner. He had broken his record and arrived by day!*

A pitch pine had been set up indoors and its boughs painted with dissolved alum to simulate frost. Hanging from the branches were wooden balls covered with tobacco tinfoil. Flakes of mica were glued to paper stars. On Christmas, Mr. Mills and Mr. Love dressed in linen collars and what Miss Waxham called "fried shirts." When Miss Waxham turned to a package from home that she knew contained pajamas, she went into her bedroom to open it.

The following day, Miss Waxham was meant to go to something called Institute, in Lander—a convocation of Fremont County schoolteachers for lectures, instruction, and professional review. By phenomenal coincidence, Mr. Love announced that he had business in Lander, too.

> *It was decided that I should go with him. I rather dreaded it. . . . I confess I was somewhat afraid of him. . . . I was wrapped up in a coat of my own with Mrs. Mills' sealskin over it, muffler, fur hat, fur gloves, leggings, and overshoes. Then truly I was so bundled up that it was next to impossible to move. "Absolutely helpless," laughed Mr. Love.*

Whatever business Mr. Love had in Lander did not in any way seem to press him. Miss Waxham stayed with Miss Davis, the county superintendent, and while other people came and went from the premises Mr. Love was inclined to remain.

> *Supper time came and Mr. Love remained. We had a miserable canned goods cold supper. Miss MacBride left, Mr. Love remained.*

> *In the afternoon, Mr. Love called. It certainly was a surprise. I explained why Miss Davis was out, but he didn't seem to mind. I said that she would be back soon. He asked if I should not like to take a drive and see the suburbs. Of course I would. . . . We went for a long*

*drive in the reservation, with a box of chocolates between us, and a
merry gossip we had. . . . He was bemoaning the fact that there is no
place for a man to spend the evening in Lander except in a saloon.
"Come and toast marshmallows," I said, and he took it as a good
suggestion.*

When she went to church on Sunday, Love was there—John
Santa Love, who had not been to church in ten years. After the service, it was time to leave Lander.

*There had been snow falling since morning, and the road was barely
visible. The light faded to a soft whiteness that hardly grew darker
when the sun set and the pale outline of the moon showed through the
snow. Everywhere was the soft enveloping snow shutting out all
sounds and sights. The horses knew the way and travelled on steadily.
Fortunately it was not cold, and the multitudinous rugs and robes
with the new footwarmer beneath kept us warm and comfortable. More
pleasant it was travelling through the storm than sitting at home by
the fire and watching it outside. When the conversation ran low and
we travelled on quietly, Mr. Love discovered bags of candy under the
robes . . . and he fed us both, for I was worse than entangled in wraps
and the long sleeves of Mrs. Mills' sealskin. The miles fell away behind us easily and quietly.*

As the winter continued, with its apparently inexhaustible re-
sources of biting wind and blinding snow, temperatures now and
again approached fifty below zero. Miss Waxham developed such
an advanced case of cabin fever that she wrote in her journal, "My
spirit has a chair sore." Even when drifts were at their deepest,
though, Mr. Love somehow managed to get through. "Much
wrapped up" on one occasion, he rode "all the way from Alkali
Butte." On another, he spent an entire day advancing his education
at the Twin Creek school.

These attentions went on in much the same way for five years.
He pursued her to Colorado, and even to Wisconsin. They were
married on the twentieth of June, 1910, and drove in a sheep
wagon to his ranch, in the Wind River Basin. It was plain country
with gently swelling hills. Looking around from almost any one of
them, you could see eighty miles to the Wind River Range, thirty
to the Owl Creeks, twenty to the Rattlesnake Hills, fifteen to the

Beaver Divide, and a hundred into the Bighorns. No buildings were visible in any direction. In this place, they would flourish. Here, too, they would suffer calamitous loss. Here they would raise three children—a pair of sons close in age, and, a dozen years after them, a daughter. The county from time to time would supply a schoolmarm, but basically the children would be educated by their mother. One would become a petroleum chemist, another a design engineer for the New Jersey Turnpike and the New York State Thruway, another the preeminent geologist of the Rocky Mountains.

In the United States Geological Survey's seven-and-a-half-minute series of topographic maps is a quadrangle named Love Ranch. The landscape it depicts lies just under the forty-third parallel and west of the hundred-and-seventh meridian—coordinates that place it twelve miles from the geographic center of Wyoming. The names of its natural features are names that more or less materialized around the kitchen table when David Love was young: Corral Draw, Castle Gardens, Buffalo Wallows, Jumping-Off Draw. To the fact that he grew up there his vernacular, his outlook, his pragmatic skills, and his professional absorptions about equally attest. The term "store-bought" once brightened his eyes. When one or another of the cowpunchers used a revolver, the man did not so much fire a shot as "slam a bullet." If a ranch hand was tough enough, he would "ride anything with hair on it." Coffee had been brewed properly if it would "float a horseshoe." Blankets were "sougans." A tarpaulin was a "henskin." To be off in the distant ranges was to be "gouging around the mountains." In Love's stories of the ranch, horses come and go by the "cavvy." If they are unowned and untamed, they are a "wild bunch"—led to capture by a rider "riding point." In the flavor of his speech the word "ornery" endures.

He describes his father as a "rough, kindly, strong-willed man" who would put a small son on each knee and—reciting "Ride a cockhorse to Banbury Cross to see a fine lady upon a white horse"—give the children bronco rides after dinner, explaining that his purpose was "to settle their stomachs." Their mother's complaints went straight up the stovepipe and away with the wind. When their father was not reciting such Sassenach doggerel, he could draw Scottish poems out of the air like bolts of silk. He had the right voice, the Midlothian timbre. He knew every syllable of "The Lady of the Lake." Putting his arms around the shoulders of his wee lads, he would roll it to them by the canto, and when they tired of Scott there were in his memory more than enough ballads to sketch the whole of Scotland, from the Caithness headlands to the Lammermuir Hills.

David was fifteen months younger than his brother, Allan. Their sister, Phoebe, was born so many years later that she does not figure in most of these scenes. They were the only children in a thousand square miles, where children outnumbered the indigenous trees. From the ranch buildings, by Muskrat Creek, the Wind River Basin reached out in buffalo grass, grama grass, and edible salt sage across the cambered erosional swells of the vast dry range. When the wind dropped, this whole wide world was silent, and they could hear from a great distance the squeak of a horned lark. The nearest neighbor was thirteen miles away. On the clearest night, they saw no light but their own.

Old buffalo trails followed the creek and branched from the creek: old but not ancient—there were buffalo skulls beside them, and some were attached to hide. The boys used the buffalo trails when they rode off on ranch chores for their father. They rode young and rode long, and often went without water. Even now, six decades later, David will pass up a cool spring, saying, "If I drink now, I'll be thirsty all day."

Even in October, a blizzard could cover the house and make a tunnel of the front veranda. As winter progressed, rime grew on the nailheads of interior walls until white spikes projected some inches into the rooms. There were eleven rooms. His mother could tell the outside temperature by the movement of the frost. It climbed the nails about an inch for each degree below zero. Sometimes there was frost on nailheads fifty-five inches up the walls. The house was clinked with slaked lime, wood shavings, and cow manure. In the wild wind, snow came through the slightest crack, and the nickel disks on the dampers of the heat stove were constantly jingling. There came a sound of hooves in cold dry snow, of heavy bodies slamming against the walls, seeking heat. John Love insulated his boots with newspapers—as like as not *The New York*

Times. To warm the boys in their beds on cold nights, their mother wrapped heated flatirons in copies of *The New York Times.* The family were subscribers, Sundays only. The *Times,* David Love recalls, was "precious." They used it to insulate the house: pasted it against the walls beside *The Des Moines Register, The Tacoma News Tribune*—any paper from anywhere, without fine distinction. With the same indiscriminate voracity, any paper from anywhere was first read and reread by every literate eye in every cow camp and sheep camp within tens of miles, read to shreds and passed along, in tattered circulation on the range. There was, as Love expresses it, "a starvation of print." Almost anybody's first question on encountering a neighbor was "Have you got any newspapers?"

The ranch steadings were more than a dozen buildings facing south, and most of them were secondhand. When a stage route that ran through the ranch was abandoned, in 1905, John Love went down the line shopping for moribund towns. He bought Old Muskrat—including the hotel, the post office, Joe Lacey's Muskrat Saloon—and moved the whole of it eighteen miles. He bought Golden Lake and moved it thirty-three. He arranged the buildings in a rough semicircle that embraced a corral so large and solidly constructed that other ranchers travelled long distances to use it. Joe Lacey's place became the hay house, the hotel became in part a saddlery and cookhouse, and the other buildings, many of them connected, became all or parts of the blacksmith shop, the chicken hatchery, the ice shed, the buggy shed, the sod cellar, and the bunkhouse—social center for all the workingmen from a great many miles around. There was a granary made of gigantic cottonwood logs from the banks of the Wind River, thirty miles away. There were wool-sack towers, and a wooden windmill over a hand-dug well. The big house itself was a widespread log collage of old town parts and original construction. It had wings attached to wings. In the windows were air bubbles in distorted glass. For its twenty tiers of logs, John had journeyed a hundred miles to the lodgepole-pine groves of the Wind River Range, returning with ten logs at a time, each round trip requiring two weeks. He collected a hundred and fifty logs. There were no toilets, of course, and the family had to walk a hundred feet on a sometimes gumbo-slick path to a four-hole structure built by a ranch hand, with decorative panelling that matched the bookcases in the house. The cabinetmaker was Peggy Dougherty, the stagecoach driver who had first brought Miss Waxham through Crooks Gap and into the Wind River country.

The family grew weary of carrying water into the house from the well under the windmill. And so, as she would write in later years:

> After experiments using an earth auger and sand point, John triumphantly installed a pitcher pump in the kitchen, a sink, and drain pipe to a barrel, buried in the ground at some distance from the house. This was the best, the first, and at that time the only water system in an area the size of Rhode Island.

In the evenings, kerosene lamps threw subdued yellow light. Framed needlework on a wall said "WASH & BE CLEAN." Everyone bathed in the portable galvanized tub, children last. The more expensive galvanized tubs of that era had built-in seats, but the Loves could not afford the top of the line. On the plank floor were horsehide rugs—a gray, a pinto—and the pelt of a large wolf, and two soft bobcat rugs. Chairs were woven with rawhide or cane.

The family's main sitting and dining room was a restaurant from Old Muskrat. The central piece of furniture was a gambling table from Joe Lacey's Muskrat Saloon. It was a poker-and-roulette table—round, covered with felt. Still intact were the subtle flanges that had caused the roulette wheel to stop just where the operator wished it to. And if you reached in under the table in the right place you could feel the brass slots where the dealer kept wild cards that he could call upon when the fiscal integrity of the house was threatened. If you put your nose down on the felt, you could almost smell the gunsmoke. At this table David Love received his basic education—his schoolroom a restaurant, his desk a gaming table from a saloon. His mother may have been trying to academize the table when she covered it with a red-and-white India print.

From time to time, other schoolmarms were provided by the district. They came for three months in summer. One came for the better part of a year. By and large, though, the boys were taught by their mother. She had a rolltop desk, and Peggy Dougherty's glassed-in bookcases. She had the 1911 Encyclopædia Britannica, the Redpath Library, a hundred volumes of Greek and Roman literature, Shakespeare, Dickens, Emerson, Thoreau, Longfellow, Kipling, Twain. She taught her sons French, Latin, and a bit of

Greek. She read to them from books in German, translating as she went along. They read the Iliad and the Odyssey. The room was at the west end of the ranch house and was brightly illuminated by the setting sun. When David as a child saw sunbeams leaping off the books, he thought the contents were escaping.

In some ways, there was more chaos in this remote academic setting than there could ever be in a grade school in the heart of a city.

> The house might be full of men, waiting out a storm, or riding on a round-up. I was baking, canning, washing clothes, making soap. Allan and David stood by the gasoline washing machine reading history or geography while I put sheets through the wringer. I ironed. They did spelling beside the ironing board, or while I kneaded bread; they gave the tables up to 15 times 15 to the treadle of the sewing machine. Mental problems, printed in figures on large cards, they solved while they raced across the . . . room to write the answers . . . and learned to think on their feet. Nine written problems done correctly, without help, meant no tenth problem. . . . It was surprising in how little time they finished their work—to watch the butchering, to help drive the bawling calves into the weaning pen, or to get to the corral, when they heard the hoofbeats of running horses and the cries of cowboys crossing the creek.

No amount of intellectual curiosity or academic discipline was ever going to hold a boy's attention if someone came in saying that the milk cow was mired in a big hole or that old George was out by the wild-horse corral with the biggest coyote ever killed in the region, or if the door opened and, as David recalls an all too typical event, "they were carrying in a cowboy with guts ripped out by a saddle horn." The lessons stopped, the treadle stopped, and she sewed up the cowboy.

Across a short span of time, she had come a long way with these bunkhouse buckaroos. In her early years on the ranch, she had a lesser sense of fitting in than she would have had had she been a mare, a cow, or a ewe. She did not see another woman for as much as six months at a stretch, and if she happened to approach a group of working ranch hands they would loudly call out, "Church time!" She found "the sudden silence . . . appalling." Women were so rare in the country that when she lost a glove on the open range, at least twenty miles from home, a stranger who found it learned easily whose it must be and rode to the ranch to return it. Men did the housekeeping and the cooking, and went off to buy provisions at distant markets. Meals prepared in the bunkhouse were carried to a sheep wagon, where she and John lived while the big house was being built and otherwise assembled. The Wyoming sheep wagon was the ancestral Winnebago. It had a spring bed and a kitchenette.

After her two sons were born and became old enough to coin phrases, they called her Dainty Dish and sometimes Hooty the Owl. They renamed their food, calling it, for example, dog. They called other entrées caterpillar and coyote. The kitchen stool was Sam. They named a Christmas-tree ornament Hopping John. It had a talent for remaining unbroken. They assured each other that the cotton on the branches would not melt. David decided that he was a camel, but later changed his mind and insisted that he was "Mr. and Mrs. Booth." His mother noted his developing sense of scale when he said to her, "A coyote is the whole world to a flea."

One day, he asked her, "How long does a germ live?"

She answered, "A germ may become a grandfather in twenty minutes."

He said, "That's a long time to a germ, isn't it?"

She also made note that while David was the youngest person on the ranch he was nonetheless the most adroit at spotting arrowheads and chippings.

When David was five or six we began hunting arrowheads and chippings. While the rest of us labored along scanning gulches and anthills, David rushed by chattering and picking up arrowheads right and left. He told me once, "There's a god of chippings that sends us anthills. He lives in the sky and tinkers with the clouds."

When in a sense it was truly church time—when cowboys were badly injured and in need of help—they had long since learned where to go. David vividly remembers a moment in his education which was truncated when a cowboy rode up holding a bleeding hand. He had been roping a wild horse, and one of his fingers had become caught between the lariat and the saddle horn. The finger was still a part of his hand but was hanging by two tendons. His mother boiled water, sterilized a pair of surgical scissors, and scrubbed her hands and arms. With magisterial nonchalance, she "snipped the tendons, dropped the finger into the hot coals of the fire box, sewed a flap of skin over the stump, smiled sweetly, and said: 'Joe, in a month you'll never know the difference.'"

There was a pack of ferocious wolfhounds in the country, kept by another flockmaster for the purpose of killing coyotes. The dogs seemed to relish killing rattlesnakes as well, shaking the life out of them until the festive serpents hung from the hounds' jaws like fettuccine. The ranch hand in charge of them said, "They ain't happy in the spring till they've been bit. They're used to it now, and their heads don't swell up no more." Human beings (on foot) who happened to encounter these dogs might have preferred to encounter the rattlesnakes instead. One summer afternoon, John Love was working on a woodpile when he saw two of the wolfhounds streaking down the creek in the direction of his sons, whose ages were maybe three and four. "Laddies! Run! Run to the house!" he shouted. "Here come the hounds!" The boys ran, reached the door just ahead of the dogs, and slammed it in their faces. Their mother was in the kitchen:

> The hounds, not to be thwarted so easily, leaped together furiously at the kitchen windows, high above the ground. They shattered the glass of the small panes, and tried to struggle through, their front feet catching over the inside ledge of the window frame, and their heads, with slavering mouths, reaching through the broken glass. I had only time to snatch a heavy iron frying pan from the stove and face them, beating at those clutching feet and snarling heads. The terrified boys cowered behind me. The window sashes held against the onslaught of the hounds, and my blows must have daunted them. They dropped back to the ground and raced away.

The milieu of Love Ranch was not all wind, snow, freezing cattle, and killer dogs. There were quiet, lyrical days on end under blue, unthreatening skies. There were the redwing blackbirds on the corral fence, and the scent of moss flowers in spring. In a light breeze, the windmill turned slowly beside the wide log house, which was edged with flowers in bloom. Sometimes there were teal on the creek—and goldeneyes, pintails, mallards. When the wild hay was ready for cutting, the harvest lasted a week.

John liked to have me ride with them for the last load. Sometimes I held the reins and called "Whoa, Dan!" while the men pitched up the hay. Then while the wagon swayed slowly back over the uneven road, I lay nestled deeply beside Allan and David in the fragrant hay. The billowy white clouds moving across the wide blue sky were close, so close, it seemed there was nothing else in the universe but clouds and hay.

One fall, their mother went to Riverton, sixty-five miles away, to await the birth of Phoebe. For her sons, eleven and twelve, she left behind a carefully prepared program of study. In the weeks that followed, they were in effect enrolled in a correspondence school run by their mother. They did their French, their spelling, their arithmetic lessons, put them in envelopes, rode fifteen miles to the post office and mailed them to her. She graded the lessons and sent them back—before and after the birth of the baby.

Her hair was the color of my wedding ring. On her cheek the fingers of one hand were outspread like a small, pink starfish.

From time to time, dust would appear on the horizon, behind a figure coming toward the ranch. The boys, in their curiosity, would climb a rooftop to watch and wait as the rider covered the intervening miles. Almost everyone who went through the region stopped at Love Ranch. It had not only the sizable bunkhouse and the most capacious horse corrals in a thousand square miles but also a spring of good water.

Fugitive criminals stopped at the ranch fairly often. They had to—in much the way that fugitive criminals in lonely country today will sooner or later have to stop at a filling station. A lone rider arrived at the ranch one day with a big cloud of dust on the horizon behind him. The dust might as well have formed in the air the letters of the word "posse." John Love knew the rider, knew that he was wanted for murder, and knew that throughout the country the consensus was that the victim had "needed killing." The murderer asked John Love to give him five dollars, and said he would leave his pocket watch as collateral. If his offer was refused, the man said, he would find a way to take the money. The watch was as honest as the day is long. When David does his field geology, he has it in his pocket.

People like that came along with such frequency that David's mother eventually assembled a chronicle called "Murderers I Have Known." She did not publish the manuscript, or even give it much private circulation, in her regard for the sensitivities of some of the first families of Wyoming. As David would one day comment, "they were nice men, family friends, who had put away people who needed killing, and she did not wish to offend them—so many of them were such decent people."

One of these was Bill Grace. Homesteader and cowboy, he was one of the most celebrated murderers in central Wyoming, and he had served time, but people generally disagreed with the judiciary and felt that Bill, in the acts for which he was convicted, had only been "doing his civic duty." At the height of his fame, he stopped at the ranch one afternoon and stayed for dinner. Although David and Allan were young boys, they knew exactly who he was, and in his presence were struck dumb with awe. As it happened, they had come upon and dispatched a rattlesnake that day—a big one, over five feet long. Their mother decided to serve it creamed on toast for dinner. She and their father sternly instructed David and Allan not to use the word "rattlesnake" at the table. They were to refer to it as chicken, since a possibility existed that Bill Grace might not be an eater of adequate sophistication to enjoy the truth. The excitement was too much for the boys. Despite the parental injunction, gradually their conversation at the table fished its way toward the snake. Casually—while the meal was going down—the boys raised the subject of poisonous vipers, gave their estimates of the contents of local dens, told stories of snake encounters, and so forth. Finally, one of them remarked on how very good rattlers were to eat.

Bill Grace said, "By God, if anybody ever gave me rattlesnake meat I'd kill them."

The boys went into a state of catatonic paralysis. In the pure silence, their mother said, "More chicken, Bill?"

"Don't mind if I do," said Bill Grace.

Some years earlier, in the winter of 1912, winds with velocities up to a hundred miles an hour caused sheep to seek haven in dry gulches, where snows soon buried them as if in avalanche. Going without sleep for forty and fifty hours, John Love and his ranch hands struggled to rescue them. They dug some out, but many thousands died. Even on the milder days, when the temperature came up near zero, sheep could not penetrate the wind-crusted drifts and get at the grass below. The crust cut into their legs. Their tracks were reddened with blood. Cattle, lacking the brains even to imagine buried grass, ate their own value in cottonseed cake. John Love had to borrow from his bankers in Lander to pay his ranch hands and buy supplies.

That spring, a flood such as no one remembered all but destroyed the ranch.

Almost immediately, the bankers arrived from Lander. They stayed for several amiable days, looked over the herd tallies, counted surviving animals, checked John Love's accounts. Then, at dinner one evening, the bank's vice-president rubbed his hands together and said to his valued customer, his trusted borrower, his first-name-basis longtime friend, "Mr. Love, we need more collateral." The banker also said that while John Love was a reliable debtor, other ranchers were not, and others' losses were even greater than Love's. The bank, to protect its depositors, had to use Love Ranch to cover itself generally. "We are obliged to cash in on your sheep," the man went on. "We will let you keep your cattle—on one condition." The condition was a mortgage on the ranch. They were asking for an interest in the land of a homesteader who had proved up.

John Love shouted, "I'll have that land when your bones are rotting in the grave!" And he asked the man to step outside, where he could curse him. To the banker's credit, he got up and went out to be cursed. Buyers came over the hill as if on cue. All surviving sheep were taken, all surviving cattle, all horses—even dogs. The sheep wagons went, and a large amount of equipment and supplies. John Love paid the men in the bunkhouse, and they left. As his wife watched the finish of this scene, standing silent with Allan in her arms, the banker turned to her kindly and said, "What will you do with the baby?"

She said, "I think I'll keep him."

It was into this situation that John David Love was born—a family that had lost almost everything but itself, yet was not about to lose that. Slowly, his father assembled more modest cavvies and herds, beginning with the capture of wild horses in flat-out all-day rides, maneuvering them in ever tighter circles until they were be-

guiled into entering the wild-horse corral or—a few miles away—
the natural cul-de-sac (a small box canyon) known to the family as
the Corral Draw. Watching one day from the granary roof, the
boys—four and five—in one moment saw their father on horseback crossing the terrain like the shadow of a cloud and in the next
saw his body smash the ground. The horse had stepped in a badger
hole. The rider—limp and full of greasewood punctures, covered
with blood and grit—was unconscious and appeared to be dead.
He was carried into the house. After some hours, he began to stir,
and through his pain mumbled, "That damned horse. That
damned horse—I never did trust him." It was the only time in
their lives that his sons would hear him swear.

There were periods of drought, and more floods, and long,
killing winters, but John Love never sold out. He contracted and
survived Rocky Mountain spotted fever. One year, after he
shipped cattle to Omaha he got back a bill for twenty-seven dollars, the amount by which the cost of shipment exceeded the sale
price of the cattle. One spring, after a winter that killed many
sheep, the boys and their father plucked good wool off the bloated
and stinking corpses, sold the wool, and deposited the money in a
bank in Shoshoni, where the words "STRENGTH," SAFETY," and
"SECURITY" made an arc above the door. The bank failed, and
they lost the money. Of many bad winters, the worst began in
1919. Both David and his family nearly died of Spanish influenza,
and were slow to recuperate, spending months in bed. There were
no ranch hands. At the point when the patients seemed most in
danger, his mother in her desperation decided to try to have them
moved to a hospital (a hundred miles away), and prepared to ride
for help. She had the Hobson's choice of a large, rebellious horse.
She stood on a bench and tried to harness him. He kicked the
bench from under her, and stepped on her feet. She gave up her
plan.

> *The bull broke into the high granary. Our only, and small, supply of*
> *horse and chicken feed was there. Foolishly, I went in after him and*
> *drove him out down the step. Cows began to die, one here, one there.*
> *Every morning some were unable to rise. By day, one walking would*
> *fall suddenly, as if it had no more life than a paper animal, blown*
> *over by a gust of wind.*

The bull actually charged her in the granary and came close to crushing her against the back wall. She confused it, sweeping its eyes with a broom. It would probably have killed her, though, had it not stepped on a weak plank, which snapped. The animal panicked and turned for the door. (In decades to follow, John Love never fixed the plank.)

Snow hissed around the buildings, wind blew some snow into every room of the closed house, down the chimney, between window sashes, even in a straight shaft through a keyhole. The wood pile was buried in snow. The small heap of coal was frozen into an almost solid chunk of coal and ice. In the numbing cold, it took me five hours a day to bring in fuel, to carry water and feed to the chickens, to put out hay and cottonseed cake for the cattle and horses.

John began to complain, a favorable sign. Why was I outside so much? Why didn't I stay with him? To try to make up to him for being gone so long, I sat on the bed at night, wrapped in a blanket, reading to him by lamplight.

Somewhere among her possessions was a letter written to her by a Wellesley friend asking, "What do you do with your spare time?"

B. J. NELSON

In "Mother's Last Request" novelist Billy Jack Nelson
tantalizes the reader while toying with the awesome request that his mother, Marie, has made of him, which
is to kill her. From that point on, the narrative is riveting, though quite uncomfortable. On the one hand,
Nelson does not want to break the law or kill a human
being, for any reason. On the other hand, Marie is bed-
bound, dying, and self-destructive. (Nelson actually
doesn't like this mother, although he says his feelings for
her are "fairly reconciled.") As Nelson plans, speculates,
imagines, and actually performs the "gruesome" act,
the reader is captivated, waiting in limbo to discover
exactly what he will do—although there is clearly no
question about his intentions—and how he will feel
afterward.

MOTHER'S LAST REQUEST

Marie wanted to die. She'd been wanting to for most of her life, I think, and wasn't it time? She was asking me. She'd been thinking about how to kill herself for months, years, especially the last few weeks. Now she knew how she would do it and was simply focusing on when. She was eighty and a couple of her teeth had recently fallen out, her stomach was swollen, food made her sick; she was in pain all over, the worst pain she'd ever had, she said, though every pain throughout her whole life was always the worst. Over the years, the hundreds of times she was sick, each time she was "deathly sick." Each pain for decades had been "the most horrible pain" she'd ever felt. You never knew. She'd turn the least matter into melodrama, managing her life neurotically, even from the beginning, I've come to believe, by pretending, by living in a world of pretense.

Anyway, she might as well just go on and get it over with, didn't I think so, too? I told her that such a thing had to be up to her, no one else. But didn't I think she might as well? What did she have to live for? She had terrible noise in her ears and couldn't hear, she'd disconnected her phone, no one called anyway, she had no friends. She had lived for fifteen years as an almost total recluse, and other than a sister she hated and another son she hadn't heard from in thirty years, there was only me. She couldn't see her soap operas except as a blur, she was shaky, trembly, she got out of breath walking from her room to the front of the house, so before being too helpless, while she could still manage, wasn't it time?

She hadn't bathed or showered in a couple of years, I think: she couldn't lift her legs enough to step in and out of the tub. She sponged off, she said. But she was still able to go to the toilet on her own, she was still feeding herself, though lately only oatmeal, buttered bread, and a little yogurt; anything else made her vomit. She was weak and getting weaker.

"No, I'm not going to the doctor," she told me. "I know what he'd do, he'd put me in the hospital and I'd be kept alive for no reason or left in a nursing home, and I don't want that. I want to lay down right here in my own bed and go to sleep and not wake up. You don't know how many times I've prayed I wouldn't wake up. Every night I go to sleep praying, dear God, please, just let me die and not wake up. So I'm going to do it. But I can't by myself. You'll have to help me."

This was Wednesday noon. She was going to take pills. Years before, she'd saved a stash of pills for the purpose, but when she couldn't afford new medicine one year, she'd used the stash instead. Recently, though, she'd gotten a prescription for one hundred Xanax, a sedative. I called in the order for her and picked up the pills from the drugstore an hour later, a regular brownish cylinder with a white cap. Marie said she was going to take them that night at about eleven or eleven-thirty, her usual bedtime, when it was quiet and peaceful. I didn't know whether she really would. She had talked suicide too often. But the pills would put her right to sleep, then all I'd have to do was slip a bag over her head and wrap it airtight around her neck with a scarf. Not rubber bands. They might leave telltale lines. She showed me the small plastic trash bag and the blue silky scarf. She'd already tried the bag on to be sure it wasn't too big. She said it wasn't. A large bag would retain too much air and take longer. She'd read that in a book from the Hemlock Society. She gave me the bag and scarf.

"Now, you just go on about your business," she said. "Tonight when I'm ready I'll call you."

I went to my room and tried to think. If this was for real, if this time she was actually going to do it, was there anything I needed to consider? Feelings, emotions? No. My feelings for Marie were fairly reconciled. I came into this world out of her body, or the physical me did, so there was that kind of blood bond, but I didn't like her as a person. I was ashamed of her as a mother. I wouldn't miss her.

In a kind of gruesome test, I slipped the bag over my head for size and found that it barely covered my neck. I could see the scarf not quite grasping enough of it to completely cut off the air and the final act getting messy. Marie would struggle, even zonked on Xanax, and she would be clawing the thing to get free, to breathe. The Hemlock Society book said that this was common. I could see myself trying to hold her hands down or, frozen, just standing there, watching. If she scratched herself or I somehow bruised her, that might look bad to a coroner. It might look like murder. And to some degree it would be. The word hung in my mind. Murder. A vague image, the word itself had no resonance. But helping to end someone's life, no matter how sick and sad and miserable, is helping to kill a human being. And in this instance, if it came about, I would be helping to kill my own mother. Could I do it? More precisely, at the last moment would I?

I drove to town and got a box of slightly larger plastic bags. If it was going to be done, the bag should be the right size, not too small. The last act should go smoothly, not with a struggle, not with my hands fighting hers, the meanness of that. I stopped at a liquor store and got a bottle of vodka. Might need something to fuzz the edges afterward. It would be my first drink in months.

It was now about three in the afternoon. I tapped at her door and went in, a rare visit. I'd been in her room perhaps three times in two years. She was sitting in her chair watching her daily soap operas. For the past two and a half years I'd provided this place for her in my house, a room perhaps twenty by twenty feet, also a sort of efficiency setup with cooking facilities, a refrigerator, and an adjoining bath. In this one room she stayed alone and kept to herself. She never left the house. She'd leave a list of the groceries and medicine she needed along with a signed check on the kitchen table, and I would shop for her. Her Social Security was just enough to pay for what she wanted. She'd show me her bank statement at the end of every month with only five or ten dollars left in her account. When we talked, it was usually when she was in the kitchen and I also happened to be there. But it wouldn't be a conversation. She might ask my opinion on the weather or some TV news item. Typically she'd say, "Do you think it's going to rain today?" I'd start to answer, "Well, no, I think—" and she'd immediately interrupt to disagree:

"That's what the weatherman says but they don't know. They

said it was going to rain yesterday, there wasn't a cloud in the sky. I don't think they have any idea what the weather's going to be. I was going to make a salad but I don't want to, I just don't have the interest. Nothing I fix tastes good anyway. I made a stew yesterday, it was like slop, I had to throw it all out. The arthritis in my hand is so bad, I took four of those pain pills, they didn't help a bit, I don't know what I'm going to do. I was going to make some macaroni and cheese but I don't even want that now. Those ratty kids next door were playing so loud, hollering and carrying on, I couldn't hear myself think. I wish that family'd move away, they're nothing but white trash. I saw the woman out in her yard yesterday wearing shorts, with big ol' fat legs, I'd be ashamed . . ."

She would talk like that forever if I listened. For about a minute I'd pretend to, then I'd simply walk away. If she began with a good word, her next word would qualify it and she'd end up carping. She didn't like herself or, worse, she hated herself, and the way it showed was depressing.

Now I stood in her room. "How 'bout a visit?" I said. She got up from her chair.

"Here, sit down."

"That's all right," I said; she only had the one chair.

"No, no, you sit here, I need to move anyway." She sat on the edge of her bed and I sat in the chair facing her. The room was dirty and cluttered. I'd offered to vacuum her carpet, but she said the noise drove her crazy and she didn't want me moving things around in there. I told her she didn't have to hear the noise, she could wait in the living room, but she said it was too bothersome. "Just leave it. I'll do it," she said. And never did. The carpet was spotted and matted where she'd spilled food.

"Well," I said, and that was all.

"It's going to be all right," she said. "Don't you worry."

She was decided. It was time. She was sick and it was probably a consumptive heart condition, that's what her father died of, and with that you don't get better, you just get worse. She'd read up on the symptoms in her medical book—it starts with a shortness of breath and your stomach, you can't keep food down. That's what was happening to her. Then it affected your kidneys and liver, they turned to mush, and you became bedridden and couldn't go to the bathroom or feed yourself—you couldn't eat anything anyway—and you'd just lie there in agony and finally die. So she was ready.

"Now, one thing I want you to do," she said, "I don't want you to tell my sister, or at least wait till you've gotten rid of all my stuff, 'cause she'll just be over here in a minute picking through all my clothes and taking everything, and I don't want her to have anything. Promise you won't tell her. Or I don't care, do what you want, but I'm telling you, I know how she'll do, you don't know how selfish she is."

And so on about how her sister had always taken and not given and had plenty of money and could afford to buy a new car every year and everything else she wanted. No forgiveness. About my brother and me, she said that she wished she'd made a home for us, that she knew she'd messed up, especially Billy, she knew he'd been the most hurt, but that it was too late now, she couldn't go back and change what happened, and she'd already cried herself out; she hadn't cried tears now in years. She'd made a mess of her own life too, but she couldn't change that either.

I'd heard it all before, the regrets, the bad times. I kept hoping she would finally declare some peace of mind or settled spirit. She didn't. I tried to remember some good moments we'd had together, some things I could mention so we could end with easier feelings. I couldn't think of one. She probably loved me the best she could, but if there was a time when I was small that she hugged me, that I felt the warmth of a mother's embrace, I couldn't remember that either. So I sat while she talked. She had lived a lifetime. But at the end of a life, after eighty years of awareness, hopes, desires, after only one chance at this world as we know it, shouldn't there be a final comprehension, a summing up, a point at least for having been? You live, for what? I wanted her to say what living had meant to her, but she was talking incidentals: her extra glasses, they were good prescription glasses someone could use, don't throw those away.

She had put a clean cover on the bed and she was going to dress in a nice clean gown. Should she wash her hair? No, she didn't need to. I could donate her clothes to charity or just burn them, but don't let her sister have any. She had already thrown away a bunch of junk and straightened the room all she could. Straightening tired her out. She said to tell Billy she was sorry but that she couldn't go back and make things different, and me, well, I could handle this, couldn't I? I told her truthfully that I didn't know. But she knew, she said, because I was always able to handle whatever came along, I never let problems bother me, did I? Well, problems are problems, I said. But she knew that I could help her die, that I wouldn't let it bother me. She was sorry she didn't stick with my father, but she just couldn't. She wanted to have fun, and then her life became such a mess. She never intended to leave us kids. She married other men so she could have a home for us, but it never turned out, she never got what she wanted, which was just to be happy and for us kids to be happy, but she couldn't help any of that now, she couldn't go back. She was just sorry about this and that and so on. She spoke, as usual, remorsefully, self-pityingly, but not exactly bitterly. It was as if she recited it all by rote: things happened, she could have done differently, but it wasn't always her fault either, and then it was always too late. After the fact, it was always too late. She voiced no new insight, no particular understanding. I felt depressed, and after about an hour I got up. I'd be back later, I said, and we could talk more then. Well, don't worry about me, she said, I'll call you when I'm ready, about eleven o'clock.

I went to my room and tried to read. It was five o'clock and I began to feel it was going to be a long night. She wouldn't do it, or she would fake it. She was involving me in another one of her emotional dramas. I might have to call the EMS. She was only going to become more disoriented, more helpless. I should probably start thinking about placing her in a nursing home.

At six-thirty she was at my door.

"I can't think about it anymore," she said, "I want to just go on and do it, is that all right with you?"

"If you're ready."

"Well, I'm ready, I keep sitting back there thinking about it. Now, you've got the bag? And the scarf—don't forget the scarf."

"They're right here."

"All right, let's get it over with."

We walked through the kitchen. She was hobbling feebly. I asked her if she'd eaten.

"Not since this morning. I'm afraid I'll throw up."

"But shouldn't you have something on your stomach, to keep the pills down? How about a little buttered toast?"

"I don't know, not buttered, maybe just a piece of dry toast."

I put a slice of bread in the toaster and followed her into her room. She sat on the edge of the bed.

"Now, here's what I'm going to take," she said. A couple of pill bottles stood on her bedside table.

"This one's fifty Wygesic, they're my pain pills, they might help. These are Xanax, the ones you got today, and I had some more. There's a hundred and thirty-eight altogether. That ought to do it if I don't get too drowsy and fall asleep before I can take them all."

"You're going to take a hundred and thirty-eight pills?"

"If I can get them down. And the Wygesic too, if I can swallow enough water. I've got a pitcherful over there, you'll have to get that for me."

She was opening the pill bottles. I felt numb.

"Wait a minute." I brought the toast from the kitchen on a napkin. "Get this on your stomach first."

She forced herself to chew several bites slowly, sipping also at a glass of water. She ate about half the toast, then immediately poured a few pills into her hand and swallowed them with water. She took another handful and another, one after the other as if on automatic. She was concentrating solely on what she was doing and not looking beyond her hands. Then her glass was empty.

"More water, more water!" Almost panicky. I got the pitcher and filled her glass.

"Hey, go slower," I said. "Take your time."

"I don't want to fall asleep before I get them down."

"It's okay, okay? Take it easy."

She drew a breath and downed several more pills. She took off her glasses and laid them on the table.

"Don't throw those away, they're good prescriptions, somebody can use them."

She swallowed more pills. I was only sitting in front of her, watching. A terrible feeling came over me, a weight of darkness. Here was this old, lonely woman actually going to die, killing herself. This was the last moment she would ever know, a worthless, measly last moment in a dismal, cluttered room in central Texas. She would never again see the two squirrels in the tree outside her window. Or the sky, the sun, the rain. This earth, this great, beautiful earth around her would be no more. She was going to die and nothing would be all. I had no words for what I felt except pity. Poor old woman.

"Marie," I said, "let me hug you."

I stood and leaned down to put my arms around her shoulders, my cheek against hers. I think she sort of patted my arm.

"I love you," I said.

"I love you, too."

I sat back in the chair. It was the first time I'd hugged her in years, and even in those years a quick hug was a mere politeness. This time was almost the same. It had not been exactly awkward but neither had it felt natural. My words, I love you, had been what, perfunctory? Hers to me had sounded the same. There had been no clutch of emotion. She immediately went back to taking her pills, hurriedly, several at a time, one swallow after another, downing them with water. I filled her glass three times. She never looked up. We didn't speak.

Then she did. "Well, that's it."

She had swallowed 138 Xanax and 20 or so Wygesic. She started to lie back on her pillow and stopped.

"Turn your back. I'm going to put a towel between my legs. The book said people lose their bowels when they're going, and I don't want to make a mess."

I turned my head. When I looked again, she was lying on her back, the end of a towel showed between her knees. She had folded her hands on her stomach.

"Now I'm going to count," she said. "That's what I do to put myself to sleep. I read that once and it works. I start at a hundred and count backwards. I never get to one. I can get to twenty, fifteen sometimes, then I'm always asleep."

She closed her eyes and started counting in a normal voice, "Ninety-nine . . . ninety-eight . . . ninety-seven . . ."

She counted as if by seconds, steadily, correctly. By eighty-five, her count had slowed, and she was several seconds between numbers. After eighty, she said seventy-eight, paused at length, picked up the slipped seventy-nine, and continued with seventy-eight, but more slowly. Her words were slurring. At sixty-six, I thought she was asleep. She'd stopped counting. Finally she managed to repeat sixty-six and that was it. She was breathing deeply and snoring intermittently with her mouth slightly open.

. . .

It was seven o'clock and beginning to get dark outside. I closed the curtains. I felt inept not to have closed them earlier. Then I didn't know how long to wait or if I should wait at all. I watched Marie breathing. If I touched her or shook her, would it rouse her? The Xanax might not have worked. She might suddenly wake. How long would it take before she was so absolutely doped there would be no chance of waking her? I imagined the moment I started to put the bag over her head, she would open her eyes. I waited perhaps fifteen minutes, then went to my room for the bag and scarf and came back. She had not moved. Her mouth was still slightly open, and she was breathing the same, softly snoring, her hands at rest on her stomach. I lifted one of them and it fell back. I nudged her shoulder. No reaction. I called her name, then louder, and shook her. No response. I walked through the house to shut the blinds and lock the doors. I took the phone off the receiver. If anyone knocked or called, I wouldn't be home. Did I need to think of anything else? I couldn't think.

The bag was not a difficulty. I lifted her head from the pillow and slipped the plastic over easily, in a single movement. I did it as gently as I could and felt no weight in her head at all. Her neck was limber, entirely relaxed. Lifting her head again, I overlapped the loose ends of the bag and wrapped the scarf evenly twice around. But not tightly. I felt an odd tenderness and sadness. Poor Marie, I thought, your whole life so damned unhappy. I felt sorry for her. I snugged at the scarf to be sure it was trapping the air.

I stood over her and watched the bag filling and being drawn back against the outlines of her face, and for a time there was nothing else. Her breathing appeared easy, but soon it was slightly harder and the bag was being sucked tighter at her mouth. Her hands started to lift and I stopped them. She didn't struggle. Her hands didn't resist mine and she didn't strain or move. There was no strength or force in her. She was only breathing harder and lying completely still. Then she quietly stopped breathing. I waited. In another moment, her chin ticked and she almost drew a half breath. That was all. The bag was collapsed and molded against her face. Her body had not convulsed or shuddered. There was no sudden absence in the room. It seemed only that she was no longer entirely present. She might have still been alive. I thought I felt a faint pulse at her wrist and under my palm on her chest the bare tremor of a heartbeat. I wasn't sure. But I needed to be sure so I waited. Perhaps five minutes. She remained absolutely inert. I loosed the scarf and pulled the bag from her head. Marie Brett had died at 7:25 in the evening, April 19, 1995. The big news that day was the bombing of the Federal Building in Oklahoma City.

I sat beside her another hour. The lines in her face were gone. It was a smoothed face and didn't look quite like the Marie I remembered. Her mouth was still ajar. She had been a dirt-poor country girl, her parents sharecroppers from Alabama who moved to Texas. She claimed she graduated from high school, I think maybe she got to the tenth grade. She was a big girl, five ten, a little hefty. Not a bad face, probably attractive. She had nice teeth, an appealing feature. Growing up, she'd worked in the fields like a man. When she was seventeen, she met my father, who was twenty. He had a job shining shoes at a barbershop. This was during the Depression. Marie would walk by the barbershop on her way home from school and flirt with Charlie, the shineboy. They went to the movies together and kissed. She'd never had a boyfriend. Charlie had never had a girlfriend. He was shorter than Marie and an introvert, a repressed soul. She was more outgoing, a girl who wanted to have fun. So they got married, each having no other choice. Charlie's mother had been domineering, and Marie was, too. She married Charlie, she said, to get away from home. She had my brother and me by the time she was nineteen. Charlie worked as a farmhand, at a service station, then at a slaughterhouse, and finally as a postal clerk, a better job than he'd ever hoped to expect. It offered security, a steady income. They made a down payment on a $1,400 house and bought furniture on credit from a mail-order catalogue. When the war came along, the world was turned upside down and soldier boys were everywhere. It was an exciting time. The world might end tomorrow. That's when Marie decided to join the war effort, so to speak. She left her husband and kids and went off to frolic with the soldiers. She became a waitress in small-town cafés. She married six times, well, seven, if you count the one she married twice, the one who regularly beat her. Billy and I lived mostly with grandparents. We would see Marie in the summers, or she would appear occasionally with small, meaningless presents and play like everybody was happy.

It's probably not possible, but I've tried to understand Marie beyond my personal resentments. What kind of person was she? The word "unfortunate" comes to mind. Not "tragic." To rise to that level, you would think a person would need first to aspire to something worthwhile, and Marie's most articulate aspiration was "just to be happy, that's all I ever wanted." This was her litany. She never learned that happiness is a matter of degree, not a permanent condition. Or she may have pretended to happiness because she knew it was nowhere, an impossibility for her, and by never finding it, she essentially confirmed her self-image that she didn't deserve to be happy. She didn't like herself, for whatever reason, and that predetermined every relationship, every single dead-end path she took. It may well have been that simple. She never understood herself, or, if she did, some truths were too hard to face. Marie began early on to live in a world of pretense. Maybe we all do. The void all around is so immense and we're so tiny, if we're scared, if we're not gritty enough to stand against defeat, then maybe pretense is a way to survive. It's also a way to get lost, and that's what happened to Marie: she pretended, she rationalized, she assumed a protective lie and became lost in a life that never happened. Except for the fallout.

To hear her tell it, most of her life was occupied with "getting a man." "I always had to have a man," she said. If she could attract a man, get a man to want her, this had to mean that she had some value, didn't it? On the other hand, by being so easy that any man could screw her and did—"screwing" is what she called it—didn't that really prove she was of the least value, a throwaway? Being little more than a fuck is being little more than faceless. Not surprisingly, when a man married her, she was immediately contemptuous of him: no doubt in her mind any man who would marry the likes of her had to be worthless, too. Of course, she only married men whom she could dominate, my father first, then the others. I was present at times when she verbally abused three of them. And they took it. But Marie would also pretend her husbands were other than they were. She said her third husband was an Air Force pilot. He wasn't. He was an enlisted man. Her fourth husband worked in a paint and body shop, but she said he was going to inherit a fortune, that his parents owned thousands of acres of prime wheat land. They didn't. They farmed about two hundred acres, of which each of their five children might one day be allotted a portion. Marie said her sixth husband was a partner in a big construction firm. He was an employee. Her seventh, she said, was a doctor, he knew a lot of medical terms. He turned out to be a nurse's aide. When Marie was no longer a waitress but a fry cook, she claimed to be a dietitian. She told each husband she'd been married only once, to my father, and that he'd died. She also told each husband she was a few years younger than she really was.

Was she smart? She never learned, she kept repeating the same mistakes, which may have been compulsive, but I believe that she was at least of average intelligence. She didn't read books, even trashy ones. Or I take that back. She read my novels and said she liked them but she wished I would write a happy book, my stories were so sad. She had no idea what I was about. She read magazines, the *Ladies' Home Journal* type, and the tabloids. She read five of those every week. She watched soap operas and game shows. She worked simple crossword puzzles and played solitaire. She never had a friend, never another woman as a friend, and men were never friends, only people she screwed. What kind of person is it who never, not once in her life, has a real friend? She set out to befriend two nieces once, then abruptly and maliciously alienated them. She alienated her sister, her two sons, all her husbands, and in the end, at sixty-five, when her last husband died and she could no longer "get a man," she became a recluse. It wasn't so much she didn't want to see people; she didn't want people to see her. She hated seeing herself.

In her last years her flesh was globs of shapeless clabbered fat. She was no longer five ten but about five seven and half-blind and deaf. She had no outside interests, no property, no money. One house she had after a divorce she simply lived in without making the mortgage payments until the bank foreclosed—and she could have made the monthly payment, it was less than rent. She had clear title to her last house and simply gave it away to a thirty-six-year-old Cuban who "promised to take care of her." She also gave him $12,000 cash, the sum of her late husband's life insurance, and signed over the title to her car. Why? I think it wasn't so much the man conned her as she very calculatingly tried to buy him. She couldn't, and probably knew she couldn't, but it was her last chance to "get a man." It was typically self-defeating and she was left with nothing, the one thing she must have felt she deserved.

So she'd finally come to the end. She didn't have a religious faith or a belief in God. She pretended she did, she talked a lot about praying, but what she said she really believed was in nothing beyond this life. When it was over, that was it, a complete stop. Now she was lying on her back in a casket position, her eyes closed, her hands folded on her stomach. She had dressed in a thin, velvety black robe. Black. She had chosen that color for her last moments. And her choice may have been determined from birth. It seemed to me Marie was probably born with an unfortunate mix of conflicting traits that gave her nature a negative cast. Unhappiness was her fix and she caused unhappiness.

Marie had tried suicide several times before. A psychiatrist might say these attempts were cries for help. I felt compelled to offer some help a time or two, which maybe sounds self-righteous, but each time I received only a kind of scorn in return. It was as if she considered help an interference. At the same time an offered kindness might make her cry, and she'd be grateful, but then she'd immediately distrust the kindness—what was it for? Her suicide attempts were in all likelihood added ways to pull others more deeply into her miasma of sorrow. Finally, if we can say it just so happens that some people are fated to live miserable lives, then Marie, perhaps, was one of those. I felt sorry for her. I felt pity for her. It's almost certain she never knew what it was to love or be loved wholeheartedly.

She said she never meant to leave us kids. But she did. After all, when you have children of your own, you find out that you don't just up and leave them after a few years and make an X for them in your life, not if you care. You don't leave your kids with a hole in their heart.

I pulled the towel from between her legs. It was not soiled. I stuffed it and the plastic bag and the scarf and the pill bottles under a wad in the trash. There was nothing else to clear away. She'd been wanting to die for a long time. When she realized she was at a point where she might be hospitalized or put in a nursing home, I think that decided it for her. She knew then that others would see her, that she would be exposed and no longer able to hide. So she would make another fantasy escape, and in her mind, if she could count on me to do the hard part, her part was merely a matter of going to sleep. She'd had nightmares all her life. She may have believed that in this sleep she wouldn't.

I opened the blinds and unlocked the doors and put the phone back on the receiver, then mixed a vodka drink and sat in my room. It was 8:30. I would wait a while to call the police. I needed to get set in my mind what I would tell them and how I would act. Anyway, it was over. I didn't feel easy. It seemed an oppressive weight might soon lift, but mostly what I felt was depressed. The drink made me lighter, but I was still tense. A friend called from Austin. I didn't mention Marie. We talked of nothing in particular, joked. After hanging up, I realized I had laughed too loudly. I would need to control myself better. I mixed another drink.

About 9:30 I called the police, said I didn't know if I should call them, but I thought my mother had died in her sleep. The police arrived within minutes and called in the coroner, a local justice of the peace. I told the coroner my mother had deteriorated rapidly in the last weeks, that she'd had a consumptive heart condition, shortness of breath, stomach problems. He took a cursory look at her, pronounced her dead from natural causes, and called the mortuary. They arrived and Marie's body was taken away. I gave the mortuary man her birth certificate and Social Security number and told him cremation. He asked about embalming. I said no. How about a service? No, none of that, I said, just the simplest, quickest way.

Then they were gone, Marie was gone, and the whole last business was finished. The house was suddenly stone quiet. I felt an odd, distant loss. Or I can't say exactly what I felt. I needed to get drunk, I thought. I poured my drink out instead. My mother, I thought, the one person I'd known my whole life, she'd given me life. But I always only knew her as Marie. I never called her mother and she never called me son.

JUDY RUIZ

Judy Ruiz's essay twists and turns in many different narrative directions: The telephone call from her brother announcing his sex change operation leads first to a college classroom and subsequently to a mysterious rendezvous on Puget Sound. There are nightmares of her creation and birth, which may be taking place in a psychiatric setting; and there is the voice of her brother, repeatedly explaining himself and his new life, and her responses, which include conversations with acquaintances and library research in a quest to understand his actions. Despite the twists and turns, the narrative remains unified, with the help of the symbolic orange, which finds a vital place in each nugget of story being told.

ORANGES AND SWEET SISTER BOY

I am sleeping, hard, when the telephone rings. It's my brother, and he's calling to say that he is now my sister. I feel something fry a little, deep behind my eyes. Knowing how sometimes dreams get mixed up with not-dreams, I decide to do a reality test at once. "Let me get a cigarette," I say, knowing that if I reach for a Marlboro and it turns into a trombone or a snake or anything else on the way to my lips that I'm still out in the large world of dreams.

The cigarette stays a cigarette. I light it. I ask my brother to run that stuff by me again.

It is the Texas Zephyr at midnight—the woman in a white suit, the man in a blue uniform; she carries flowers—I know they are flowers. The petals spill and spill into the aisle, and a child goes past this couple who have just come from their own wedding—goes past them and past them, going always to the toilet but really just going past them; and the child could be a horse or she could be the police and they'd not notice her any more than they do, which is not at all—the man's hands high up on the woman's legs, her skirt up, her stockings and garters, the petals and finally all the flowers spilling out into the aisle and his mouth open on her. My mother. My father. I am conceived near Dallas in the dark while a child passes, a young girl who knows and doesn't know, who witnesses, in glimpses, the creation of the universe, who feels an odd hurt as her own mother, fat and empty, snores with her mouth open, her false teeth slipping down, snores and snores just two seats behind the Creators.

News can make a person stupid. It can make you think you can do something. So I ask The Blade question, thinking that if he hasn't had the operation yet that I can fly to him, rent a cabin out on Puget Sound. That we can talk. That I can get him to touch base with reality.

"Begin with an orange," I would tell him. "Because oranges are mildly intrusive by nature, put the orange somewhere so that it will not bother you—in the cupboard, in a drawer, even a pocket or a handbag will do. The orange, being a patient fruit, will wait for you much longer than say a banana or a peach."

I would hold an orange out to him. I would say, "This is the one that will save your life." And I would tell him about the woman I saw in a bus station who bit right into her orange like it was an apple. She was wild looking, as if she'd been outside for too long in a wind that blew the same way all the time. One of the dregs of humanity, our mother would have called her, the same mother who never brought fruit into the house except in cans. My children used to ask me to "start" their oranges for them. That meant to make a hole in the orange so they could peel the rind away, and their small hands weren't equipped with fingernails that were long enough or strong enough to do the job. Sometimes they would suck the juice out of the hole my thumbnail had made, leaving the orange flat and sad.

The earrings are as big as dessert plates, filigree gold-plated with thin dangles hanging down that touch her bare shoulders. She stands in front of the Alamo while a bald man takes her picture. The sun is absorbed by the earrings so quickly that by the time she feels the heat, it is too late. The hanging dangles make small blisters on her shoulders, as if a centipede had traveled there. She takes the famous river walk in spiked heels, rides in a boat, eats some Italian noodles, returns to the motel room, soaks her feet, and applies small band-aids to her toes. She is briefly concerned about the gun on the nightstand. The toilet flushes. She pretends to be sleeping. The gun is just large and heavy. A .45? A .357 magnum? She's never been good with names. She hopes he doesn't try to. Or that if he does, that it's not loaded. But he'll say it's loaded just for fun. Or he'll pull the trigger and the bullet will lodge in her medulla oblongata, ripping through her womb first, taking everything else vital on the way.

In the magazine articles, you don't see this: "Well, yes. The testicles have to come out. And yes. The penis is cut off." What you get is tonsils. So-and-so has had a "sex change" operation. A sex change operation. How precious. How benign. Doctor, just what do you people do with those penises?

News can make a person a little crazy also. News like, "We regret to inform you that you have failed your sanity hearing."

The bracelet on my wrist bears the necessary information about me, but there is one small error. The receptionist typing the information asked me my religious preference. I said, "None." She typed, "Neon."

> *Pearl doesn't have any teeth and her tongue looks weird. She says, "Pumpkin pie." That's all she says. Sometimes she runs her hands over my bed sheets and says pumpkin pie. Sometimes I am under the sheets. Marsha got stabbed in the chest, but she tells everyone she fell on a knife. Elizabeth—she's the one who thinks her shoe is a baby— hit me in the back with a tray right after one of the cooks gave me extra toast. There's a note on the bulletin board about a class for the nurses: "How Putting A Towel On Sometime's Face Makes Them Stop Banging Their Spoon/OR Reduction of Disruptive Mealtime Behavior By Facial Screening—7 P.M.—Conference Room." Another note announces the topic of remotivation class: "COWS." All the paranoid schizophrenics will be there.*
>
> *Here, in the place for the permanently bewildered, I fit right in. Not because I stood at the window that first night and listened to the trains. Not because I imagined those trains were bracelets, the jewelry of earth. Not even because I imagined that one of those bracelets was on my own arm and was the Texas Zephyr where a young couple made love and conceived me. I am eighteen and beautiful and committed to the state hospital by a district court judge for a period of one day to life. Because I am a paranoid schizophrenic.*
>
> *I will learn about cows.*

So I'm being very quiet in the back of the classroom, and I'm peeling an orange. It's the smell that makes the others begin to turn around, that mildly intrusive nature. The course is called "Women and Modern Literature," and the diaries of Virginia Woolf are up for discussion except nobody has anything to say. I, of course, am making a mess with the orange; and I'm wanting to say that my brother is now my sister.

Later, with my hands still orangey, I wander in to leave something on a desk in a professor's office, and he's reading so I'm being very quiet, and then he says, sort of out of nowhere, "Emily Dickinson up there in her room making poems while her brother was making love to her best friend right downstairs on the dining room table. A regular thing. Think of it. And Walt Whitman out sniffing around the boys. Our two great American poets." And I want to grab this professor's arm and say, "Listen. My brother called me and now he's my sister, and I'm having trouble making sense out of my life right now, so would you mind not telling me any more stuff about sex." And I want my knuckles to turn white while the pressure of my fingers leaves imprints right through his jacket, little indentations he can interpret as urgent. But I don't say anything. And I don't grab his arm. I go read a magazine. I find this:

"I've never found an explanation for why the human race has so many languages. When the brain became a language brain, it obviously needed to develop an intense degree of plasticity. Such plasticity allows languages to be logical, coherent systems and yet be extremely variable. The same brain that thinks in words and symbols is also a brain that has to be freed up with regard to sexual turn-on and partnering. God knows why sex attitudes have been subject to the corresponding degrees of modification and variety as language. I suspect there's a close parallel between the two. The brain doesn't seem incredibly efficient with regard to sex."

John Money said that. The same John Money who, with surgeon Howard W. Jones, performed the first sex change operation in the United States in 1965 at Johns Hopkins University and Hospital in Baltimore.

Money also tells about the *hijra* of India who disgrace their families because they are too effeminate: "The ultimate stage of the *hijra* is to get up the courage to go through the amputation of penis and testicles. They had no anesthetic." Money also answers anyone who might think that "heartless members of the medical profession are forcing these poor darlings to go and get themselves cut up and mutilated," or who think the medical profession should leave them alone. "You'd have lots of patients willing to get a gun and blow off their own genitals if you don't do it. I've had several who got knives and cut themselves trying to get rid of their sex organs. That's their obsession!"

Perhaps better than all else, I understand obsession. It is of the mind. And it is language-bound. Sex is of the body. It has no words. I am stunned to learn that someone with an obsession of the mind can have parts of the body surgically removed. This is my brother I speak of. This is not some lunatic named Carl who becomes Carlene. This is my brother.

So while we're out in that cabin on Puget Sound, I'll tell him about LuAnn. She is the sort of woman who orders the in-season fruit and a little cottage cheese. I am the sort of woman who orders a double cheeseburger and fries. LuAnn and I are sitting in her car. She has a huge orange, and she peels it so the peel falls off in one neat strip. I have a sack of oranges, the small ones. The peel of my orange comes off in hunks about the size of a baby's nail. "Oh, you bought the *juice* oranges," LuAnn says to me. Her emphasis on the word "juice" makes me want to die or something. I lack the courage to admit my ignorance, so I smile and breathe "yes," as if I know some secret, when I'm wanting to scream at her about how my mother didn't teach me about fruit and my own blood pounds in my head wanting out, out.

There is a pattern to this thought as there is a pattern for a jumpsuit. Sew the sleeve to the leg, sew the leg to the collar. Put the garment on. Sew the mouth shut. This is how I tell about being quiet because I am bad, and because I cannot stand it when he beats me or my brother.

"The first time I got caught in your clothes was when I was four years old and you were over at Sarah what's-her-name's babysitting. Dad beat me so hard I thought I was going to die. I really thought I was going to die. That was the day I made up my mind I would *never* get caught again. And I never got caught again." My brother goes on to say he continued to go through my things until I was hospitalized. A mystery is solved.

He wore my clothes. He played in my makeup. I kept saying, back then, that someone was going through my stuff. I kept saying it and saying it. I told the counselor at school. "Someone goes in my room when I'm not there, and I *know* it—goes in there and wears my clothes and goes through my stuff." I was assured by the counselor that this was not so. I was assured by my mother that this was not so. I thought my mother was doing it, snooping around for clues like mothers do. It made me a little crazy, so I started deliberately leaving things in a certain order so that I would be able to prove to myself that someone, indeed, was going through my belongings. No one, not one person, ever believed that my room was being ransacked; I was accused of just making it up. A paranoid fixation.

And all the time it was old Goldilocks.

So I tell my brother to promise me he'll see someone who counsels adult children from dysfunctional families. I tell him he needs to deal with the fact that he was physically abused on a daily basis. He tells me he doesn't remember being beaten except on three occasions. He wants me to get into a support group for families of people who are having a sex change. Support groups are people who are in the same boat. Except no one has any oars in the water.

I tell him I know how it feels to think you are in the wrong body. I tell him how I wanted my boyfriend to put a gun up inside me and blow the woman out, how I thought wearing spiked heels and low-cut dresses would somehow help my crisis, that putting on an ultrafeminine outside would mask the maleness I felt needed hiding. I tell him it's the rule, rather than the exception, that people from families like ours have very spooky sexual identity problems. He tells me that his sexuality is a birth defect. I recognize the lingo. It's support-group-for-transsexuals lingo. He tells me he sits down to pee. He told his therapist that he used to wet all over the floor. His therapist said, "You can't aim the bullets if you don't touch the gun." Lingo. My brother is hell-bent for castration, the castration that started before he had language: the castration of abuse. He will simply finish what was set in motion long ago.

I will tell my brother about the time I took ten sacks of oranges into a school so that I could teach metaphor. The school was for special students—those who were socially or intellectually impaired. I had planned to have them peel the oranges as I spoke about how much the world is like the orange. I handed out the oranges. The students refused to peel them, not because they wanted to make life difficult for me—they were enchanted with the gift. One child asked if he could have an orange to take home to his little brother. Another said he would bring me ten dollars the next day if I would give him a sack of oranges. And I knew I was at home, that these children and I shared something that *makes* the leap of mind the metaphor attempts. And something in me healed.

A neighbor of mine takes pantyhose and cuts them up and sews them up after stuffing them. Then she puts these things into Mason jars and sells them, you know, to put out on the mantel for conversation. They are little penises and little scrotums, complete with hair. She calls them "Pickled Peters."

A friend of mine had a sister who had a sex change operation. This young woman had her breasts removed and ran around the house with no shirt on before the stitches were taken out. She answered the door one evening. A young man had come to call on my friend. The sex-changed sister invited him in and offered him some black bean soup as if she were perfectly normal with her red surgical wounds and her black stitches. The young man left and never went back. A couple years later, my friend's sister/brother died when s/he ran a car into a concrete bridge railing. I hope for a happier ending. For my brother, for myself, for all of us.

My brother calls. He's done his toenails: Shimmering Cinnamon. And he's left his wife and children and purchased some nightgowns at a yard sale. His hair is getting longer. He wears a special bra. Most of the people he works with know about the changes in his life. His voice is not the same voice I've heard for years; he sounds happy.

My brother calls. He's always envied me, my woman's body. The same body I live in and have cursed for its softness. He asks me how I feel about myself. He says, "You know, you are really our father's first-born son." He tells me he used to want to be me because I was the only person our father almost loved.

The drama of life. After I saw that woman in the bus station eat an orange as if it were an apple, I went out into the street and smoked a joint with some guy I'd met on the bus. Then I hailed a cab and went to a tattoo parlor. The tattoo artist tried to talk me into getting a nice bird or butterfly design; I had chosen a design on his wall that appealed to me—a symbol I didn't know the meaning of. It is the Yin-Yang, and it's tattooed above my right ankle bone. I suppose my drugged, crazed consciousness knew more than I knew: that yin combines with yang to produce all that comes to be. I am drawn to androgyny.

Of course there is the nagging possibility that my brother's dilemma is genetic. Our father used to dress in drag on Halloween, and he made a beautiful woman. One year, the year my mother cut my brother's blond curls off, my father taped those curls to his own head and tied a silk scarf over the tape. Even his close friends didn't know it was him. And my youngest daughter was a body builder for a while, her lean body as muscular as a man's. And my sons are beautiful, not handsome: they look androgynous.

Then there's my grandson. I saw him when he was less than an hour old. He was naked and had hiccups. I watched as he had his first bath, and I heard him cry. He had not been named yet, but his little crib had a blue card affixed to it with tape. And on the card were the words "Baby Boy." There was no doubt in me that the words were true.

When my brother was born, my father was off flying jets in Korea. I went to the hospital with my grandfather to get my mother and this new brother. I remember how I wanted a sister, and I remember looking at him as my mother held him in the front seat of the car. I was certain he was a sister, certain that my mother was joking. She removed his diaper to show me that he was a boy. I still didn't believe her. Considering what has happened lately, I wonder if my child-skewed consciousness knew more than the anatomical proof suggested.

I try to make peace with myself. I try to understand his decision to alter himself. I try to think of him as her. I write his woman name, and I feel like I'm betraying myself. I try to be open-minded, but something in me shuts down. I think we humans are in big trouble, that many of us don't really have a clue as to what acceptable human behavior is. Something in me says no to all this, that this surgery business is the ultimate betrayal of the self. And yet, I want my brother to be happy.

It was in the city of San Antonio that my father had his surgery. I rode the bus from Kansas to Texas, and arrived at the hospital two days after the operation to find my father sitting in the solarium playing solitaire. He had a type of cancer that particularly thrived on testosterone. And so he was castrated in order to erase his pain and to stop the growth of tumors. He died six months later.

Back in the sleep of the large world of dreams, I have done surgeries under water in which I float my father's testicles back into him, and he—the brutal man he was—emerges from the pool a tan and smiling man, parting the surface of the water with his perfect head. He loves all the grief away.

I will tell my brother all I know of oranges, that if you squeeze the orange peel into a flame, small fires happen because of the volatile oil in the peel. Also, if you squeeze the peel and it gets into your cat's eyes, the cat will blink and blink. I will tell him there is no perfect rhyme for the word "orange," and that if we can just make up a good word we can be immortal. We will become obsessed with finding the right word, and I will be joyous at our legitimate pursuit.

I have purchased a black camisole with lace to send to my new sister. And a card. On the outside of the card there's a drawing of a woman sitting by a pond and a zebra is off to the left. Inside are these words: "The past is ended. Be happy." And I have asked my companions to hold me and I have cried. My self is wet and small. But it is not dark. Sometimes, if no one touches me, I will die.

Sister, you are the best craziness of the family. Brother, love what you love.

RAYMOND CARVER

The simplicity of Raymond Carver's words and the brief clarity of his observations are what make this memoir of his father so plain, yet so powerful. A myriad of images broadside the reader: in less than a half page of prose, Carver bombs the outdoor toilets of his neighborhood with rocks—or sets them on fire; deludes his third-grade teacher to take him to a different house out of shame for where he lives; hefts the cast-iron colander with which his mother has just smashed his father's head; watches his mother dispose of his father's whiskey, then subsequently immerse his father's hand into a warm pan of water in order to make him divulge information in his sleep. His minimalistic prose is lean, spare, bleak—and astonishingly and relentlessly powerful.

MY FATHER'S LIFE

My dad's name was Clevie Raymond Carver. His family called him Raymond and friends called him C. R. I was named Raymond Clevie Carver, Jr. I hated the "Junior" part. When I was little my dad called me Frog, which was okay. But later, like everybody else in the family, he began calling me Junior. He went on calling me this until I was thirteen or fourteen and announced that I wouldn't answer to that name any longer. So he began calling me Doc. From then until his death, on June 17, 1967, he called me Doc, or else Son.

When he died, my mother telephoned my wife with the news. I was away from my family at the time, between lives, trying to enroll in the School of Library Science at the University of Iowa. When my wife answered the phone, my mother blurted out, "Raymond's dead!" For a moment, my wife thought my mother was telling her that I was dead. Then my mother made it clear *which* Raymond she was talking about and my wife said, "Thank God. I thought you meant *my* Raymond."

My dad walked, hitched rides, and rode in empty boxcars when he went from Arkansas to Washington State in 1934, looking for work. I don't know whether he was pursuing a dream when he went out to Washington. I doubt it. I don't think he dreamed much. I believe he was simply looking for steady work at decent pay. Steady work was meaningful work. He picked apples for a time and then landed a construction laborer's job on the Grand Coulee Dam. After he'd put aside a little money, he bought a car and drove back to Arkansas to help his folks, my grandparents, pack up for the move west. He said later that they were about to starve down there, and this wasn't meant as a figure of speech. It was during that short while in Arkansas, in a town called Leola, that my mother met my dad on the sidewalk as he came out of a tavern.

"He was drunk," she said. "I don't know why I let him talk to me. His eyes were glittery. I wish I'd had a crystal ball." They'd met once, a year or so before, at a dance. He'd had girlfriends before her, my mother told me. "Your dad always had a girlfriend, even after we married. He was my first and last. I never had another man. But I didn't miss anything."

They were married by a justice of the peace on the day they left for Washington, this big, tall country girl and a farmhand-turned-construction-worker. My mother spent her wedding night with my dad and his folks, all of them camped beside the road in Arkansas.

In Omak, Washington, my dad and mother lived in a little place not much bigger than a cabin. My grandparents lived next door. My dad was still working on the dam, and later, when the huge turbines producing electricity and the water backed up for a hundred miles into Canada, he stood in the crowd and heard Franklin D. Roosevelt when he spoke at the construction site. "He never mentioned those guys who died building that dam," my dad said. Some of his friends had died there, men from Arkansas, Oklahoma, and Missouri.

He then took a job in a sawmill in Clatskanie, Oregon, a little town alongside the Columbia River. I was born there, and my mother has a picture of my dad standing in front of the gate to the mill, proudly holding me up to face the camera. My bonnet is on crooked and about to come untied. His hat is pushed back on his forehead, and he's wearing a big grin. Was he going in to work or just finishing his shift? It doesn't matter. In either case, he had a job and a family. These were his salad days.

In 1941 we moved to Yakima, Washington, where my dad went to work as a saw filer, a skilled trade he'd learned in Clatskanie. When war broke out, he was given a deferment because his work was considered necessary to the war effort. Finished lumber was in demand by the armed services, and he kept his saws so sharp they could shave the hair off your arm.

After my dad had moved us to Yakima, he moved his folks into the same neighborhood. By the mid-1940s the rest of my dad's family—his brother, his sister, and her husband, as well as uncles, cousins, nephews, and most of their extended family and friends—had come out from Arkansas. All because my dad came out first. The men went to work at Boise Cascade, where my dad worked, and the women packed apples in the canneries. And in just a little while, it seemed—according to my mother—everybody was better off than my dad. "Your dad couldn't keep money," my mother said. "Money burned a hole in his pocket. He was always doing for others."

The first house I clearly remember living in, at 1515 South Fifteenth Street, in Yakima, had an outdoor toilet. On Halloween night, or just any night, for the hell of it, neighbor kids, kids in their early teens, would carry our toilet away and leave it next to the road. My dad would have to get somebody to help him bring it home. Or these kids would take the toilet and stand it in somebody else's backyard. Once they actually set it on fire. But ours wasn't the only house that had an outdoor toilet. When I was old enough to know what I was doing, I threw rocks at the other toilets when I'd see someone go inside. This was called bombing the toilets. After a while, though, everyone went to indoor plumbing until, suddenly, our toilet was the last outdoor one in the neighborhood. I remember the shame I felt when my third-grade teacher, Mr. Wise, drove me home from school one day. I asked him to stop at the house just before ours, claiming I lived there.

I can recall what happened one night when my dad came home late to find that my mother had locked all the doors on him from the inside. He was drunk, and we could feel the house shudder as he rattled the door. When he'd managed to force open a window, she hit him between the eyes with a colander and knocked him out. We could see him down there on the grass. For years afterward, I used to pick up this colander—it was as heavy as a rolling pin—and imagine what it would feel like to be hit in the head with something like that.

It was during this period that I remember my dad taking me into the bedroom, sitting me down on the bed, and telling me that I might have to go live with my Aunt LaVon for a while. I couldn't understand what I'd done that meant I'd have to go away from home to live. But this, too—whatever prompted it—must have blown over, more or less, anyway, because we stayed together, and I didn't have to go live with her or anyone else.

I remember my mother pouring his whiskey down the sink. Sometimes she'd pour it all out and sometimes, if she was afraid of getting caught, she'd only pour half of it out and then add water to the rest. I tasted some of his whiskey once myself. It was terrible stuff, and I don't see how anybody could drink it.

After a long time without one, we finally got a car, in 1949 or 1950, a 1938 Ford. But it threw a rod the first week we had it, and my dad had to have the motor rebuilt.

"We drove the oldest car in town," my mother said. "We could have had a Cadillac for all he spent on car repairs." One time she found someone else's tube of lipstick on the floorboard, along with a lacy handkerchief. "See this?" she said to me. "Some floozy left this in the car."

Once I saw her take a pan of warm water into the bedroom where my dad was sleeping. She took his hand from under the covers and held it in the water. I stood in the doorway and watched. I wanted to know what was going on. This would make him talk in his sleep, she told me. There were things she needed to know, things she was sure he was keeping from her.

Every year or so, when I was little, we would take the North Coast Limited across the Cascade Range from Yakima to Seattle and stay in the Vance Hotel and eat, I remember, at a place called the Dinner Bell Cafe. Once we went to Ivar's Acres of Clams and drank glasses of warm clam broth.

In 1956, the year I was to graduate from high school, my dad quit his job at the mill in Yakima and took a job in Chester, a little sawmill town in northern California. The reasons given at the time for his taking the job had to do with a higher hourly wage and the vague promise that he might, in a few years' time, succeed to the job of head filer in this new mill. But I think, in the main, that my dad had grown restless and simply wanted to try his luck elsewhere. Things had gotten a little too predictable for him in Yakima. Also, the year before, there had been the deaths, within six months of each other, of both his parents.

But just a few days after graduation, when my mother and I were packed to move to Chester, my dad penciled a letter to say he'd been sick for a while. He didn't want us to worry, he said, but he'd cut himself on a saw. Maybe he'd got a tiny sliver of steel in his blood. Anyway, something had happened and he'd had to miss work, he said. In the same mail was an unsigned postcard from somebody down there telling my mother that my dad was about to die and that he was drinking "raw whiskey."

When we arrived in Chester, my dad was living in a trailer that belonged to the company. I didn't recognize him immediately. I guess for a moment I didn't want to recognize him. He was skinny and pale and looked bewildered. His pants wouldn't stay up. He didn't look like my dad. My mother began to cry. My dad put his arm around her and patted her shoulder vaguely, like he didn't know what this was all about, either. The three of us took up life together in the trailer, and we looked after him as best we could. But my dad was sick, and he couldn't get any better. I worked with him in the mill that summer and part of the fall. We'd get up in the mornings and eat eggs and toast while we listened to the radio, and then go out the door with our lunch pails. We'd pass through the gate together at eight in the morning, and I wouldn't see him again until quitting time. In November I went back to Yakima to be closer to my girlfriend, the girl I'd made up my mind I was going to marry.

He worked at the mill in Chester until the following February, when he collapsed on the job and was taken to the hospital. My mother asked if I would come down there and help. I caught a bus from Yakima to Chester, intending to drive them back to Yakima. But now, in addition to being physically sick, my dad was in the midst of a nervous breakdown, though none of us knew to call it that at the time. During the entire trip back to Yakima, he didn't speak, not even when asked a direct question. ("How do you feel, Raymond?" "You okay, Dad?") He'd communicate, if he communicated at all, by moving his head or by turning his palms up as if to say he didn't know or care. The only time he said anything on the trip, and for nearly a month afterward, was when I was speeding down a gravel road in Oregon and the car muffler came loose. "You were going too fast," he said.

Back in Yakima a doctor saw to it that my dad went to a psychiatrist. My mother and dad had to go on relief, as it was called, and the county paid for the psychiatrist. The psychiatrist asked my dad, "Who is the President?" He'd had a question put to him that he could answer. "Ike," my dad said. Nevertheless, they put him on the fifth floor of Valley Memorial Hospital and began giving him electroshock treatments. I was married by then and about to start my own family. My dad was still locked up when my wife went into this same hospital, just one floor down, to have our first baby. After she had delivered, I went upstairs to give my dad the news. They let me in through a steel door and showed me where I could find him. He was sitting on a couch with a blanket over his lap. *Hey,* I thought. *What in hell is happening to my dad?* I sat down next to him and told him he was a grandfather. He waited a minute and then said, "I feel like a grandfather." That's all he said. He didn't smile or move. He was in a big room with a lot of other people. Then I hugged him, and he began to cry.

Somehow he got out of there. But now came the years when he couldn't work and just sat around the house trying to figure what next and what he'd done wrong in his life that he'd wound up like this. My mother went from job to crummy job. Much later she referred to that time he was in the hospital, and those years just afterward, as "when Raymond was sick." The word *sick* was never the same for me again.

In 1964, through the help of a friend, he was lucky enough to be hired on at a mill in Klamath, California. He moved down there by himself to see if he could hack it. He lived not far from the mill, in a one-room cabin not much different from the place he and my mother had started out living in when they went west. He scrawled letters to my mother, and if I called she'd read them aloud to me over the phone. In the letters, he said it was touch and go. Every day that he went to work, he felt like it was the most important day of his life. But every day, he told her, made the next day that much easier. He said for her to tell me he said hello. If he couldn't sleep at night, he said, he thought about me and the good times we used to have. Finally, after a couple of months, he regained some of his confidence. He could do the work and didn't think he had to worry that he'd let anybody down ever again. When he was sure, he sent for my mother.

He'd been off from work for six years and had lost everything in that time—home, car, furniture, and appliances, including the big freezer that had been my mother's pride and joy. He'd lost his good name too—Raymond Carver was someone who couldn't pay his bills—and his self-respect was gone. He'd even lost his virility. My mother told my wife, "All during that time Raymond was sick we slept together in the same bed, but we didn't have relations. He wanted to a few times, but nothing happened. I didn't miss it, but I think he wanted to, you know."

During those years I was trying to raise my own family and earn a living. But, one thing and another, we found ourselves having to move a lot. I couldn't keep track of what was going down in my dad's life. But I did have a chance one Christmas to tell him I wanted to be a writer. I might as well have told him I wanted to become a plastic surgeon. "What are you going to write about?" he wanted to know. Then, as if to help me out, he said, "Write about stuff you know about. Write about some of those fishing trips we took." I said I would, but I knew I wouldn't. "Send me what you write," he said. I said I'd do that, but then I didn't. I wasn't writing anything about fishing, and I didn't think he'd particularly care about, or even necessarily understand, what I was writing in those days. Besides, he wasn't a reader. Not the sort, anyway, I imagined I was writing for.

Then he died. I was a long way off, in Iowa City, with things still to say to him. I didn't have the chance to tell him good-bye, or that I thought he was doing great at his new job. That I was proud of him for making a comeback.

My mother said he came in from work that night and ate a big supper. Then he sat at the table by himself and finished what was left of a bottle of whiskey, a bottle she found hidden in the bottom of the garbage under some coffee grounds a day or so later. Then he got up and went to bed, where my mother joined him a little later. But in the night she had to get up and make a bed for herself on the couch. "He was snoring so loud I couldn't sleep," she said. The next morning when she looked in on him, he was on his back with his mouth open, his cheeks caved in. *Graylooking,* she said. She knew he was dead—she didn't need a doctor to tell her that. But she called one anyway, and then she called my wife.

Among the pictures my mother kept of my dad and herself during those early days in Washington was a photograph of him standing in front of a car, holding a beer and a stringer of fish. In the photograph he is wearing his hat back on his forehead and has this awkward grin on his face. I asked her for it and she gave it to me, along with some others. I put it up on my wall, and each time we moved, I took the picture along and put it up on another wall. I looked at it carefully from time to time, trying to figure out some things about my dad, and maybe myself in the process. But I couldn't. My dad just kept moving further and further away from me and back into time. Finally, in the course of another move, I lost the photograph. It was then that I tried to recall it, and at the same time make an attempt to say something about my dad, and how I thought that in some important ways we might be alike. I wrote the poem when I was living in an apartment house in an urban area south of San Francisco, at a time when I found myself, like my dad, having trouble with alcohol. The poem was a way of trying to connect up with him.

PHOTOGRAPH OF MY FATHER IN HIS TWENTY-SECOND YEAR

October. Here in this dank, unfamiliar kitchen
I study my father's embarrassed young man's face.
Sheepish grin, he holds in one hand a string
of spiny yellow perch, in the other
a bottle of Carlsberg beer.

In jeans and flannel shirt, he leans
against the front fender of a 1934 Ford.
He would like to pose brave and hearty for his posterity,
wear his old hat cocked over his ear.
All his life my father wanted to be bold.

But the eyes give him away, and the hands
that limply offer the string of dead perch
and the bottle of beer. Father, I love you,
yet how can I say thank you, I who can't hold my liquor
    either
and don't even know the places to fish.

The poem is true in its particulars, except that my dad died in June and not October, as the first word of the poem says. I wanted a word with more than one syllable to it to make it linger a little. But more than that, I wanted a month appropriate to what I felt at the time I wrote the poem—a month of short days and failing light, smoke in the air, things perishing. June was summer nights and days, graduations, my wedding anniversary, the birthday of one of my children. June wasn't a month your father died in.

After the service at the funeral home, after we had moved outside, a woman I didn't know came over to me and said, "He's happier where he is now." I stared at this woman until she moved away. I still remember the little knob of a hat she was wearing. Then one of my dad's cousins—I didn't know the man's name—reached out and took my hand. "We all miss him," he said, and I knew he wasn't saying it just to be polite.

I began to weep for the first time since receiving the news. I hadn't been able to before. I hadn't had the time, for one thing. Now, suddenly, I couldn't stop. I held my wife and wept while she said and did what she could do to comfort me there in the middle of that summer afternoon.

I listened to people say consoling things to my mother, and I was glad that my dad's family had turned up, had come to where he was. I thought I'd remember everything that was said and done that day and maybe find a way to tell it sometime. But I didn't. I forgot it all, or nearly. What I do remember is that I heard our name used a lot that afternoon, my dad's name and mine. But I knew they were talking about my dad. *Raymond,* these people kept saying in their beautiful voices out of my childhood. *Raymond.*

HILARY KOSKI

"Stream of consciousness" writing is an illusion. It sounds loose and nearly out of control, simulating real-life spontaneity, but hidden within this flow is an unmistakable narrative direction (frame) and an unwavering thematic agenda (focus). As is so deftly demonstrated in "The Beauty Parlor" by Hilary Koski, every seemingly random thought and image has a definite connection: hair, furniture, friends, dress codes, unfullfilled loves (and lusts), shattered dreams. You can see the connections in her subtle, roundabout transitions: from the story of the sofa in the beauty parlor to her mother's manic behaviors; from the evolution of the school dress codes to hair coloring; from her haunting lost love, Carl, to the concepts of memory and invention and her own coming of age.

THE BEAUTY PARLOR

The whole time I was growing up I never knew the real color of my mother's hair. Once a week she would go to the beauty parlor where I'd sit and wait for her, amid funny smells and creams and big bubble dryers like spaceships.

The waiting room was near the front, and the windows at the two front walls were floor to ceiling; you could see right in. Men with big fat stomachs would come to get their wives, and when their wives weren't ready they would sit and wait, resigned and happy, not finding it the least bit odd that their wives would leave the beauty parlor looking no more beautiful and usually much funnier than they did when they walked in.

I would sit there too, and wait for my mother, and watch the strange, ugly ladies be escorted by the hand one by one to the dryers. The beautician would lead them over—the girl, they called her—drop their hand for a moment while she opened the flying saucer hatch at the top of the dryer, and then push them under. You could usually catch a glimpse of the pale, pasty faces, half-smiles starting around the red-gash mouths, just as they were swallowed up by the big bubble hood. This was the best part of my wait at the beauty parlor; I looked forward to it every week as I sat and waited for my mother. Never before had I seen anything quite this wonderful, nor, come to think of it, have I since. Repulsed as I was by these fat, horrid women, I, too, wanted to be taken by the hand by the chummy girl who would tell me all her secrets as I would tell her mine, and position me under that dryer. An hour of deafening noise in there and you'd come out changed. People would try to talk to you, they'd scream sometimes, but you just couldn't hear them. I saw it all the time; nothing touched you in that bubble. I could come out changed. I wanted to come out changed. But it wouldn't work, somehow. My eighty pounds just wouldn't fill the chair and press against the sides of it like the flesh of those women did; my head was much too small and much too low. And if the girl had pushed me under she would have knocked me down.

But oh, to look. How I loved to look. Until one day when I looked down and saw that the long, wide couch I was waiting for her on was the very same couch from our living room. That she had sold. She'd do things like that, my mother, sell the couch right out from under you. And then I had to look straight ahead, not even at Egbert, my favorite spaceship dryer, to avoid the looks of the fat-stomached men sitting next to me who knew. My mother came out laughing; she always did, her new hair stiff, and she'd steal glances in the rear-view mirror all the way home.

She said she went grey early, at thirty-five or so, so I would have to have seen it; the grey. But I remember thick brown hair, a soft, light color, healthy looking, and I realize now that she was going there not only to have it washed and set but dyed.

I color my hair too. For about six months now, since the grey stopped looking sexy. I have just turned forty and cannot afford to go to the beauty parlor. I use Clairol Color Mousse; Honey Gold Brown. Clairol Color Lotion of the same exact shade is much too dark, as is Light Warm Golden Brown. Clairol has the secret, you know. It's true. They will not divulge what's in the stuff. There are ingredients not listed on the package. You can call, write, break into the computer; it's Classified. One can only speculate. Their plant up in Stamford has one of the tightest, most advanced security systems in the country—which we pay for with our tax dollars. And this fascinates me, truly.

My hair, like my mother's, has had a few past lives. I was blonde 'til I was fourteen or so, then it turned gradually darker until a year ago, when the streaks of grey came in. A guy I was seeing asked me why my hair was three different colors and he didn't believe me when I told him I didn't dye it. And I didn't—until about a month after that, when I got sick of explaining my hair to people and looked in the mirror one day and thought the grey was just horrible and that I'd lost something I could never get back—the color of my hair!—and I shivered it hurt so much—like that time on my couch. She never told me she had sold it. I found that out sitting on it, waiting for her there at the beauty parlor. And I never brought it up.

I would wait for her a lot, at least it seems that way now, and miss her; and I don't mean long for her; I'm talking about timing. Once she came to visit me at lunchtime; a lot of the mothers did, but this was the one time I remember her coming. I was out on the playground, hiding, as I always did, from dodgeball. I saw the black and white Chevy from a distance and I ran to meet it, I ran really hard and fast, but she drove off before she saw me. I watched her through the chain link fence, watched her drive away, and I was exhausted—and ashamed—of what I couldn't have said—and the thing I remember most, aside from her calm, straight profile be-hind the wheel—laughing—was the fence; the exact curve of the metal, the intertwining links, its symmetrical diamond pattern, precision and strength. I didn't mind it, the fence. You might have thought I would have. But I think I found it calming, solid. Tim-ing is a funny thing. The moment you start to go grey, the very first monkey in a millennium of monkeys to stand upright, the long, long wait to call someone who doesn't want to talk to you; not too long and not too soon. Timing. She had me at thirty-five. Which was like fifty in those days. Which is not so unusual today.

The very latest study on hair dye proves, once again, that it does not cause cancer. Endless analyses of hair coloring, reems of data, have all arrived at the very same verdict: Harmless. The FDA protests too much. Lethal, Malignant—Brain Tumors; that's what I think (like saccharin, which gives you bladder cancer; fast-growing tumors in rats and humans, both. Sweet 'n Low reintroduced years later as aspartame in blue packets this time instead of pink, and re-named, quite accurately, Equal). Brain tumors from hair dye, that's what I think; tumors that make you crazy.

But at the beauty parlor I didn't know crazy. Not yet, anyway. There at the beauty parlor, for a moment in time, she was still my mother, and I was her daughter, and as different as we were from the others there—and from each other—I was still a daughter waiting for her mother at the beauty parlor. The couch was the be-ginning of crazy, the very beginning, I know now. Soon after that came the armchair and curtains, and the broken TV so the fat-stomached men would have something their dead eyes could land on. The loveseat she'd keep. I remember its embroidered satin roses as she bumped it, lunging towards me in the living room. And how I ducked and punched her back afterwards, how easy this was to do; she was tiny. How I disappeared for a week and when I came home we never brought it up. I just sat there the very next day at the beauty parlor—on the couch that used to be mine—and dreamed of an hour with Egbert. Did I mention she was pretty? And smart. And crazy, so crazy. But you've probably got that by now. My mother was crazy. The week I was gone I stayed at Shelly's, and we had one big slumber party. We stayed up every night and watched Million Dollar Movie and ate Breyer's vanilla bean ice cream (with real vanilla beans; you can't get it anymore) and made phony phone calls to every teacher we ever had. And Shelly's parents knew. That was the best thing about it. They knew and they just let us. It was so cool. It was like because my mother was crazy, we had permission. They were kind, her parents. And they never brought it up.

No one did, ever, not even Shelly. The thing about two loners being friends is that they respect each other more than two other people might. There were secrets, not to be divulged. Ingredients not listed on the package. One could only speculate. Shelly had hers, too; some talk about her mother like a sister—to this day I'm not quite sure—but we sensed them in each other early on, our secrets, and we deferred to them, gently.

There were other kindnesses, too. Like the day we were hauled down to Mr. St. Mary's office, hysterical. I mean we just couldn't stop laughing. Mrs. Aygree, the librarian, had showed up in a brand-new shirt. Usually we'd take bets on which of her three shirts she would wear that day; palm trees, panda bears or donuts, each tucked into the constant long black skirt—and then one Wednesday she comes in in giraffes—and they look just like her; that was the thing. I mean they both had the very same head and neck. We both saw it at the same exact second and made the big mistake of looking at each other, and then it was all over. Shelly doubled over squealing and I couldn't catch my breath; I mean there was no air at all left in my lungs and my stomach was killing me; it was sheer panic. We were wailing and we couldn't stop, and she dragged us out and into his office. She stopped the class and everything, and when he took us into the room with PRINCIPAL on the door and sat us down, he looked at our faces, back and forth, first Shelly's and then mine, and then his face cracked and he started laughing so hard I thought he might burst something; I mean fifty looked pretty old in those days—and the three of us sat there looking at each other, just laughing and laughing, until he finally coughed "Get out of here!" between hiccups. Then it was all right, somehow; like maybe I wasn't really her after all. Like maybe every time I laughed I might not hear her laughing. He was all right; Mr. St. Mary. He didn't act like everyone else did; like someone like me should be the last one laughing—though maybe that was true. He was okay. Maybe he had secrets, too. He must be eighty years old if he's a day now, if he's alive at all, that is. I wonder what he looks like; I can still see his face with his thick black hair; laughing, unable to stop. I wonder if he dyes it now. A lot of men do these days, even men that old; especially men that old. But I kind of doubt it.

Kids'll dye their hair too, especially around here where I live now, Greenwich Village—though that's a whole other category—and they did back in school, too. I was never one of those kids, nobody I really knew was. They were the hoods, the Wrong Side of the Tracks kids. I was in love with one of them. Carl, his name was. From Art Club, and he rode a motorcycle. Which was no small thing then. Pale, skinny Carl with his watery eyes and straight black hair. He dyed it. They were making him take Art Club as punishment—and to graduate—he'd been left back twice, I think. He just wanted out. You could see it in his face; the glassy stare, resigned, the way he'd let his body fall into his seat. He'd stare at me, completely calm, and my fingers would fumble tubes of oil paint and sometimes send one flying from my hands to the other side of the room I was so nervous. And my eyes would dart. The calmer he looked the more nervous I became. I never succeeded in meeting his gaze. I tried, all winter long, but I never could do it.

They let us wear jeans that March; we were the very first class not to freeze in stockings and skirts, and Carl would watch me in my stiff new Levis, trying hard to look cool. We were vanguard, cutting edge. That year was the very last year for garter belts too; after that it was all pantyhose. We came of age in that change; the moment we were old enough for stockings they switched it to pantyhose. Timing. She was real bad by then. I distinctly remember the smooth white button descended from elastic with the hook that would slide right over it, and exactly where it hit on my thigh—and then the sleek one-piece stockings with the built-in panties, too. I came of age in that change; embarrassed, confused. The day I switched to pantyhose I imagined Carl watching. I was wild for him. But I never could meet his eyes. He wanted out—of everything. Which is maybe why I couldn't. Because it would have taken anything, anything at all, to make me want out too—though you'd never have guessed it if you'd noticed me then. And because when I think of him now, beautiful Carl with his chiseled face that I had wanted to sculpt if I'd only known how, I'm sure he got what he wanted: I think of him dead. He was so sad, Carl. Which is maybe why I loved him.

But I'm not yet ready to bury it all—the secrets, the laughter, the years of wanting nothing but to be invisible—and I'm certainly not ready to bury Carl. Not just because he saw me when no one else could, or because he gave up so early—but because I still haven't made up my mind. Whether to go with him or not. I still don't know if he was wise or weak. Or both. I never knew his last name. Or the real color of his hair. So I don't know how to find him, I don't know where he is. Or if he is. And I can't let him go. He still stares at me, you know. Most of the time.

Ghosts. There are lots of them. Like another one I know. We used to sit at the table, before he moved away, seven o'clock, dinner time. That's when he'd get home, always at seven. But he wasn't there. He would sit, and sit, and stare. The face showed nothing. I didn't know where he was, who he was. Once, early on, I tried to figure it out. I was clever. I hid a radio behind the one we had and tuned it to the same station. The news. The news was always on at dinner time. I asked him to turn it off. He did. The radio behind it kept on playing. And his face showed nothing. The news was on and I found out nothing. She tossed her head back then, with the new, stiff hair that didn't move, that I never knew the color of—and she laughed. I gave up trying to figure it out right about then. He's gone now. But he still floats around me. The nothingness, the never knowing.

Maybe we invent it all, just make it all up. I mean we choose, we all do, what to hold onto, what to let go of. Remembering, forgetting. One isn't any easier than the other. They're both just about impossible, and you pay a price for both. But I'm not going for heroics here; I'm just trying to make it through the day. What is a memory, anyway? What makes a memory? How do you remember something, someone you never even knew? And what is knowing? Too many questions, I guess. But I just can't help it. And I'd really like to know. Right now, anyway. Most of the time I actually don't. Most of the time I entertain them when they come to call, just answer the door when they knock, play games with them when they're restless. These ghosts; like spoiled children. I shouldn't be home when they drop by. But it's hard. Because they're always around and they're always bored. They have no lives except through me. Vicarious thrills. Pathetic, don't you think? But they're in me, a part of me, like the colors of my hair. Always changing, they're relentless. And they just don't let me be. I can hold them back for weeks sometimes, or longer, but deathly white, they move back in and take me, piece by piece. They'll capture me, these ghosts. They'll steal me. Until I'm one of them.

But I am not afraid; I know them well. And I can make them wait. I can buy them a few weeks, a few months at a time. Of Time. Clairol Color Mousse; Honey Gold Brown. I can be the girl—I have been the girl—and take my own hand, lead me to the mirror where she tells me all her secrets as I tell her all of mine, where a face that's not invisible, that maybe never was invisible—a face not strange or ugly—just looks back. Clairol Color Mousse; Honey Gold Brown. They can wait, these ghosts. And they'll wait as I waited for my mother; at the beauty parlor.

PHILLIP RICHARDS

Phillip Richards, "a black professor of English at a small 'elite' university in upstate New York," uses scenes and stories to effectively shape and contrast "the folk" of his past with "the folk" of his present, which is the focus of this very provocative and dramatic essay. Richards's persona is provocative as well; he shares insights about himself, but his parents and students dominate the narrative.

LEAVING THE FOLK

I am a black professor of English at a small "elite" university in upstate New York. In this tiny town the shoe-store owner, newspaper vendor, and garbagemen wave hello to me as I walk to the gray stone campus buildings where I work. My family leaves our doors unlocked—neighbors sometimes come into the empty house to return a casserole dish—and I am currently in possession of a lawn mower that I borrowed three weeks ago. I spend most of my time teaching and writing about literature. My presence here is not accidental. My parents attended Hampton Institute, a small black college in Virginia, where they studied under white New England teachers who were themselves educated in schools such as the one at which I now teach. My mother grew up idealizing the crisp abolitionist air that I have breathed for much of my professional life. My life here is, in fact, the fulfillment of her dreams.

At my university, I am frequently called upon to give moral and psychological support to the black students who attend this predominantly white school. No one had ever demanded this of me; it is implicit in my existence here. Many of the black students I encounter feel deeply alienated from the very institution that provides them with a free $25,000-a-year education; they are distrustful of whites and often cannot handle the schoolwork. In class they tend to stick together. In public their faces are impassive. Their speech to outsiders is often laconic and ironical. They have shielded themselves emotionally from an academic and social environment that they find profoundly threatening. Beneath their stony exteriors is a trauma that outsiders cannot know.

Those black students who mingle with their white classmates have probably gone to upper-middle-class suburban high schools or private schools. One immediately recognizes the exceptional black students on campus: their faces tend to be relaxed, they are likely to say hello, as is the community manner and—I will not let this pass—they tend to be light-skinned. They look like my parents, say, might imagine a black student at such a school to look. They belong *at the school* rather than *in the school's black community.* The very best of them are making a break that every black intellectual, in his own way, makes—away from the world of the folk and into the realm of ideas. And I suspect that despite their excellent manners they are more than a little uneasy.

Five years ago, along with a psychologist and a historian, I taught an interdisciplinary course on racism. Although my colleagues gave informed lectures, what I remember were the moments of psychodrama and rage exhibited by the black students huddled in groups in our large, sunlit classroom. From time to time the black students confronted the whites with evidence of the racism they found embedded in every aspect of academic life at the college. At one point I asked why the blacks remained at such a despicable place, why they did not walk out. The unofficial spokesman for the black group, addressing me in a tone one uses with overeducated dummies, told me that they were there for the scholarship money.

My students' behavior paralyzed me for the rest of the day. I felt that I should have had some prepared response, for, as I have said, part of my academic function is to provide guidance to black students. All I have to offer by way of explanation is the sense that the impasse between me and my black students is not extraordinary. It has repeated itself often in my life and in the lives of my parents, and perhaps in the lives of their parents as well. My black students are living black America's central but largely unacknowledged reality: division by class. They are entering the impasse in which I came to know the world.

I was born in 1950 in Cleveland, Ohio, where my father came to work in the steel mills and auto factories after World War II. He and my mother moved from neighborhood to neighborhood there, in a pattern that led from Glenville to Mt. Pleasant to Lee

Harvard and finally to Forest Hill, the once-exclusive section of Cleveland Heights. There was nothing distinctive about this journey; it had been followed in different forms first by middle-class Jews and later by middle- and, finally, lower-class blacks. The consequences of the demographic shifts on Cleveland's East Side do not encourage sentimental attachments to old neighborhoods. I would not, for example, get out of the car now to inspect the studio apartment in Cleveland's Glenville where my parents first lived. A few years ago, however, I drove into Mt. Pleasant to show my wife and children the shingled three-bedroom house on the leafy street where I'd grown up. In front of what had once been the Reverend McKinney's sycamore-shaded lawn, I paused behind a large, white Cadillac. From the house that had once belonged to the Reverend McKinney ran two young black men. Although I saw them pass a small packet into the Cadillac's window, it took me much longer than my wife and thirteen-year-old daughter to recognize what had happened—in the broadest sense. When we returned to my family's house in Cleveland Heights, my father, now eighty years old, gave me a look when he heard that I had driven my wife and children in a Volvo station wagon down Kinsman Street to East 137th Street—then he broke out into his broad, incredulous laugh, amazed that anyone could be so stupid.

Forty years ago, around 5:00 P.M. on Saturdays, in front of the house on East 137th Street, my father would stand in the driveway and hose the stray grass down into the street. The loose cuttings streamed down the asphalt to the gutter, where they flowed into the sewer. My father stood there erect for a good half hour, moving slowly down the drive, his jaw set, his eyes placid with thought. By that time in the day he had cleaned the entire house and often had worked on whatever car we owned (we always had a large American station wagon that my father held together for six or seven years). He was then in his early forties and worked, by my count, sixty and sometimes seventy hours a week as a custodian in the Cleveland public schools. In one of those significant parental acts that no child can fathom, he kept me, his eldest son, by his side for most of Saturday, telling me tales of his early life. Before he became the rather self-satisfied black burgher that he seemed to me at nine years old, he had been an undertaker's assistant in Kentucky, a drifter, a shipmate working on the great aircraft carriers as they were being built in Newport News during World War II, and a lackluster student in auto mechanics at Hampton Institute, where he had sung spirituals and blues. When I was old enough to ask why he wandered across the country at nineteen with neither money nor kin, he replied that something had said go, and he went.

I was a slender, bookish boy who lived in my imagination; I appalled my father, much of whose experience consisted of watching disasters overtake heedless people like myself. And many of the stories he told on those Saturday mornings and afternoons were about such disasters. He remembered, for instance, the typhoid fever that had struck his hometown in Kentucky, killing most of the black children his age. When their temperatures went past 102, he said, they usually died. Working on an aircraft carrier, he had watched as two men killed a third by playfully sticking an air hose up his anus. In one of the factories where he had worked, he had seen men electrocuted. His own father had worked in the mines in Kentucky and died of stomach ulcers, howling on his bed while his wife and children listened, utterly unable to comfort him.

My father told these stories in an enormously calm manner, with no change of expression. He rarely maintained eye contact with me but instead looked off into the distance, much as my black college students do when I question them too insistently about their studies. After finishing the lawn, my father would walk me around the neighborhood and chat with the neighbors, Mr. Beasely and Mr. Gregory. At first the men would solicitously ask me questions about school and current events, but inevitably the talk settled into the same placid tones of voice, the same faraway looks—the signs of shared understanding that this world was full of suffering, expected and unexpected. The great unending trauma demanded endurance—the set lips and impassive gaze with which black men learn to confront the world. (It has taken me years of working with black students to understand that it is this same stern faculty of endurance I inevitably encounter in their silences and quizzical glances. They have the nihilistic attitudes of the folk, but secondhand, by way of the rappers on MTV and the buffoons on black situation comedies. Nevertheless, their postures seem to carry authentic weight.)

My mother would often angrily interrupt my father's story-telling in the driveway in order to redirect him to his work. He loved to talk, and my mother saw his talk as a kind of intolerable irrationality, a luxury that kept the family from further achievement. My parents had acquired what little they owned only through her frugal budgeting, her fierce restraints upon my father's spending habits, and the utter suppression of any kind of pleasure that cost money. His stoic worldview accompanied a present-mindedness that allowed him to draw pleasure from the very world that confined him. In defiance of my mother, for example, he would buy handfuls of fruit candy when we went downtown to shop.

Lacking my father's self-possession, my mother was never satisfied with our circumstances. She was forever on the move; even in repose she was not still. Had my father not been so unshakably rooted, he might have been disturbed, but he looked on her with a certain amusement. Seated on the gray sofa, he watched her the way one might observe a newly caged cockatoo. Her friends were the left-wing teachers at Park Synagogue, the only white nursery school in Cleveland willing to hire a young black woman in the late 1940s. She had pounded the streets of the East and West Sides past mobs of pushing, poking, babushkaed, newly arrived immigrants. She now had the job of teacher and was renowned in Cleveland's cultured Jewish society for her skills with her students, children of wealthy Jewish families. She had seen the boom of prosperity that gilded the postwar lives of her students and their parents (the synagogue designed in the international style by Eric Mendelsohn, its Chagall-like air of old-world modernism amid what was still a woodsy Cleveland Heights), and she grimly discerned the world of black middle-class Cleveland from the vantage point of the flowering possibilities of Shaker Heights and Beachwood. It is easy now to stereotype the vulgarity of suburban life in the Fifties, but that way of life represented an essentially green American spirit of promise. My mother grasped a springtime sense of the world's fluidity, which in that moment seemed to be symbolized by the movement of successive groups through the Canaan of Cleveland's East Side, and it was there that she wanted to move from East 137th Street.

. . .

I now live in what I have to come to recognize as a distant offshoot of my mother's world. The age of leftist black and white cooperation in which she lived is now gone. Most of my students come from upper-class families in New York City and its surrounding suburbs in Connecticut and New Jersey, and although I used to know all of the cultural signs of the left, I am now bewildered by the improbable collage of styles and shapes that pass through my classroom. When I read my students' papers, it occurs to me that I am teaching the children of the generation of postwar toddlers my mother taught. My closest friend in prep school once showed me a Park Synagogue nursery school report written by my mother and still kept by his family. It was a two-page note closely written in a determined and meticulous hand. Its focus was a lengthy analysis of the way in which my friend played with his class's pet animals. I try, and fail, to imagine my mother at age thirty-one or thirty-two, observing the habits of wealthy Jewish children with hamsters. Her efforts, I suppose, are little different from my own as I watch my wealthy white charges' attempts at comprehending Jonathan Edwards, Nathaniel Hawthorne, and Toni Morrison. The deep irony of black life, which my mother had noticed already in the Fifties, was that the greatest intellectual fulfillment for blacks is to be found in atypical places, in unexpected connections and unimagined conditions. But although my students have inherited the same deep promise of American life that drove my mother to her remarkable accomplishments as an educator and parent, many do not recognize me as a brother. In their eyes I am the beneficiary of obscene privileges that will be denied them. They regard me skeptically at the beginning of each semester, and over the course of the term cautiously watch one another across the newest ethnic fault line in American life.

So unlike were my father and mother that one had to remind oneself that they were both black. Only during the rituals of Saturday morning breakfast did one come to understand the complicated set of anxieties, hopes, and satisfactions that had brought them together. At the breakfast table they told and retold the story of their unexpected union, and there, for brief moments, I realized that my parents had been young once: my mother a light-skinned, long-haired girl, madly in love with my father at Hampton, giving up a fellowship to the Bank Street School in New York City for the fall of 1947; my father a factory worker and erstwhile mechanic, a failed sociology and physical education student at all-black Kentucky State. On the face of it, they were an unpromising match: she was nineteen, with her future before her; he, a good twenty-nine, with bad prospects. At Hampton, they rowed together in boats, fished for eels, and plotted a life in which their differences made no difference at all.

The black middle class is now in the process of constructing a romance around the history of its black colleges, but Hampton Institute was a tough, bitter place for my parents, even though both had come from difficult backgrounds. Whenever I complained about racial discrimination, my father would wryly observe that it was particularly bad among black people. My mother, he knew, had been hurt in ways that only one who held black middle-class aspirations could be. Her father, himself a mulatto child of a slave-master father, had, through hard work, thrift, and the leeway given racially mixed people in her part of Virginia, built a large successful farm, which he lost in a horrifying apocalyptic fire when my mother was seven. Raised by her older and well-off married cousins, she bore, as an orphan, the brunt of the family's legacy of decline. To attend Hampton as a disadvantaged student despite what my cousins called her "blow hair" (hair long and straight enough to blow in a fan) must have been an enormous trauma. A poor grind, she was looked down upon despite her light skin (something that took some doing in the Hampton of the Forties). Even though she was an excellent student, she gave up a scholarship to Howard, fearing the snubs that the children of black doctors, lawyers, and undertakers reserved for their fellow blacks. At Hampton she concentrated on her studies while working nearly forty hours a week. My father, misplaced in the trade school, was working almost equally long hours, exploited by teachers who on more than a few occasions called him out of bed to repair defunct wartime cars. Under autocratic professors, amid snobbish classmates, my parents could never escape their backgrounds in dirt-poor rural Virginia and Kentucky. Indeed, when I encountered the black academic world, their pasts would shadow me.

However much my parents respected the New England culture that the white missionary professors had brought to Hampton from Massachusetts, New York, and Connecticut, they despised its appropriation by an academic black middle class eager for a glory and a social standing that the transplanted New Englanders went out of their way to disdain. My parents saw these black academics and their Phi Beta Kappa children attending Dartmouth and Columbia as the very embodiment of ruthless black status-seeking arrogance. My father's first dean at Kentucky State, who was black, had dismissed him from school, admonishing him to go home and find a job cleaning for the white people. My father was fond of imitating a young black martinet who had just received his Ph.D. from Indiana University. Standing in overalls in the garage, my father would mock the black professor (as he was called), holding his finger like a candle. "I am Dr. Mark," he said in a falsetto voice, "and I will fail you."

My home was filled with pious respect for what black students at my college now disparagingly call white Western culture, a respect whose perfunctory signs were ragged paperback editions of Freud's writings and Shakespeare's tragedies. Oblivious to my parents' real relationship toward the cultural world into which they pushed me, I dutifully read the books they gave me, practiced for the piano lessons they arranged at the Cleveland Institute of Music, studied French at Western Reserve's summer school, and earnestly observed what I saw at the Cleveland Museum of Art. Yet even the haphazard cultivation available to a black boy on Cleveland's 137th Street inevitably led me to discover that my parents' respect for culture had little to do with their actual lives. Like everything else they possessed, they held their enthusiasms in trust for their children's future. I can qualify this generalization only by noting their appreciation of the great African American singers they had heard as college students at Hampton in the Forties. The names of Paul Robeson, Roland Hayes, and Marian Anderson were mentioned with nothing less than religious awe. And some of the fiercer arguments at the Sunday dinner table concerned the tempos with which spirituals had been sung that morning at Antioch Baptist Church, a question ultimately turning on a deeper dilemma; namely, whether the great slave hymns were, as my parents felt, the self-pitying moans they had become among the urban black lumpen of the North or were, in fact, what W. E. B. Du Bois and James Weldon Johnson claimed they were: the American Negro's most dignified and profound contribution to the culture of the West.

This passion perhaps explains my contact with a spinsterish, wire-haired, eccentric black woman in her late sixties named Mrs. Apple, a teacher discovered by my parents at the Cleveland Institute of Music. One afternoon, on the pretense of being frustrated by my inept performance of a Chopin prelude, she spent over an hour playing Chopin, Liszt, and Brahms for me, discoursing all the while on Romanticism as I listened, spellbound. It had never occurred to me before that this music, along with the foreign-language texts on her desk, was part of a world of thought, time, and place. I wondered with whom she discussed her love and knowledge of music and literature, this apparently secret treasure that she had clearly hoarded for herself. In her ramblings I had the first premonitions of the life abroad not only in music but in the books and names in the dull gray library at 140th Street and Kinsman.

At the end of those Saturday morning breakfasts, my parents basked in the reminiscence of their intention to come to Cleveland because it was a place where they could educate their children in good schools and museums and live in the relatively inexpensive large homes of Wade Park, Glenville, and Mt. Pleasant. These neighborhoods eventually turned into ghettos, but even now their vast fronts convey the promise Cleveland offered its postwar immigrants from Europe and the South. If my father possessed these dreams, he had taken them from my mother, even as she had appropriated his placid assurance that this middle-class utopia could, in fact, be reached. The Cleveland they arrived in looked more like what one expected of Warsaw or Prague than a Midwestern American city on Lake Erie. As a young boy I noticed that more people on the buses read Polish, Hungarian, or German newspapers than the lackluster morning *Plain Dealer* or the sensationalist *Cleveland Press*. In this new world, my parents had created an unlikely romance. Once, deep into a Saturday afternoon, my father showed me two packets of letters wrapped in pink ribbon, their correspondence when my father came to Cleveland to find work in the factories while my mother stayed in Hampton after their marriage. It was hard to imagine that my parents, who had spent many of their nights arguing over the bills, had once been enthralled with their new fortunes. But it is clear from the letters that

Cleveland would be an escape from the endless color snobbery of Hampton Institute, from my maternal relatives (who thought the marriage such an obvious disaster for this bright young girl with a scholarship), and (this point being even farther from the surface) from the restrictions of the color line that imprisoned them outside the middle-class black world. Their deepest, most pleasurable memories had a pastoral simplicity: riding the pedal boats in the Wade Park lagoon, my mother reading alone in the library on 106th Street, and the long walks they took through then green Glenville, dreaming of the bourgeois life and happiness that they would one day possess.

This happiness rapidly ran afoul of the prejudices held by the blacks my parents came to know in Cleveland. Although my mother's skin color, her education, and her social aspirations might have qualified her for an upper-class black church such as the Euclid Avenue Congregational Church, my father's job as a janitor suited him only for the storefront churches along Cedar Avenue. They compromised and attended Antioch Baptist Church, where they were roundly snubbed by the elite of doctors and professionals and assigned to the lower class of maids and laborers.

Their minister, the Reverend McKinney, belonged to a light-skinned Mississippi family. The son of a sharecropper, he had nevertheless attended Morehouse College. In the sanctuary of the pulpit, he flaunted his class privilege by reprimanding members of the congregation who responded aloud to him during his sermons. In a nasty bit of class consciousness, he made fun of the large, expensive leather purses carried by a number of elderly black women. These women were maids, and for them, as for many lower-class people in Antioch, church attendance afforded a show of dignity denied them in their employers' homes in Shaker Heights and Beachwood. My mother was the last person to romanticize lower-class blacks, but even she was struck by the utter cruelty of McKinney's frequent jibes.

All the same, church was the ideological pivot of our lives. The sermon was the first literary form that carried the structure of ideas for me; the sacraments, my first encounter with mystery in the form of metaphor. The church's articulation of mystery allowed me to feel for the first time what I could not adequately explain to myself. To go to a black Baptist church in Cleveland in the late Fifties and early Sixties was to encounter the deepest hopes and aspirations of black people at a propitious time in history. My parents attended morning and early afternoon services, teaching Sunday school in between. The songs of the young adult choir were often spirituals. There was a junior church for older children and young adolescents. At Communion, Christians were served a sweet undiluted portion of Welch's grape juice; I can still feel its stickiness on my tongue. Music was provided by a choir, to which I belonged. There, for the first time, I heard "We Shall Overcome," sung by three girls who crossed their arms and joined hands. Theologically, we were exposed to the Reverend McKinney's interests, which I now understand were those of a typical nineteenth-century evangelical. I recall little emphasis on hellfire, but I came to know in a powerful way that life would end. What would death look like? Perhaps the bright glimpse of green that I caught under water during my baptism, by full immersion, in the church's glass-walled font.

The eschatological slant of the service persisted into our Sunday dinner. Frequently, Mrs. Watkins, a tall, elderly black woman, was invited from church to eat with my grandmother, a small, wizened woman nearly eighty years old. Mrs. Watkins, I now realize, was a common black churchgoing type, relatively rare in our congregation. Sitting on the gray sofa above the thinning, scrupulously vacuumed carpet, she held forth. She would spend long hours discussing the apocalypse with my grandmother, who knew extraordinarily lengthy passages of the Bible by heart. Mrs. Watkins, as such people will, mistook my close attention for a certain kind of religious potential and began indoctrinating me with her visions of the end. And on one Sunday afternoon when I was about eleven years old, I ran from room to room convinced that I heard God calling my name.

My father, however, was not interested in conversation about the apocalypse. His close acquaintance with disaster had made him unmoved by talk that touched bottom. My parents had friends who had recently come up from the South and thus were familiar with bankruptcy, garnished wages, and failed credit. Not only would the world end, as Mrs. Watkins claimed it would; a world *was* ending, the coming of some final day being in evidence all around us. My parents worked deep in the city of Cleveland, where signs of an approaching end, at least as they conceived of it in their provincial Southern way, were hard not to see. And Sunday dinner—with its fried chicken, iced tea, and lemon meringue pie—was a time for stocktaking. Although the inner-city schools—huge, dank, drab prison-like buildings where my father worked—would take on apocalyptic terrors in the Sixties, a dismal foreshadowing was already visible in the Fifties. In the mornings after church, I accompanied my father to check a school building and watched him repair the windows broken by stones that lay on the classroom floors. Even more ominous were the growing thefts of typewriters and business machines that increasingly required my father to rise from bed at three in the morning after the school alarms had been tripped and the police had been called. The crimes were nothing compared with the outright violence of the world of the street, a world utterly removed from my view but available for inspection in the lurid tales of black-on-black murder and rape reported in the *Cleveland Press* and the local black newspaper, *The Call and Post*.

As the Sixties passed, my parents encountered increasing signs of social collapse, and by the time of the riots in the summer of 1966, no one could accuse my father, who by then had been a custodian for nearly fifteen years, of being naive about black urban life. After one of his schools was burglarized in Hough, Glenville, or Collinwood, he would drive there and wait in his car until the police gave him the all clear to approach a huge dark building that they themselves were only too happy to leave. But even the routine destruction of the windows that he fixed on Sunday, the maliciously stopped-up toilets, and the casually strewn excrement did not prepare him for what he began to see in the late Sixties and early Seventies. The stories he brought home about his workday were gradually marked less by outrage than by incredulity as he described how, day after day, eighteen-, nineteen-, and twenty-year-olds (the Cleveland school system being what it was) routinely kicked in doors and ripped thermostats from walls. He was similarly amazed by the young pregnant women who were violent in the face of perceived and imagined insults, not only from boys and men but from other girls like themselves. As time progressed, both groups were increasingly ignored by teachers and principals, and especially by custodians, who had no wish to be shot by people for whom they had no responsibility. By the Seventies, the daily schedule of violence was taking place amid the aura of marijuana, floating from the bathrooms to the halls and, finally, like the yellow fog in "The Love Song of J. Alfred Prufrock," everywhere.

My father's perspective was also informed by his commerce with the black working man. In his schools he supervised crews of twenty and thirty laborers, cleaning women, and various repairmen. The people drawn from the lower-class black community traditionally brought to their jobs the tricksterism and cynicism bemoaned by conservative social scientists and social pathologists and now celebrated by major black critics in the Modern Language Association as the spiritual heart of African American culture. Cleaning large schools with such people required a sharp tongue, a stern hand, and calculated shows of force designed to impress people who had been deconstructing white patriarchal rhetoric for some time. Yet even my father was amazed as their habitual resistance to work began to take on new forms. His men had no interest in the traditional route from laborer to fireman to custodian (a route taken by my father under the supervision of an older generation of Polish custodians deeply suspicious of his ability to learn the intricacies of shoveling coal) and were, increasingly, individuals best represented by a young man who each day dressed in a new bizarre wardrobe—one day a suit, the next day African dress.

The same tale was told from another point of view by my mother, now an administrator in the Cleveland Head Start office. She had dealt first as a teacher and then as a supervisor with the children of the violent young men and touchy girls now carefully avoided by my father in the schools. Predictably, the young parents' rage continued at home—that is, in the unlikely instance that both were home. By the early Seventies, this rage had begun to take on surreal manifestations that made my mother, already hardened by years of ghetto work, wince. Cigarette burns, severe welts, and broken limbs, freely and casually admitted by the three-year-old victims to be the work of "daddy," now appeared regularly. A successful gardening project that my mother had started some years earlier had withered away along with the plausibility of the bourgeois values of thrift, autonomy, and self-respect that had sustained it.

Long an advocate of continuing education, my mother arranged with a local community college to place teacher-educators in an associate degree program for early childhood education. By the end of the first term, these students would be receiving mostly Ds from young white radical and liberal professors who were constantly on the phone with my mother, asking whether they might give these students a grade below C. By the next semester, now perfectly aware of their status in the university, these students cruised through the spring with D averages. Afterward, they inevitably dropped out of Cuyahoga Community College, Head Start, and public life itself, only to be seen briefly by my mother in silk dresses, stepping out of new Elektra 225s on their way to marathon card games played in ghetto apartments before huge new Sony color TVs. The emergence of this new leisure class was a continuing mystery to my mother—she, after all, had given up a graduate fellowship to the Bank Street School to work full time and raise a family. More puzzled than angered—why would these people, who clearly were given *everything,* quit school?—she began to ponder an emerging white liberal explanation for this phenomenon: that work, social mobility, respectability—indeed the entire gestalt of the American middle class—meant nothing to these people. But this was an explanation that she would never accept. She rejected it over and over again in increasingly fierce arguments with privileged liberal suburbanites whom she began to suspect of a cynicism deeper than anything out on the already nihilistic streets.

This world continued to come apart. Young pregnant students would bring their smallest children to school; their fathers would bring guns. When I was a child it was hard for me to make out the exact dimensions of this world, but they were revealed by the few inner-city children in my Sunday school class; already they were brazen, their mouths set, their faces impassive, and their minds scarred with a cynicism that defined the way in which they engaged life. Shortly after a space launch, my Sunday school teacher, Dr. Toney, an orthodontist who taught at the Western Reserve School of Dentistry, asked one of my classmates what he thought of the American space program. The boy, who was no more than ten, replied quickly and unequivocally that there was already more than enough trouble on earth for white people to attend to. I remember Dr. Toney's flinch.

. . .

In time, my parents escaped the coming terrors of urban wrath, and, in a typically middle-class black journey, they progressed from a one-room apartment in Wade Park to a duplex in tree-lined Glenville to their first single home on 137th Street in Mt. Pleasant to a slightly larger house on 173rd and Intermere in Lee Harvard to, finally, the woodsy, once-enclosed gardens of Forest Hills, where, three years later, as an elderly couple fearing robbery and assault, they decided not to open the door of their $90,000 house on Halloween.

The vision of the city left behind shadowed us and received considerable reflection at the Sunday dinner table. In the midst of their accounts of the trials of black life as it was lived in Cleveland from 1947 through the Sixties, my parents brought up the same quarrel with almost ritualistic frequency. The prosperous North Carolina farm my mother grew up on had been surrounded by dirt-poor sharecroppers who had remained on the land of their antebellum masters. The sharecroppers had never moved, and they exerted only minimal energy in attending to their own needs. Late in the winter, when their thin stores of canned vegetables disappeared, these people—perhaps the wife and a young child—would come to my grandparents' door and ask for a "mess of beans." My grandmother readily acceded to these requests, only to rage at the sharecroppers' indolence long after their emissaries had gone. At the dinner table, my mother continued her mother's rage, now directing it at the urban poor who kept my parents awake at nights, busy on Sundays, and enervated every day of the week. My father had a different line of reasoning. He argued quietly and firmly that these people were not to be condemned for what they did, that their seeming indolence made a kind of sense, although he did not say what this was. His view only enraged my mother further; she argued that *this* was what was wrong with the race in general: "no gumption." Her father, denied any money by his white father, had as a young man hopped a freight train in North Carolina and landed in New York, where he bellhopped until he made enough money for a down payment on a plot of land between Roanoke Rapids and Weldon, where Route 95 now runs.

Here my mother would pause. Her father had died of pneumonia after the great house, the embodiment of all his dreams for his family and himself, burned down. She and her mother had been plunged into a life of dependence and poverty, albeit genteel for a black family during the Depression. But without gumption, she insisted, the race would accomplish nothing. Her exchanges with my father would continue through the last piece of lemon pie, until my father picked up the Sunday paper and went upstairs, silently, to the bathroom. In the kitchen, my mother would fume.

My father's view now haunts me wherever I go in this ambition-ridden life. I suspect that he and the sharecroppers of my mother's childhood were well acquainted with the void into which their fragile livelihoods might collapse. What did he mean when he said that the sharecroppers were perfectly *right* to sit there in all of their begging indolence? Moreover—and this was the heart of the matter—what peace could they have made with themselves after having encountered my grandmother's icy contempt? What did it mean that their way of life was justified? My father seemed to be as deeply committed to the family's fierce mobility as my mother, yet in his stoic acceptance of a final emptiness I found an ironic counterpoise to the hustle and bustle of her middle-class zeal.

The deepest lesson of my life is contained in the impasse between my parents on those Sunday evenings. African American culture may be grounded not in one impulse but in two: the world of intellectual and social accomplishment embodied by my mother; and the world of the folk, the world of my father, a world defined by its endurance of the harsh realities of deprivation, pathology, and racism.

This latter world—the world of the set jaw of my father—is now chillingly inhabited by my black students. Born in the Seventies, they are perhaps the first generation of African Americans to confront the deep terrors of urban black existence with little more to sustain them than the nihilistic ironies of the ghetto. The profound destructiveness and rootlessness that seeped into middle-class black life during the Fifties and early Sixties is now their cultural style, its fragmentation and alienation commodified and legitimated by corporate interests. This commercialized world of the folk provides the explanations with which many young black people confront the experience of oppression. And, to an unprecedented extent, it is the context in which black intellectual life is now formed.

The life of intellectual aspiration, however, requires an aloofness from the world of the folk. This is the distance my students are trying to calibrate, to articulate for themselves. This is why they consider me sullenly across the space of my classroom or endure stony conversations with me during walks across campus. No black of aspiration—especially today—can abandon the tragic vision of the folk, especially as they pass through their valley of destruction in today's urban holocaust. Yet I hope that the very best of my black students will, like the best of African American intellectuals, find a self and a consciousness that exists—however fleetingly—above this nation's cauldron of racial despair.

JACK CADY

In "Welcome Sweet Springtime" Jack Cady introduces his neighbors—common, ordinary people he describes as heroes because they have survived difficult lives, stayed together through most of the twentieth century, and supported each other and prevailed during the hard times of the Great Depression, two wars, and now age and loss. The sweet simplicity of the lives of the people Cady portrays is captured in the sweet simplicity of his prose, the strength of this essay—which, Cady states, "is a celebration of the greatness of people who do not think of themselves as great and who are rarely noticed by our busy world." Cady demonstrates how writers may discover incidents to dramatize and themes for essays in the most mundane events.

WELCOME SWEET SPRINGTIME

As winter turns to spring the woodpile gets to looking small and lost and lonesome. Wind still humps along this northwest coast, bringing snow and rain from Alaska. People still hunch before stoves while admiring the thought of daffodils. Sometimes even the oldest heads and hands get caught with knowing we've got more winter than they've got woodpile. That's what happened to Mitchell around crocus time, and a month before the daffodils.

You'd think the man would blush. He's been at this business of living for eighty-four years, and he's shoved enough fir and pine and alder into stoves. He's toasted his shins with heat from maple, cherry, pear, and apple. During the Great Depression he even heated with dry corn mixed with rabbit droppings. The man has seen his share.

He still got caught, though, and had to go out hunting; which, when you're eighty-four, means firing up the rusting pickup and chugging down to Water Street which runs long and pretty empty this time of year. Mitchell doesn't much hold with chainsaws, but doesn't mind buying wood from men who do. In this small town there won't be many jobs until spring tourist season. Our young guys rob timber company slash piles, then park their trucks on Water Street. People walk along checking the loads. A good mix of seasoned fir and madrona brings the highest price.

So Mitchell went out shopping, and probably told himself and everybody else that they don't grow firewood like they used to. He likely fussed and poked and prodded and thumped like a man adrift in a melon patch. He'd never stoop to haggling, but you can bet he claimed prices were mighty dear. Anyway, he comes home in triumph, trailed by a wideside pickup full of wood. The youngster driving is grateful and hiding it. Cordwood brings ninety dollars, and the kid sure needs ninety dollars. You can tell by looking at his truck.

The whole business turns out sort of liberating. Winter around here tucks us into our houses. We wave across wet or snowy lawns as we trundle to the woodpiles. There's Dave and Sally's small place, and it couldn't be more clean and tidy if it was Dutch. Across the street sit the disabled apartments where social workers put up folks who need a lift. There's my place next to them, and Mitchell across from me. Christine and Ed live in the apartments and kind of make the place a point of interest. Ed is blind and in a wheelchair, but he's got a good mind for stories. He records them on tape for others who have his problem.

And there's the crazy lady, Sarah Jane, who cranks up volume on her record player and dances before her front window, usually wearing clothes. She owns a good heart, though. Mostly. But that's getting ahead of the story.

Just as the wood truck backs into Mitchell's yard, along comes a break in the clouds. The snow is nearly melted after rain, and it's like nature spoofs Mitchell who got nervous and bought wood. It's like nature says, "Mitchell, old son, I've tricked you all over again, because here comes a warm spring."

The break in the clouds is just enough so everyone can get out and superintend the wood truck, plus catch up on all the happenings. I go over, my new pup bought before Christmas trails along; the new dog in the neighborhood.

Ed and Christine's dog is Shadow, but Shadow doesn't live here anymore except in memory; which we all have lots of. I'm the youngster in this neighborhood, being only sixty-one.

The pup makes a hit with the kid, and of course that takes time from unloading. The black-haired kid and the brown-furred pup go skylarking off somewhere, and I ease up to the firewood with a critical eye. Mitchell stands looking proud and shamed; proud because he's bought well-seasoned fir, and shamed because he had to in the first place.

"It looks real good," I tell him. He grunts, still standing tall as a ladder, but bent like a warped board, and ready to change the subject. His hands are larger than his thin arms say they ought to be.

He'll be two days stacking that wood. Maybe Dave and I will help, if Mitchell's pride can handle it.

Dave and Sally step from their house and walk toward us, Dave walking straight, like the soldier he once was; Sally wearing a red scarf and looking pretty frail. If Dave did not check the load he'd bust.

From out of a stand of scraggly weeds the pup pops loose in that jack-rabbity way pups have. The kid comes back to his truck, breathing deep but not winded. Now we've got a crowd. The kid starts to unload. Balks of fir fly, hit the ground, thump and roll.

We talk about firewood and pups. Then we talk about Sarah Jane who went to the hospital yesterday. Sarah Jane didn't take her medicine, and that made her get a butcher knife and go after Christine. Christine ducked in the house and called 911. Ed couldn't see a blamed thing, being blind, and, being in a wheel-chair, in no shape to tussle a knife.

This business about Sarah Jane is news because sometimes I forget to open my drapes. When 911 came I missed it. I tsk and tush and figure something will happen next.

The kid has his load coming off thumpity-thump. I'm holding the pup so she won't dance under a flying hunk of fir. Christine comes from her apartment. She's still a pretty woman, but care-worn. She has her hardships, but still congregates real easy. It isn't the firewood draws her, but the first meeting of the neighborhood this spring.

A squincy lot of snow still lingers among some weeds, and Christine has to get enough together so the pup can chase her first snowball. Christine throws the ball about eight feet, and the pup does what we expect. She jumps after the snowball and gets all confused when the thing falls apart. In between dead weeds a little green is starting to perk, and that's a good sign of early spring, and a good sign Mitchell's been bamboozled.

"She's going to look like a beer keg on stilts," Christine says about the pup, who is half Lab and half spaniel.

"But with a very fine smile," I tell her. The break in the clouds disappears, and gray northwest mist sits high in the trees.

"I dread the day when we lose ours," Sally says, and everybody is polite. Dave and Sally have a mutt who is nobody's favorite, being a bad-tempered loudmouth, and rowdy. Sally just got over a dead-serious bout at the hospital, and now she'd got to make it through spring; because, have you ever noticed, how, if old folks are going to slide, they do it just before spring?

"I couldn't bear to get another dog," Sally says, and everybody thinks the same thing but nobody talks. Dogs live ten or twelve years. There isn't a mother's son or daughter in the neighborhood with a real long chance of outliving a pup, even though it's a responsibility; something I'd better think about.

The kid bangs his fingers between a couple hunks of wood, and cusses under his breath but not loud. That means he's had some raising from somebody.

"Things got sort of exciting yesterday." Sally says this noncommittal in case Christine doesn't want to talk about it, but Christine does.

"I hope she's going to be all right," Christine says. "I worry over Ed. He feels helpless as it is."

"Sarah Jane's okay when she takes her medicine." Dave thinks Sarah Jane is a nut, but defends her. Defending folks is what Dave does best.

We stand around thinking about all this. The doctors say Sarah Jane is paranoid schizophrenic, and it's probably something wrong with her system and not her brain. She talks to herself a lot, but, hell, *I* talk to myself a lot.

"I honestly don't know whether I hope she comes home or not." Christine looks kind of guilty. "We have our own problems. I feel like a hypocrite."

"It's cheaper to buy wood midsummer," Mitchell murmurs. He's not wandering, exactly. He's trying to change the subject because Sarah Jane scares the spit out of him. When his wife died, Mitchell got defensive. Nobody was around to stand between him and reality. Mitchell's one of those dreamers without the steam to make dreams happen. He's just cruised these many years. Then he lost Mary, and Mary is now like Shadow; living here just in memory.

The pup wiggles in my arms. The last of the wood flies off the truck. The kid has broken a good sweat, a tall kid and kind of skinny. The pup wiggles harder. She's found a new friend, and she's ready for more skylarking.

"The state people might not let her come back," Dave says about Sarah Jane. "Those government people don't like inconvenience."

"Nothing to feel guilty about," Sally tells Christine. She touches Christine's hand, kind of sympathetic, then holds onto Dave's arm.

I set the pup on the ground. Sarah Jane has her own personal grocery cart that she pushes four blocks to the store. The store manager puts up with it. I wonder if 911 returned the grocery cart. Meanwhile, Mitchell heads toward his house to get money for the kid. Sally and Dave and Christine sort of drift away. Sally leans a little on Dave, her red scarf a spot of color on this gray northwest afternoon. Skylarking starts up between pup and kid. A breeze comes by, promising the temperature will hit sixty.

It looks like all of us will make it through another spring. I look at the heap of wood, knowing that winters and woodpiles and lives never come out exactly even; but the red and golden fir is beautiful to see. Young creatures are beautiful. I watch the kid and pup. The kid throws a stick. The pup knows exactly what to do. It's easy to understand why Sarah Jane goes crazy, but I'm not sure my reasons and her reasons match.

JULENE BAIR

In her essay, which captures the lives of a Kansas farming family of the 1950s—her family—Julene Bair portrays a dichotomy in which women are "interior creatures" compared to men, who labor in the fields and whose sweat and blood maintain the family equilibrium. Men, not women, are expected to be angry, moody and distant, victims of the whims of the weather and the national economy. Throughout, Bair's details are raw and realistic, definitively demonstrating her intimacy with her material, from the clumps of dried mud on the shop floor with sticker and Kocha weeds embedded in them "amidst pools of oil and spilled grain" to "ants nibbling away chunks from the carcasses of grasshoppers or beetles rolling balls of dung toward the stairs."

HOUSEWIVES, FIELDHUSBANDS

I stir my box of Lincoln Logs with one of the long, half-round pieces. Finally, the chimney appears, wedged under the gritty flaps at the bottom of the box. The red balsa cutout settles like a breath on the peak of the green roof. My cabin is complete and ready for transport to its sacred spot at the center of the blue-glass coffee table.

Not wanting my mother to wander by and see my shrine, I pull the wide, paneled door out from the wall between the dining and living rooms, cringing at the noise made by the concealed rollers overhead. I then close the Venetian blinds. The mauve-tinted, floral-carpeted room glows dark and violet. This would be perfect, except I want the wind to stop. It moans through the eaves and whistles through the sashes of the windows, filtering fine dust onto the sills.

Dad said this morning, "If it blows again like yesterday, we'll be cutting tomorrow." I know all of the High Plains country counts on this south wind to ripen the wheat, but it robs mornings of promise and makes July afternoons a weary trial. Outside our windows, the branches of the old elms and locust trees creak and bob, on the verge of breaking. The leaves toss, revealing their gray undersides. Dust devils churn up and down the gullies in the summer fallow across from the house. Thistles and devil's claws—the thready, dual-pointed pods of wild gourds—roll across the farmyard. To go outside requires wearing one of the stale-smelling cotton scarves that hang from the hooks on the porch because, otherwise, my fine blond hair would tangle and fill with dirt. I would have to wear jeans too, in the 90-degree heat, because of blowing yard sand. Even inside, I feel as if I'm under siege—my skin and hair getting dirtier by the minute.

Using Mom's spray bottle I took from beneath the kitchen sink, I squirt vinegar water onto the coffee table glass and wipe it clean. Imagining the cabin being carried like the Ark of the Covenant on the shoulders of Israelites, I lower it gently onto the table. The glass is French blue, my mother tells me—the deep, irresistible cobalt of Evening of Paris perfume bottles. As a toddler, I used to lie across this table, spreading my arms wide. I remember in the tender skin of my belly and shoulders how cool and smooth the glass was. I used to draw my lips between my teeth and rub my mouth back and forth, then watch transfixed as the fog I'd breathed onto the surface evaporated.

I hold the flashlight beneath the glass and shine it upward. With my chin on the mahogany table edge, I stare through the cabin's windows at the indwelling light. I hear Mom walk past the closed door behind me. On the verge of being discovered at worship, I press my hand over my lips and hold my breath, but her steps fade toward the kitchen. I imagine this is my house and I am 20, married to Adam, the most rakish and dangerous of Ben Cartwright's sons. Twenty seems a terribly long time to wait, but that's how old my mother was when she married. Adam has built me this house in the center of a lake on the Ponderosa, in Montana, where a clean wind, instead of lifting field dirt, rushes through tall pines.

I don't wonder why I feel shame; I just do. I have closed out the real day and replaced it with manufactured light. This is the softest room in the house, even though the easy chair and couch are covered in an abrasive pile weave, and even though the carpet is wool, doesn't reach the walls and has no pad under it. The colors are elegant and muted, and the light filters around the edges of the blinds through the white sheer curtains, which, my mother tells me, are spun fiberglass. I always come to this room to fantasize, to imagine a future. Maybe thinking about an alternate life in another place induces guilt, as if growing up were a betrayal of my parents and the present. Or maybe I'm already subconsciously ashamed of domesticity, thinking it inferior to outdoor life. In this room, alone, the door pulled closed, the shade drawn, I revolve in the very womb of withdrawal.

Suddenly, men's voices rattle along the wide door panels and along the back of my own rib cage. I flick off the flashlight and shove it under the couch, where it rolls noisily off the edge of the carpet onto the pine floor. I pick the cabin up and wreck it into the box, which I hide behind the lounger. I open the blinds and, lacking any other exit, loudly shove the door back into the wall, hoping the noise will mask my embarrassment.

The men are standing with their backs to the living room, looking out the big bay windows. My brother Bruce, my father, and the hired men—Hank, Uncle Raymond, Elmer—are in their stocking feet, having removed their boots on the work porch. But they still wear all their other armor—heavy denim jeans or overalls, blue or gray work shirts, leathery dark forearms and necks. I notice that the house has darkened and Mom has turned on the overhead lights. The wind has stopped and, punctuated by the sound of distant thunder, rain patters on the roof. The scents of cool air and dampening dust freshen my outlook on not just the afternoon, but life. My mother and I will run our rags over all the furniture, where the gleam of wood and glass will last, at least until the fields dry out and the dust begins to blow again.

I wedge myself between my dad and Bruce to stand before the middle window. I expect Dad to place the flat of his palm on my head and press; I expect the usual playful teasing, but his focus is outward. Something inside me trills along with the mounting force of the wind as it returns in earnest, from the north now. Lightning snaps. We are negatives, our forms inscribed on the surface of the single bright instant. I hunch reflexively, trying to shelter myself from the immediate thunder. But there is no hiding from such noise. I look around and above us, sure to see our house shaken to rubble, just as I destroyed my log cabin. Beside me, Dad hasn't flinched. He's standing with his arms dangling, slightly bent at the elbow. His muscle-rounded shoulders seem to tilt even more forward than usual. His striped overalls hang off him as if he were a statue.

Mom stands on the other side of Bruce, a dishtowel draped over her shoulder. She embroidered the towel last winter. It has a fanciful design of two puppies frolicking, one brown, one black. They are tugging on a red rope, its ends looping prettily and tied off in frayed knots. She wears a housedress, which she also made. Her legs are bare except for white anklets and the brown Ace bandage she wraps daily to prevent varicose veins. Another bolt, and the electricity goes out. The dark afternoon moves into the house itself, the air suddenly chill. We are all lined up here—brother and sister, mother and father, the hired men—all equally dependent on what the sky does. Bruce and Julene, Jasmin and Harold, Elmer and Hank. Uncle Raymond sits behind us at the dining table, seemingly unaware of the storm.

The rain isn't just falling anymore, but driving southward in a sheet. We watch the front move past the barn and into the sumac south of the house, where the stalks bend before it. Dad is untouchable now. His jaw is set and angry. I notice he has forgotten to remove his battered work hat. I can't bear to be near him, in this position I've always fought Bruce for. I retreat and draw a chair up to the dining table beside Uncle Raymond.

Raymond is my cousin Vicki's dad. They came back from Florida a year ago, where Dad says he "just piddled," losing all the money he inherited from Grandpa Bair. Now they live in Grandpa's old place, five miles west of ours. Raymond hires on to help my father during the busiest times. He'll be driving truck this harvest, if there is a harvest.

The hail starts sporadically, a slow death of hope, one "thunk!" of ice against the roof, then two within the same instant, stones hurled by something that isn't God, my dad knows. Whatever "shits" these stones—that's his word—doesn't think and doesn't care. We watch the hail bounce off the sidewalk, pelt the trees. Soon we can no longer see the barn through the white downpour. The tempest puts a brilliant end to a day of wind and dirt, thrilling me even as the leaves are being stripped from Mom's locust trees, even as every wheat bud, at least in the nearby fields, is being pounded into the ground.

My father and the men linger after the hail has moved on. No one owns rain slickers in Kansas. It rains seldom enough that we just wait it out. The lights don't come back on, so Mom goes into the kitchen to find the candles. Even though it's only 4 p.m., the sky is still dark, and we all want something, some flame to hover around. I hear her rustling through the sink drawer. "Well, criminetly," she says. "Where's the flashlight?" Soon she carries four candles in, and she and I drip wax onto saucers.

Dad sits in his lounger at the far corner of the room. I've never seen him so removed. I look back and forth between his under-lit face and Uncle Raymond's, whose broad cheeks are even wider in the light. The candles cast undulating shadows up around his eyes, and two tufts of kinky gray hair bloom off the top edges of his shiny scalp. There's an odd energy about Raymond, despite his frozen posture. He's mulling something—some old hurt. I've heard Dad say that Grandpa was cruel to him. "He always told him he was worthless." Then Raymond went wild in his teens, landing in jail several times after drinking brawls. "Mom always bailed him out," Dad says.

I can see Dad's chest heaving; he's breathing purposefully, huffing almost, as if to exert will at least over this much of nature, himself. I can feel the slackness inside his cheeks, as if I were inside him, my own jaw hanging slightly open beneath closed lips, the spit forming faster than normal, an adrenal drenching. His jaw and brown eyes have released the anger, and he is only worried now, computing how to recover. He is figuring already, 10 minutes after the storm, what it will take in manpower, in time, in machinery, in seed, to disk the wheat under and plant millet, the only crop that might "make" this late if the first frost comes no earlier than the usual Sept. 20. After a rain like this, it'll be four days at least before he can get back in the field. Dad is a born farmer. When he was only 10, Grandpa had him driving teams of six horses in the fields. He'll persevere. We all depend on this. Tiptoeing past his easy chair, we let him sit and stew. Hank and Elmer go out the dining room door to stand on the porch. Raymond gets up absently and follows them. We immediate family members carry our candles into other rooms.

Subconsciously, on afternoons such as that one, I knew that while my mother and I might suffer deprivations due to the storm, we were lucky not to be male. A man had to keep moving, out in the void of the bigger world. Kansas was not the Midwest, where there were hills, trees and rivers. The landscape was not soft and feminine, nor the air moist. The climate of western Kansas was harsh, the sky huge and daunting. It fell to men to wage enterprise across that distance. A man had to keep spinning, like a gyroscope, the force of his energy keeping his family in balance. If he lost heart; if the emptiness of the plains got inside him, slowing his movements till he shuffled over the dirt like Uncle Raymond rather than stomped like my father; if the heat and hugeness wearied him until he craved the cool interior of the house; if he couldn't face a shattered crop, but sat and let weeds take the field; if he failed to spin, he and his family would topple. My father never contemplated slowing down. He never allowed any pain to enter his consciousness, where it might distract him from the field task at hand.

For the most part, my mother lived inside, walled in by equally rigid, but less demanding, expectation. Dad had a life and liveliness she did not. She depended on him to go out and reap, to bring not only cash but joy back inside. He was always just in from outside, and power and energy accompanied each entrance, as if sunlight and wind came in with him.

"Yass-min," he would call, with exaggerated lilt as he leaned in the kitchen doorway, his hands dripping water from the work porch sink onto the linoleum. "Oh Yass-min! Towel, Yass-min." It wasn't that his German ancestry still carried over in his speech; he just enjoyed poking fun at Mom's Swedish heritage, and he liked the slightly off-color sound of "Yass."

"Ooohhh, damn it," my mother would come cussing from a far corner of the house where she'd been immersed in some chore, perhaps ironing sheets on the big roller ironer, the mangle, as it was incongruously called. All seriousness, angry with herself, she would scurry into the washroom behind the kitchen and reemerge. "Here," she would say. "Here's the damned thing. I forgot to put it out I guess."

"Thank you, Yass-min," Dad would say, his voice melodic.

After the hail, I knew my father wouldn't be in a teasing mood for months. From my perspective, that would be the hugest cost of the storm—the loss of my father's light.

My mother wasn't entirely an interior creature. Sunlight ran in all our veins, and she had many outdoor chores. She milked the cow, raised chickens and vegetables, and tended an immense, beautiful flower garden. During summers, after my brother Bruce began working with the men, I would often sleep in. On waking, I would look out my east window first thing. It reassured me to see my mother in the yard, bent over her hoe, weeding the roses or her irises. What I liked most, I think now, was how the sun poured over her, affirming her. To protect her skin, she always wore garden gloves, a bonnet, and a long, light-colored cotton blouse over her housedress. Even though dressed protectively, she appeared completely confident and managerial. When the weather cooperated, she shaped beautiful life out of the dirt, as if her hoe were a wand and she a magician. The yard belonged to her, she to it, just as the house and she co-owned each other.

I would go downstairs, pour myself a bowl of cereal to eat at the dining room table, and in she would come, swinging the dining room door open before removing her bonnet and stomping her feet on the mud porch mat. "Phew," she would say. "It's getting hot out there." Energized by the morning and her work, she would stride over to flip the switch on the window air conditioner.

After rinsing my bowl, I would leave it in the sink and go outside to stretch in the warmth. I strolled past the flowers, their purples, reds, and pinks intense under the sprinklers Mom had left going in the beds. I said good morning to all the yard animals and ventured up past the chicken coop and granary to the shop. Sometimes I visited when the men were working. Amidst their cussing, they would look my way and correct one another with glances. Often they'd be welding and would warn me to close my eyes or turn my back so as not to be blinded. All activities would involve a lot of pounding. Bang, clank, clank—hammers on steel. Generally vacant, though, the shop only echoed the presence of the men.

Dad made no pretense at cleanliness. He left his tools scattered over the workbenches, which were coated in a half-inch layer of dust and grease. Big clumps of dried mud, fallen off implements, lay on the shop floor amidst pools of oil and spilled grain. The clods had sticker and Kochia weeds embedded in them, and numerous bugs roved about, ants nibbling away chunks from the carcasses of grasshoppers, or beetles rolling balls of dung toward the stairs leading down into the shop basement. The basement still housed the implements Grandpa Carlson had used—plowshares and harness trees, all blended to yellow-brown in color by a coat of dust and condensed oil. Sometimes I would take a step or two down the stairs and peer in. Just enough dim light fell through the south window to highlight a complex city of spider webs, many belonging to black widows, common in our region. A jumbled mass of old boxes, chains, gears, fan belts, tubing, and scrap iron competed for both floor and wall space. I had often seen Dad saunter down the stairs into the cavern to retrieve a piece of iron for welding, but before long, standing there, the dank air breathing up at me, I would begin to imagine salamanders and spiders crawling up my ankles. I would scamper back up the steps, stamp my feet, and swipe my hands over my clothes and through my hair.

Back in the house, when it had become too hot outdoors for both of us, my mother entered into her comfortable, unquestioned and unquestioning routine. At 10 in the morning, she might be rolling out cinnamon roll dough. Once monthly she waxed the dining room floor, disturbingly cutting me off from trespass. I didn't like not having my house. For it was my house, almost more than anyone's. I owned it in the manner of a luxuriating house cat. I was free to wander the rooms, loll in any of them, sit on the kitchen counter while nibbling crackers, build forts under the dining room table, do headstands against the walls, or ride pillows down the un-carpeted hall stairs. When the wax dried, its sheen captivated me, offering me yet another pastime—gliding up and down the fake wood planks in my socks. The linoleum looked like real wood flooring, and Mom bragged about how it had fooled many a visitor.

My mother's and father's realms seldom intermingled. Even though her parents had handed our farm down to her, Mom never set foot in the shop her father, John Carlson, had built. She would send me "up there" to get a pair of pliers or her hoe, which Dad had taken up to sharpen on the grinder and had forgotten to return. Although she loved working in her garden, on the rare occasion when she came in contact with grease or machinery, I could almost see her begin to wither, like Superman before kryptonite. I inherited my childhood dislike for wind from her. "Confounded wind! Cussed dirt!" she would say, coming in from an errand up at the chicken house or in her yard. During wheat harvest, when the big combines moved through all the surrounding fields like giant, robotic insects, Mom would take dinner out to the very edge of the cut wheat in the trunk of her car. These were the only times I ever saw her in the field. She sprang the trunk lid, then lifted the tablecloth off her Corning Ware. She served fried chicken, green beans, dinner rolls and my favorite potatoes, cut in large hunks that she first boiled, then fried in butter. The combine and truck drivers, sitting on a blanket Mom had placed in the scant shade of the biggest wheat truck, inhaled the scrumptious food in shifts. The noon sun re-flected off the stubble as if it were real gold, causing us all to squint as we watched the progress of the harvest in our own and neighbors' fields. Summer thrummed up out of the ground. But Mom didn't enjoy the picnic much herself. The wind lofted the combined smells of engine grease and fried chicken across the wastes while she, having little appetite under the circumstances, swatted at flies and, in response to the dust kicked up by passing trucks, said "ooh-ugh!"

Coming into the house, the men, on the other hand, entered civ-ilization, at ease. The farmstead, with its windbreak of elms, the house at center, formed a rare oasis in a landscape where farms were two or more miles apart. After the big light of the outdoors, the house's interior was refreshingly protective—cool in the summertime, warm and emanating baking aromas in the winter. In the summer, the men came in just before dinner and collapsed into easy chairs in front of the window air conditioner, their knees splayed, their turned feet resting on the edges of their Red Wings. Their guards came down once they were inside; they relaxed with abandon. My brother Bruce always made a show of this, throwing his arms wide, letting his cap hang from one hand. A red hat ring circled his forehead.

Everyone tacitly understood that through the men's magnanimity, we females were allowed our luxuries. We could take naps in the cool house, while the men struggled on through the heat of the day. Then, on the first Friday of each summer month, my mother and I zoomed past the fields where Dad and the men, a phrase that included my brother from the age of twelve on, made slow, tedious rounds in the open-air tractors. On these charmed days—club days—I didn't envy my brother his importance, but counted the minutes until my mother and I entered the immediate and exotic world of someone else's garden.

It is the first Friday of August, club day. Mom and I arrive at the Berkholders' behind the Demig car. Mabel Pittman pulls in behind us. We all sit for a moment with the windows rolled up to let the dust settle. Then, if the scene could be witnessed from an invisible, floating blimp sent to revisit the era, the passengers' and drivers' doors of our square-bumpered, two-toned cars would be seen opening and discharging women and children, all girls, or boys deemed too young to work with their fathers. You would see us greeted at the yard gate, then led on the ceremonial walk through the flower garden.

This is the monthly meeting of the Sunny Circle Home Demonstration Unit. I walk behind my mother on the narrow path, lined with big quartz rocks that Rudy and Vonna Berkholder haul back in the trunk of their Plymouth each late September, when, after the winter wheat is planted, "We finally get to take a vacation," Vonna says. "We go fishing at Estes Park. He fishes. I relax."

"I wish Harold would cave in and take a vacation," my mother says. "But no. He's just sure the whole place will collapse if he leaves for more than a day."

"Well, that's Harold for you," says Mabel Pittman. She is a round woman, and a little stern. Her own husband, Ernest, got a taste for travel in the Navy, though they can seldom afford a vacation, the way my family could if Dad weren't so tight. This is the subtext, but Mabel is a practiced diplomat. She conveys her main message, then sweetens it. "I just love your dress, Jasmin. Where did you buy it?" Mabel knows my mother made the brightly colored, polished-cotton print dress. It has the scalloped neckline Mom's been fond of for the last two years now and the full, eased skirt. Mabel works half-time in town at the ASCS, the federal agency that oversees crop support payments to farmers. This job away from home grants her an unusual worldliness; she's accustomed to ruffling then smoothing all sorts of feathers.

I follow behind my mother, admiring her turquoise high heels, the toes round enough to kiss, and her stockings, which have a tantalizing straight black seam down the back. Soon, I will be wearing heels, I remind myself, and I can hardly wait. My mother is among the prettiest of this dozen or so women, wearing their finest for one another. She is "well kept up," meaning her figure is trim and her skin still soft and pale. Some of the women are rail-thin, while the ample flesh of others is fallen, hanging from their underarms, collected in sagging paunches under navy blue or brown, nylon-print dresses. A few, like Mabel, are large, tubular women, neckless, chinless, the typical absence of smiles more frightening in them. They pour their amplitude into straight skirts and cap-sleeved blouses. Their stride is mincing, dressed such. The wind ripples the thin fabric of all the women's clothing, and some hold their hair, as if, dressed for town, they've actually become town women, unaccustomed to the weather of a typical afternoon. Their bodies and attire are all part of the demonstration unit. My mother insists we dress up nice whenever we go anywhere. For today, I'm wearing a print dress blooming with muted morning glories. The fabric enchanted me when I first saw it in Twila's two weeks ago. Now, like all the dresses my mother makes me, it doesn't quite live up to the sophisticated vision I had in mind. The low slung waist with the narrow, violet belt is supposed to ride on my hips. Except I have no hips. "Oh, Julene, look at this one!" Mom says, lifting the face of a huge, white peony for me to admire. "And those poppies!"

I smile, pretending awe over the ragged, blowing scarves of pink and orange.

"These are about all the flowers I've had this year," says Vonna Berkholder. "Lost the earlier ones."

"Oh, I know," says Angela Calahan. "The hail stripped my garden bare." Those women whose gardens survived the storm make mental notes to bring Angela some of their canned beans and tomatoes. The Calahans live close to the bone in a basement house, dug the year they were married, the upper floor never completed, as Emmet had promised Angela it would be. Angela looks twice her age, her skin wrinkled and loose on her bony frame. The Calahans have five kids, "all living in that hole," my mother often says. Three of them—Junie, Alice, and Todd—are here today. I try to act ladylike, which is to say, tamped down, controlled, as I exchange glances with them and the Pittman kids, LuAnn and Alfred. We are all shy amidst the promenade of women, but that will change as soon as our mothers begin their meeting.

Stepping into the just vacuumed and dusted living room, the women pat their hair and say, "My gracious! That wind!" Like blossoms, their perfume floral, they settle onto the mint-green sofa and chairs. I love Vonna Berkholder's drapes. They have huge vines over a gray background. Yellow bamboo shoots weave squares behind the leaves, and the big windows in this newer house frame a gorgeous lawn, where the sprinkler is running.

After all the woman are settled into the folding chairs that circle the living room, I leave to change my clothes in the pink-and-black-tiled bathroom. I run my fingers over the cool squares, breathing deeply the scent of rose soap. The Berkholders are the only family in our part of the county with a nicer house than ours. I figure we'll have about an hour and a half to play. Normally the women would hear a short talk on some domestic topic—pressure cookers, the food groups, or garden pest control—but today they must plan their fair booth. Farm safety was last year's topic. They decorated the booth in green and yellow crepe paper to match the model John Deere tractors they used. One was upturned in a bar ditch, a pair of denim clad legs sticking out from underneath. In another scenario, a Ken doll lay on the ground behind his tractor implement, a blue fold-down disk. The women had painted his chest with red fingernail polish. I'd always wanted one of those disks to pull behind a toy tractor in the yard dirt, and I ogled it with a pang of regret over being 10 going on 11, too old for such playthings. In my favorite scene, a tinfoil lightning bolt pointed at the head of a third farmer, still driving his tractor. Across the top of the booth, stenciled letters read, "The 3 C'S OF D-isaster: Carelessness Causes Casualties."

Outside, I feel set free, wearing last summer's faded pedal pushers, a plain white sleeveless blouse and canvas sneakers. We older kids forget our dignity and dance an energetic shuffle with the little ones. I don't even mind the wind today. We are all so excited that we can't decide what to do first—investigate the kitten nest in the machine shed as Wanda Berkholder wants to do, run through the yard sprinklers, climb to the roof of one of the neat, green-roofed outbuildings to point out our own farms and the grain elevators in Ruleton and Goodland, ride the tire swing over the hay loft, or, as Alfred Pittman suggests, play strip poker in the windbreak. LuAnn and I object simultaneously.

"Alfred!"

"Gol!"

"Yuck!"

A couple summers ago, I taught Alfred and LuAnn the game, which my brother Bruce had just taught me. But I chickened out as I began to lose, just as I had with Bruce. My parents say Alfred is slightly retarded; that's why he still comes to the ladies' parties, although we share a birthday, and I know he recently turned 12. I'm still astounded that he doesn't know any better than to announce our shame to the entire neighborhood. Hasn't he noticed the bumps on LuAnn's and my chests? Or perhaps he has, and that's why he wants to play. The thought causes me to shudder. We opt for the lawn sprinkler, then a dirt clod fight in the windbreak, which has been recently plowed. We capture granddaddy grasshoppers and smear their tobacco juice on one another's arms. Wanda Berkholder, who hasn't changed out of her dress, and who has a habit of pressing her rhinestone-studded glasses against her nose, coyly disappears before any of these rowdy games begin. Every so often, I glimpse her standing on the porch, pretending not to notice us. She'll be starting junior high in the fall, I then remember.

When a sixth sense tells us it's time for refreshments, we tumble in and suddenly contain our energy to stand politely behind our mothers' chairs. We expect to answer the usual boring questions, but also to enjoy the attention of so many civilized and orderly women. Instead, they all gasp and begin to laugh. Until Mabel rails, "LuAnn Margaret Pittman, what sort of lady have I raised? You get your little behind back out there and stand under that garden hose. Alfred, you see that she does it, and when we get home, it's a lickin' for you, letting your sister get all filthy!"

My mother, less inclined to remonstration, says, "Julene, you need to wash up too." I'm mortified. How had I forgotten who I was, who I was becoming?

Angela merely looks at her kids, not expecting much one way or the other, and nods. Vonna Berkholder says, "Wanda, go onto the laundry room porch and get some towels." I look down at the dried mud on my calves and arms. I'm too big for these pedal pushers, and I realize that my hair, which Mom combed back into a pert ponytail before leaving home, must now look straggly and windblown.

But once again outside, in the sunlight, I find the hose bath delicious and thrilling. Wanda administers it, standing in the grass in her patent leather shoes, raising and lowering the nozzle, giggling for the first time all afternoon. I'm not even bothered knowing that all our mothers have come out on the front steps to oversee us and to be sure we use the towels that, unlike the ones we have at home, match. Then Mrs. Berkholder brings us refreshments—apricot nut squares and Kool-Aid. I pick the coconut off the cookies and toss it in the evergreen hedge beside the porch, feeling lucky that we didn't have to undergo the usual routine, us girls being asked if we've been helping our mothers this summer, Alfred and Todd if they've been helping their dads, if we're ready for school to start yet, or if we're entering anything in the fair. I can visualize the women inside, sipping their coffee and nibbling the dessert off the transparent pink-tinted china, handed down from Wanda Berkholder's grandmother, for whom there was a big funeral last winter. "Will she really whip you?" Wanda asks Alfred.

"Nah," Alfred says.

"Might," LuAnn says hopefully.

Although laughter would often ripple through the living room during refreshments, the women weren't very good visitors as a rule. After the dessert was praised and the dishes stacked in the kitchen, they would sit politely on, but I could see that they did so unwillingly. They folded one arm across their stomachs and rested the knuckles of the other hand against their chins. The business meeting completed, they could barely tolerate idle hours within another woman's domain. The women drifted out of the conversations, their eyes staring into space as they dragged the back of a thumbnail over their lips. Excited to have the rare opportunity to play with other kids, I couldn't understand my mother's anxiousness to get back home. I would beg to stay another half-hour and she would sometimes defer, but reluctantly. "I've go to put supper in the oven," she would say.

Over supper, re-ensconced in her own house, Mom would tell Dad the latest news from the neighbors. Behind each woman's name—Angela Calahan, Vonna Berkholder, Mabel Pittman, Violet Demig, Emma Cossman, Muriel Hooper—lingered the image we conjured of their men—Emmet Calahan, Rudy Berkholder, Ernest Pittman, Norm Demig, Wilmet Cossman, Raymond Hooper. With each of these men, we associated land and the characteristics of the way he farmed it—straight or crooked rows, weedy or clean, cloddy or smooth, planted on time or late, good stands or poor, to the road edge or just to the telephone poles. About those men he most respected, my father would say, "He's a doer." For Ernest Pittman, our nearest neighbor, he had a modicum of respect, because he "does get out there early." Ernest had been in the Navy and had fought in World War II, while my dad took advantage of the farmer's exemption, a subliminal bone of contention between us and the Pittmans. Having lived elsewhere myself now, I suspect that Ernest's glimpse of other cultures and his life on shipboard liberated him from the rigid customs of his neighbors. He stripped down to his boxer shorts and white Navy cap when he drove his tractor hot summer afternoons. If Mom was planning a shopping trip to town, Dad would say, "Close your eyes when you drive by the Pittmans', Jasmin. Naked Ernie is sowing wheat."

The women were judged by how well they kept their houses and by their own appearance. In both cases, the adjective of praise was "well-kept." To be fat or to have, as my dad often said, "a rear end as broad as a barn" was a sin in women, whereas men's weight was seldom referred to. If, when he visited a neighbor's house, he saw newspapers and clothes strung around, dishes still on the table at 1:30, lint in the corners, or cats on the counters, my father would exclaim after he left, "Gawd! What a trash heap," referring not just to the house, but to its wife. It never occurred to him to be ashamed of the way he kept his own shop; his worthiness was judged by another standard.

The men were as oblivious to raising kids and to putting meals on the table as the women were to the preventive maintenance on tractor engines, but the women rested in the lap of the men's world, not the other way around. Without husbands, quite simply, the women would have no food to serve, no home to demonstrate, no car to drive. What men provided—money—and the place in which they worked—the whole, huge world—were more essential than what women provided—home.

Even though I disliked the inequality I witnessed around me— the way boys, men, and their work were deemed superior—even though I gave voice to rebellious notions—that I would myself do the most esteemed "men's work" someday, as a nuclear physicist, astronomer, or vet—and even though I got good grades in all my classes, including science, the actual practice of any of these occupations was inconceivable to me. Each would involve the use of alien, complex tools. There would be huge cyclotrons, observatories, or austere operating rooms. Aesthetics wouldn't figure into the picture at all. There would be nothing to decorate; even I would have to dress unbecomingly. The notion of atoms fascinated me, but the elements, the whole exterior world of substance and chaos beyond the domestic, belonged to men. Perhaps I could apply myself, understand and succeed; but those occupations really seemed foreign and uninteresting. As a vet, there would be scalpels and formaldehyde and ether and unforgiving responsibility and manure and saliva and fleas and filth. I didn't really want to be a vet or physicist or astronomer; I just wanted to be able to say I was one. And I didn't truly expect to earn my own living. I wanted the luxury of womanhood, but wished to avoid the lower prestige.

I was preparing to be a housewife, despite my disdain for that term. I laughed at my friend Helen when she showed me, on her bed at home, how she had learned in home ec to fold the sheet under the mattress in crisp "hospital corners." I was a good student, had a philosophical nature, wondered about religious issues, was disturbed by political injustice, but it never occurred to me that I might make a living through thought. I had no models for this; no academics lived in my community or anywhere nearby.

Even though I talked about college, both Helen and I knew that my real purpose there would be the classic one, for women.

During the weeks following the hail, my mother must have slept poorly next to Dad, that powerful man who had lost his wheat and feed crops. Would she even dare to place a hand on his shoulder as he lay, himself a mountainous, frozen storm? Would she dare say anything?

By day, my dad responded to his losses with goals and purpose. My mother was a servile planet to which he returned evenings. She steadily prepared and put nourishment before him. It wouldn't be until next summer, and a good crop, that he would sneak into the kitchen again, after washing up on the work porch, and swat her bottom as she stood rolling out biscuit dough at the kitchen counter.

Mom had planned a trip for that fall, a vacation in Arkansas, where my father's sister Alta lived. "Oh, we won't go now," she said, as school approached and I began to wonder where I'd stay while they were gone. Mom longed to get away, to do something fun. As far as Dad and travel went, though, he was like my horse, Fancy, who would choose some common object to shy away from. The hail provided a righteous-seeming excuse. Yet by October, the winter wheat would all be in the ground, the sheep would still be out to pasture, and the hail had left him no feed to cut. "We could go if he really wanted to," Mom said.

Her energy abandoned her more often than usual that summer, and she took advantage of her prerogative to rest. "I'm so ti-i-red," she would say, the end of the sentence sliding down into the depths of baritone complaint, last vestige of a family drawl my father teased her about and which she'd worked hard at abolishing. She would lie down on the couch in the living room. "You should take a nap now, too," she would say, and I would sit for a while in the prickly easy chair and watch the lines of light along the outer edges of the Venetian blinds filter through the curtains. The threads in the sashed, white, fiberglass drapes glimmered like translucent tubes. Beneath her need to rest lay an assumption about the physical frailty of women, as compared to men, a frailty I could also choose to give in to, but I resisted. The living room waited. The blue-glass coffee table. The Plaster of Paris collie that I'd ridden when I was 2. The olive-black screen of the Zenith TV.

On one such afternoon, the house ticked with the passing seconds and finally pushed me outside. I wandered the farmstead alone, except for the animals, and most of them were drowsing also. Finding Penelope, my favorite cat, drinking water that had dripped from the window air conditioner into Mom's hollyhocks, I picked her up and kissed her on the head. She dangled mutely. Overhead, clouds floated by. I trailed sticks along the walk, a circuit I'd followed a thousand, million times. How many would that be, I asked myself, how many zeroes—nine—one billion. I'd been doing it since long before I was 6, when I marched up and down the walk with dead Christmas trees, or stalks of dry dill plant, singing "Onward Christian Soldiers."

I gathered the energy to catch and saddle my horse. The enterprise required a lot of effort. First, I had to go back inside, tiptoe up the stairs and pull on jeans and boots. In the barn, I filled a grain bucket with oats and carried that and the halter as I climbed the corral fences. I trundled out into the huge pasture, the grasshoppers clacking, the sun firing the part in my hair. Due only to the heat, Fancy allowed herself to be caught. Back in the barn, her tail flicked me along with the flies as I got the saddle down off the stall divider. I completed the cinching, the bridling, then led her back out into the afternoon.

We ambled out the road, bordered by REA power poles on the left, telephone lines on the right. Magically, out of nowhere, I could hear a radio station playing tinny music and, every so often, an announcer—just the cadence and tone of his voice, never distinct enough to pick out words. Looking over my shoulder, I watched the house's chimney, as red and as perfect as the one in my Lincoln Logs, bounce until it disappeared behind a hill in the road. Somewhere in the bright distance, in a world I was trying to figure out how to animate with my own energy, tractors crawled over the fields. I could hear their engines below the phantom announcer, whose voice hypnotized, as did the violet, indwelling light I'd left behind in the living room.

Both my parents' realms seemed underwritten by supernatural forces, but on that hot, unalloyed afternoon, I wanted to ride out from under their spells. I pretended, with my mother asleep behind me in the big box of a house that held only her, my brother among the men in plow traces beyond me, that I was as wild as the weeds, as wild as the rattlesnakes and badgers that peered from the ditch banks. And that I could choose who I would be.

BOB COWSER, JR.

Bob Cowser, Jr., uses baseball to focus this essay about adolescence, growth, and despair in a colorless and uninspiring part of the country. In an essay, the best kind of focus is narrow and specific. Note that the reader learns a great deal about Cowser and his life within the confines of baseball and his own feelings of inadequacy, which are interconnected. As the narrative proceeds, other stories subtly emerge: a sudden suicide, an alienated brother, and a father's literary legacy passed on to this isolated teenage narrator, Cowser himself.

SCOREKEEPING

We live two lives: one restless in our bodies and one beyond that, which saves us. That's a fortune cookie platitude I came to all by myself the summer I finished eighth grade and turned 14, the summer my brother's grade school friend took a revolver from his father's rifle cabinet and shot himself in the head. I knew it was a plain thought even as I composed it, laying on my back in my bed the nights after the kid killed himself. I had made it deliberately plain, piecing it together word by word. I did not want the echo of Scripture to complicate what I thought was the barest truth of things.

This was 1984. My brother Jimmy and I lived with our family in the rural West Tennessee town of Martin, two hours up the Mississippi from Memphis, along the same stretch of the river Huckleberry Finn and another Jim are said to have traveled. Martin was a railroad town established in 1873 on land originally ceded from the Chickasaw and was named for a Mr. William Martin, who donated considerable acreage in order that the Illinois Central Gulf tracks might be routed through the area's creek bottoms. A boy's life there was mostly slow but also oddly brutal, something our parents had not known to prepare my brother and me for, having transplanted themselves and their family to rural Tennessee from other places. But the hollow report of that revolver had jarred all of us into a new awareness. I struggled to get my mind around the notion of two lives at first, though it had been my own idea originally. I couldn't imagine in any detail a life beyond my bodily one, beyond the grief I found when I came to that body's limits. Maybe we don't find that place beyond our bodies until we are in dire need, which is the one time we can trust ourselves to learn anything, need being such a fine teacher.

Just what was going on in the larger world that summer I'm not sure. I always think how the 60s offer so many defining events—lunar landings, police actions, assassinations and rock group breakups—that might serve as backdrop for the story of a life. The Chinese curse of interesting times. But this was the 80s, which most people I know can't yet think of as really being "the past," and history hasn't dignified us with any such curse. Even if I could put a finger on what the world was like when I turned 14, I know the people of Martin were not paying it any mind, were in fact resisting most of the larger world's conventions, time among them. To leave I-55 near Cairo, Illinois and head east across the river into Tennessee on one of the ribbon-like, two-lane country highways that intersects the interstate (which you have to do to find Martin) is at least to step *out* of time, if not to step *back* in it.

It is entirely possible that I never gave one thought to what was going on in the world beyond me that summer. I believed, right up to the time my brother's friend killed himself, that I had my own mess of a life to deal with. My seventh-grade history teacher had told me in front of our entire class that I was a "bad advertisement" for my parents, though I had tried, almost in spite of myself, to make myself presentable to the adults in my life. I was a compulsive talker, pudgy and flat-footed, who'd had braces cemented to his teeth the previous winter, and who was quite bitter that, at 14, his body had begun, in so many ways, to betray him. When my eyesight started to go around that time, I took it for an omen, the last straw, salt in the wound.

My eyesight left me gradually at first. Earlier that spring, I had been unable to read the chalkboard from my desk in the last row of Mr. Cole's American History class. I did my best to explain that fact away and refused even to talk about the possibility of wearing glasses. "It's the glare," I told my parents. But I was also struggling that summer, as I always had, to play baseball, and Junior Babe Ruth ended the excuse-making abruptly. In my first 17 at-bats that summer, I had either struck out or rolled weakly to the second baseman. I wasn't seeing the ball. It was like a cartoon aspirin whizzing toward me, and it was all I could do to chip it to the right side of the infield—the surest sign, my coach said, that a hitter is picking the ball up late.

"He's afraid of the ball," I heard Ronnie Powell tell the other grimy ballpark urchins between the pitches offered me. He stood behind the plate while I batted, his shirt open and his rake-like ribs pressing against the chain link backstop. But he spoke the truth. I knew, standing in the soft clay of the batter's box, that the summer night loomed somewhere out past the infield, hung like a curtain, deep and velvet black and utterly beyond me. Base hits went out there, and I could hit nothing into that. I eventually broke down and made an appointment with my mother's optometrist, who told me that while I was not going blind, neither would my eyesight get any better—only gradually worse.

Rather than swing myself out of my slump, like the big-hearted boys in baseball novels I found in the juvenile section of the public library, I quit the team. The same week I quit, some of the older players on our team had held my friend Leland Bracknell down before practice and shoved a dead bird—a crow—in his mouth. This never happened in baseball novels. The older boys had gone after Leland *particularly* because he lost one or two fly balls in the ballpark lights the night before, but they went after him *in general* because he was from Chicago and was thus different, as in not like them. They chased him like rodeo handlers after a roping calf, around the bases and then in circles in the outfield.

When they caught him behind one of the dugouts, Jeff Wright held his legs and Tom Jones his arms, while Rip Jones pried Leland's mouth open with one hand and stuffed the bird in it with the other. "Don't," Leland was saying, "Don't, goddammit!" Leland's family had moved down from Chicago when he was 4 or 5, and Leland brought quite a mouth with him. He shouted curses that day that I had never heard before, Chicago curses I was sure.

It was hard to watch Leland writhe there in the red dirt of the bullpen pitcher's mound, the bird's beak disappearing into the dark of his throat. I walked into one of the dugouts. The Bracknells lived in a brown mobile home just below our backyard, and Leland visited our house every day, so he was like family. He would have come over more often, my mother used to joke, but for another neighbor's wire pen full of yelping Dobermans that stood between Leland's yard and ours. My parents drove him to every baseball practice and to all the games, and though they would never say so, I think they grew to love him. I didn't particularly like Leland—in many ways he frightened me—but he held some fascination for me. Chicago seemed terribly exotic to me then, and Leland loved to regale me with stories about it, particularly about the food you could get there and the greasy delicatessens where you bought the food—Reuben sandwiches and meatball subs, dripping with sauce. Martin had no delicatessens. "Someday, we'll take the train up there," Leland would tell me. I suppose he was (aside from my brother) the closest thing I had to a real friend when I was 14, and as I get older, I am beginning to realize that actually liking our friends is a luxury not all of us can afford. If delicatessens are all you have in common with somebody, there you are. Leland did not wait for a ride home that last day but walked alone before practice ever began. I stayed for practice that afternoon, but I was so sick to my stomach I could hardly hold a bat. I returned to Harmon Field only once more, several days later. As a means of making my quitting official, I had my mother drive me to the field an hour or so before one of our games so I could surrender my uniform. It was early evening. The players' shadows were still long on the infield as they warmed up. I dragged myself toward my coach, who stood in the gravel on-deck circle near the visitors' dugout, about 100 yards from where my mother parked. He was a tire builder out at the Goodyear plant, a strong man but quite short. Over my shoulder, I slung the green uniform my mother had cleaned and pressed and placed on a clothes hanger.

On the drive from our house to the field, Mom and I had rehearsed an honorable bit about quitting and being sorry for leaving the coach shorthanded, and upon reaching him, I delivered it by rote. "Be respectful," my mother had said to me as I climbed out of our Gran Torino wagon, "even if you have to fake it." I heard her as I talked. It went rather well, all in all, though I don't remember a word of what I said. It probably lasted all of 45 seconds.

The coach's rhetoric came next. "If I had a body like you, hell, son," he said, exasperated, "I could push houses over." He didn't say anything else, his eyes fixed on some distant point beyond the outfield fence. I wasn't listening anyway. That kind of talk had always seemed full of riddles to me. I hung the curved neck of the clothes hanger carefully in the chain link of the high dugout fence, so that the breezes blowing around the ballpark caught the uniform from time to time, holding the pants aloft like a long, green flag. Then I turned from him and walked toward my mother's car, thinking only of the maggoty crow in Leland's mouth.

"Do you think I'm a wimp, Mom?" I asked matter-of-factly as I got back in the car.

"No," she said, turning the Torino on and beginning to drive away. "Leland will always remember that you were loyal."

It made me uneasy, the way my mother treated my quitting like it was a *non servium* straight out of Joyce. I hadn't quit as much out of loyalty to Leland as I had out of a well-founded fear that the fate which befell him would befall me if I continued to play, and I guess my mother knew it. But it was her way to offer her children alternative perspectives to the choices they made, "enlightened" perspectives she called them. She told me that she understood my decision to give up the game, that in an odd way she was proud of me for quitting, and she took the opportunity presented by my predicament to tell me once again what a literally Godforsaken place she thought Martin was. Life there was so unlike her upbringing in suburban Cleveland, an upbringing that she could represent as humble (they were poor) or remarkably dignified, depending on her rhetorical needs at the time. "I'll lay a bet they never fed crows to the students at the St. Augustine Academy for girls," my Dad might say to her, quite sincerely. "No, Bob, they didn't," she would tell him, leaving the room or closing a door or lighting a cigarette for emphasis. My Dad had grown up in rural Hopkins County, Texas, where people did things like stuff crows in boys' mouths and feed meat mined with shards of glass to family dogs, so he deferred to Mom on matters of civility.

I was more or less resigned to the quitting. I never bought, and still don't buy, any of that crap about quitters never winning, though I think I hear it about once a day. I searched earnestly in those years for words that I might live by, accepting no proverb without testing it against others I put my faith in. The line of bullshit about quitting directly contradicts a pair of aphorisms I clung to tightly, out of necessity more than anything: that I couldn't "win them all," and consequently that, as my mother had always said and said again that day, I had to "pick my battles."

Still, a part of me hated to quit baseball, growing up as I had in a house immediately next to Martin's Little League park on Christine Street. I knew I stunk at baseball, but I hadn't always stunk. Baseball was one thing I had grown up expecting to do. My family had always suppered in summer over the din of infield chatter across the street. "Batter, Batter, Batter," the boys sang—then

"SWING," and then we heard the crack of the bat or the percussion of the catcher's mitt. The sound of that chatter was maddening sometimes—it was supposed to be, like a plague of singing locusts. Yet on quiet Wednesday nights, when all of Protestant Martin was at church (we Cowsers were one of the few Catholic families in town) and no games were played, especially toward the end of the summer and the Little League season and the beginning of school, my brother and I stood in the front yard and guessed the silence of the empty park was the loneliest sound we had ever heard, and wished for the chatter to come back.

I was in freefall after that. There was no life for a boy in Martin who wasn't playing baseball. The game brings a young life order, not just the scheduled games and practices but the game itself. There is an order in it, an order transcending clocks and time. Even the act of pitch and catch connected me to something, to someone beyond myself. But I had turned my back on that. Instead, I woke late in the day, after my parents had gone to teach summer school and my sister Mary had taken off for band practice and my sister Ruth for babysitting, after my brother left on his bike to do whatever it was that cool boys did in summer (I, of course, had no idea). The house was dark when I crawled from bed—my parents kept lights off in the summer to keep the house cool—and I would haunt the place until the family returned, sneaking frozen mini-donuts and half-frozen Girl Scout cookies from the deep freeze and watching baseball and reruns and soap operas on television. We got Cubs and Braves games on cable. I think my dad was very worried about me, because he followed me around with suggestions about what I might do with myself. He'd not done that before. "Go to the library" was one suggestion he made over and over, just to give you an idea.

Some evenings, Leland Bracknell and his "chain-ganger friends," as my prim sister Ruth liked to call them, showed up at our back door to urge me outside into the streets with them. And some nights I went, up Clearwater to McGill Street then up Summer Street, where the nice girls lived in the old homes, houses as old as Martin was. Leland played Quiet Riot on his boom box while we walked down the middle of those quiet streets with a generic but very real sort of defiance. Now that all that's passed and I've pretty much abandoned Leland, my sister laughs and asks me if I can believe I was a chain-ganger. I don't know, but I guess I can believe it.

I had the vaguest sense of dread about my life then. High school waited for me at the end of the summer like something big and messy and difficult, something that counted and would matter later in my life. I was not ready for things that mattered. That sense creeps back into my life from time to time even today (with particular frequency since I got married and enrolled in graduate school): the sense that though I appear 19 or 22 or now 25, I am in fact still only 14 on the inside and am biding my time until someone in a position of authority figures me out. Now, I have some perspective and can see life beyond my "permanent record," but in those awkward years, I could not see beyond my school days to a better time and had only my parents' word that such a time would ever come.

I did quit baseball in enough time to reclaim my position as scorekeeper and announcer for the Little League next door, something I had hoped to do and something my poor eyesight did not affect. The summer before, for $7 a game, I'd sat in a makeshift press box keeping official score and announcing the batters for the Pee-wee League games. "Now batting so-and-so," I would say. "So-and-so on deck." Occasionally I'd vary things a little, add something I picked up from all the baseball I watched on television. But the parents and coaches grumbled when I did that.

The job seemed to fit me, like nothing else in my life. The money was fine for a boy my age, "walking around money" Mom called it, and I could work alone, which seemed important at the time. The job also involved pretty much constant talking—another key. And the fact that my little brother Jim played baseball so well made the job rewarding in other ways. Jimmy had moved up to Little League that summer, to the Argo Collier Astros, and he had taken up pitching. It seemed no one could hit him. Pee-wee players batted against a pitching machine, but Little Leaguers faced a live arm, and Jim had discovered since moving up that his arm was very live.

While most of the other boys threw overhand, Jimmy brought side-arm pitching back to the Martin Little League, and all the Little League fathers agreed he was something to watch. He would bring his arms and striding leg very close to his body as he began his windup, then dip his shoulder deeply so that he held the ball just above the ground. He released the ball from that point—about 7 o'clock—as he brought his arm whip-like across his body and stepped toward the plate, often with such force that the cap popped off his head. The sun setting orange behind him (as it often was on those evenings), my brother Jim must have appeared to the young hitters an illusionist. There was sleight of hand to what he did. I loved to watch the strikeouts line up as I recorded them on the scorebook's tiny ball diamonds, K after K. I wrote them carefully, deliberately.

In a real way, Jim's pitching made my summer, the simple beauty of it, and I know it pleased my parents, too. They no longer walked across Virginia Street to the ballpark as they had done faithfully the years I struggled through Little League; Jim had become too superstitious and forbade them to come. But on the nights he was slated to pitch, Mom and Dad would pull lawn chairs out under the giant magnolia in our side yard to sit amid the fireflies and watch their boy throw. He was too dazzling to miss altogether. It is ennobling to do even the smallest thing well and gracefully, and Jim's dedication to pitching and sheer skill at doing it taught me that, though I don't think I quite understood it that summer. And I found real satisfaction in witnessing and recording my brother's grace. It connected me to the game and its order, though, again, it has taken me some years to figure that out.

The night we found out about the suicide, I was across the street working a ballgame. My mother and father were both waiting for me to return from the ballpark. It was odd for my father to be up that late—11 or so. I found both my parents' faces in the porch's lamplight. Hearing it open, they had both started for the door.

"Lee has killed himself," my dad said coolly as I walked under the arm he'd opened the door with, "shot himself." I stopped dead. Dad took it upon himself to be the head of the house in times like that—not in a loud way, but diplomatically, almost reluctantly. I always heard more duty in his voice than anything.

Mom explained that Jimmy had been told. "Take it easy with him," she said. Mom and Dad were going to do that. They did not know how he would take it. I suppose it is a story how he *did* take it.

Jimmy and this kid were fourth-grade classmates. I had only

met my brother's friend a few times. He was blonde and blue-eyed, smallish and still cherubic, a compulsive talker like myself and beautiful, like my brother. Jimmy thought he was terribly funny, which threatened me somehow. His father was a wildly successful auctioneer, one of the most important men in our county. In that respect, as the son of schoolteachers, my brother had nothing in common with the dead boy. But both boys were bright and clever and, most of all, convinced of their toughness. That made them friends. Many days after school, the two boys had gone to his father's realty office on one of Martin's main drags, where they had gotten into liquor cabinets and all other sorts of mischief. Jim had never gotten in much trouble at home for any of that, and my brother pretty much gave up drinking altogether by the time he was 13, jaded as he was. But we learned later that his friend had paid dearly.

The day he shot himself, he had received his final fourth-grade report card. I never heard what the grades were, but at 11, this child was convinced that he would rather be dead than wait for the rope-whipping he was sure he had earned at his father's hand. Before his father returned from work, he took one of his father's many revolvers, closed his mouth around it, and delivered himself from his body. My mother's friends say it was his father who found his body a few hours later and who, of those who survived the boy, was most wounded by that shot, most confused. The words "Mouth of the South" were chiseled into the back of his gravestone. His father insisted on that.

I do not recall sleeping or not sleeping the night I found out. I met my brother in the kitchen the next morning. He was slopping through a bowl of Corn Pops at the kitchen table.

"I hate it when Dad buys me the wrong goddamned cereal," he said to me vacantly. He had a mouth like Leland's, even then. Of course, it was my sister Mary who ate Corn Pops. I went for a bowl in a cupboard behind Jim. He became gravely serious then.

"I can't pitch, Bobby," he said to me, in a sadder voice than I ever heard from him. "I can't pitch, man."

And indeed he could not. A photographer from the "Weakley County Press" snapped him on the mound later that night, and the "Press" ran the photo in the lower right corner of the front page a week later. Jim is striding toward the plate in the picture, his red stirrup socks out of his shoes and flying and his cap about to pop from his head. He is a beautiful boy, but he is tired and grieved, with a man's grief. You can see that.

It would be poetic for me to tell you here that it was his friend's death which ruined Jim as a pitcher. It may be so. I only know Jim was not the same pitcher after that night. What had made him a good pitcher remained. But what had made him beautiful, an illusionist, was gone.

In fact, he was an altogether different boy after that gunshot. A few nights after the boy died, the police woke my parents very late to say they had my brother in a squad car, that he looked very bad, like he hadn't slept, and that they'd found him pacing one of the ballpark's dugouts across the street an hour or so before. The police thought he was much too young to be out at that hour. Jimmy told my parents the dead boy had come and "talked to him" that night, and that he'd snuck out the window and gone to the dugouts to think awhile. I still don't know if he believed his friend, dead four days by then, had appeared to him, or if he'd made it up to save his skin. I would put almost nothing past my brother. I do know he hadn't slept in four days because I had been awake myself at all hours of the night, lying face up in my bed, and I had heard my brother banging around the house.

Jimmy never played baseball another summer but began to take odd jobs during the summer months instead—scrubbing 18-wheelers, baling and hauling hay, painting houses. He became more like a boarder in my mother's home than a brother or a son. Jimmy still ate with us and allowed my mother to make his bed and wash his clothes. He bore us no ill will. Jim was still preternaturally cool. But some part of my brother became solemn. Not gloomy, simply solemn and reverent in the most natural way. The experience of his friend's death set Jim apart, and he could no longer consider himself a part of our family, and sometimes he said as much. There was a span of years around that time, in fact, during which my brother appeared in no family pictures. He had carved out a space next to himself, so that for a time there was no room for us. I think now the space he had carved next to himself was Lee's place, and that space is where he kept him. I cannot begrudge him that space, all things considered. He was looking for that place beyond his body. We were all doing that.

. . .

Certainly my brother had learned to do that from our father, who always allowed life to happen at one or two removes from himself. I lived my whole life with the sensation that my father was one room away, behind a half-closed door in a farther room, enjoying a silence and stillness I could never approximate. He walked every night up and down the wide streets around our house for the hour or so before my mother served dinner, and as I grew up, I had always guessed he was visiting on those walks the people he kept closest to himself, the colorful characters from his Texas hometown who he told us about: his parents, his dead sisters, his younger brother R.L. For many years, I misunderstood this. I sometimes thought he hadn't gotten the family he had bargained for, that he would have enjoyed having one of the quieter, more studious boys in my class for a son. But he'd lived a whole life, more than 35 years, before we came along, and he knew grief before he knew us. I know now it tempered him. My brother had joined my father in that farther space, for a while at least, and, ironically, I began to understand them both a little better.

I spent a lot of the time I was alone in our house the rest of that summer with my hands in my father's top drawer. He kept a roll of quarters there, among his undershirts. I often stole two and rode Jim's bike or my sister Mary's down the hill and through the yards behind our house—not pedaling, just coasting—past the frothing Dobermans and Leland Bracknell's trailer to the Akin-Jackson Motor Company on the Dresden Highway, where I would buy a Pepsi. My father must have known I was taking the quarters, almost two a day, but he never said a word. One afternoon about two months after my brother's friend died, I found in that drawer a poem my father had written and titled "On the Suicide of an Eleven-Year-Old." Dad had just begun to publish poems then. I think he was 51. Journals that included his work began to appear unannounced around the house—things like "Cape Rock," "Zone 3," "The American Literary Review"—but I had never thought to read them. This poem I read, because I felt a part of it.

Though we were told he was a hunter,
Skilled already in the use of firearms
(We know he held the pistol true),
Much game survived the boy's brief career.

The squirrels and the grey dove
Continued their feeding
Hours after the sudden shot,
And the doe is grazing now
Near the cedar brakes.

On that night the Earth
Did not waver from its course
Nor was the moon's ring related
To the grief we endured.

How still and perfectly the words lay there. I wanted to follow my father around the house and quote him to himself. " 'The grief we endured': Yes, Dad, yes! Perfect." Here was my Dad scorekeeping, after all, ordering his grief. This—writing—was the small, ennobling thing he did, alone and quietly. I was on fire to talk to him about it, but thought better of doing so.

Months later, that poem appeared in "The Sulphur River Review," and though it has been years since he wrote it, and though he has written much more in the meantime, I remain convinced it is the best thing my father ever wrote. I realize it is odd for a boy to say he was raised by a poem, even 100 poems, but the fact that my own place in the world was made clearer to me precisely as I discovered that poem is, I insist, no coincidence. Readers can understand what I mean: What writers you love have said of the world must frame experience for you in some small sense, must have become a part of what life is. So it was for me.

My dad's poems taught me to honor—if not wholly love—space and distance. Their words are so still, so precise, move so close to what we all feel that I despair of them coming closer. Then the words ebb away, as if they respect the distance between themselves and what Dad means, and wants them to mean. It seems the poem pulled me out of that awful year, allowed me to compose myself. I found, or made, a life beyond my body. After that summer, I thought it no longer necessary that my father fill the spaces we sometimes found between us with talk, talk that must have seemed to him so idle. He loves and grieves in measured tones.

My brother has not written about the suicide yet, and he may never do it. For Jim, life is its own calling. Jim had more of the boy than Dad or I did and so has kept that solemn place next to himself empty for his friend, as it should be. It is a division of labor: Life happens to Jim; I do the scorekeeping.

ALICE HOFFMAN

Addressing her reader in the voice of her deceased grandmother, Alice Hoffman skillfully tightropes the blurred gray line between fiction and nonfiction. The reader knows that Hoffman's grandmother, Lillie Lulkin, is actually not writing this essay. But Hoffman hears her voice echoing in her heart and makes a conscious literary decision: to not filter or taint her grandmother's persona and to allow this charismatic woman to speak directly to the reader.

ADVICE FROM MY GRANDMOTHER

When crossing the street, never trust the judgment of drivers. They may not stop for you. They may roll over you, and keep on going. In fact, never trust anyone. They're not your family, their blood is not half as thick as water, why would you take their advice? Do they have your best interest at heart? Not one bit, and frankly, neither do most of your own relatives. It's dog eat dog, it really is, although what can you expect? Life is hard. Life is a battle. Life is what you make of it. Be prepared with a career. Retail is good—people are always buying. Everything could be burning down around them, and they're buying. You can call this sort of behavior foolish, but it's human nature. It's hope.

All people are created equal—black, white, Chinese, Moroccan, it doesn't matter. Equal. Everyone. All the same, whenever there's a murder, check the newspaper to make sure the culprit isn't Jewish—you'll breathe easier if you do. Then double-check and make sure the murderer isn't from New York—you'll breathe easier still. Give to charity, but don't tell your relatives that you do. Keep secrets well. Don't lie, but never tell the whole truth. That sort of thing is too hard to swallow, honey. That's what fiction is for.

Anything served in a fancy restaurant can be equaled in your own kitchen. As a matter of fact, everything can be made out of potatoes—bread, soup, pancakes, cake. Alone on a desert island, all a person really needs is a bag of potatoes and a toaster oven. Forget planes, jets, cars, TV. Without a doubt, a toaster oven is the finest invention of the twentieth century. It broils, it bakes, it toasts, it sits on your counter, small as a mouse. Always read labels. What? You're surprised it's so full of chemicals? You think these companies have your best interest at heart? But a potato. There's nothing evil they can do to it. No additives or red dye or msg there. A potato is a hundred percent pure. It is what it is. Unlike most things.

Between men and women, love is not only blind, but stupid. Oh, sure, love has a sense of humor, but the punch line is usually sex, money, despair, or kids, and none of these are particularly funny. Here's how you test if love is real. Broil a chicken (with a side dish of potatoes, naturally) and invite him over. Cook badly. Even if you're already a bad cook, make it worse. Trust me, it's easy. Throw in anything you want. Too much salt, too much pepper. Feed him and see what he says. A complaint means he's thinking about himself, and always will. A compliment means he'll never make a living. But a man who says "Let's go to a restaurant," now he's a real man. Order expensive, and see what he's got to say then. Kiss him good-night. Go ahead, don't be afraid. Do you hear your blood in your head moving too fast? Are you faint? Do you need a Tylenol? Are you sick to your stomach and shaky in your knees? That's love all right, so don't fight it, honey, because in such matters, no human is immune. Not even you.

Don't kid yourself—nothing lasts forever. This can be both a plus and a minus. A plus if you buy on credit and drop dead before payments are complete. A minus if you purchase an item, a horse, for instance, or a washing machine, and it either dies or breaks down and there you are, still paying out monthly installments. This philosophy can be applied to marriage and to life in all its forms. When something doesn't last forever, you can wail and moan or thank your lucky stars. After all, would you rather be stuck with a bill for a dead horse or cheat the seller from your grave?

Sleep is overrated. Who needs it? Do you know how much you could accomplish while all those idiots out there are asleep? You could be first in your class, you could write twenty novels, you could polish your furniture, which I notice you've never before considered. And, after all, it's true that with sleep come dreams. Sometimes when I wake up I look in the mirror and expect to see a girl of sixteen, and I'm shocked by the stranger looking back at me. I dream about my mother, who made a sour-cherry pie that was so delicious people said angels must have been beside her in the kitchen. Don't ever do what I did and throw caution to the wind. Don't marry for love. The one I picked, when I fixed the chicken and potato dinner to test him, he simply pushed his plate away. He was so lovesick he didn't eat! I should have seen him for who he was. I should have known that this kind of man would wind up sleeping on sunny afternoons, stretched out on the couch, and that the smile on his face would be so sweet no woman with half a heart would dare to wake him.

Try it and you'll see I'm right. If you stay awake, you'll hear the cockroaches and be ready for them with some spray or a shoe. You'll be prepared to throw a book at those mice who think they're so smart as they run along your counter. You'll see the morning star and the way the sky looks like heaven when it's still so early daytime itself seems like a dream.

Wear an apron when you cook. Put on heels when you go out to dinner. Buy your cemetery plot with a group—you get a better deal that way. Stay in school. Don't eat pork. Don't even look a pig in the eye, or you'll get dizzy. Always go to at least two doctors when you're sick, so you get a second opinion, and when you're given a prescription, only take half. They always want to overdose you, and half is plenty. Usually, a scarf around the neck, tea and lemon and whiskey will cure anything. For a broken heart, eat ice cream. For your wooden furniture, olive oil, plain and simple, and it doesn't have all those lousy chemicals they're always pushing off on us.

Women can do anything men can do and more, but is this any reason to tell men the true story? Let them think what they think. Do they believe the proper use of a screwdriver means a higher intelligence level? Fine, if they do, let them. Good luck to them. When you have a baby you will know a secret that no man can ever know. You may forget it later, but for a little while you will know that within yourself you hold another's life. This puts the ability to use a screwdriver in its proper place. Nowhere. Unless you've got furniture you need to put together.

If you ever lose a child, the way I did, then you'll know the other side of the truth. You'll understand what it means to be destroyed and still get up every day and fill the kettle with water. You will see steam from the kettle and weep. Insist nothing is wrong. A piece of dirt flew up and lodged beneath your eyelid. That's all. On the street, tears will fall onto the sidewalk and fill up your shoes. Say the sun is in your eye. Maybe you have pink-eye. If you show your grief, it won't go away. If you keep it secret, it won't go away. It is with you forever and ever, but there may be an hour when you don't remember. An evening when the sky is blue as ink. An afternoon when your daughter runs after a cricket she will never catch. Whisper your baby's name. Then be quiet. If you're lucky you'll hear the name said back to you every time you close your eyes.

Always accept apologies. It won't hurt you to be gracious, and no one knows what you're really thinking, inside your head. Wear black for all occasions, including weddings, bar mitzvahs, and funerals. When I die, bury me quickly. Don't be afraid to leave me in the ground. I'm not frightened, and I never have been. Not about those sorts of matters. Wear low shoes on most occasions and a warm coat. Don't be so snotty about putting on a pair of gloves in cold weather or taking food home from restaurants. Why do you think doggie bags were invented? When you have a rent-controlled apartment to sublease, give it to a relative.

Don't think that good deeds go unforgotten. Don't think that is the point of good deeds. Some people believe that the more you do for others, the quicker your spirit flies, or the better you sleep at night, which is fine if you believe in such things.

Bathing on a cold day is worse for your health than a little dirt will ever be. Spit on the ground when you hear gossip, so you can listen in peace without fear of slander seeking you out. Stay away from spiders. Wash your face with oatmeal. Take long walks, but not after dusk. Once, when I was little, I went where I wasn't supposed to go at twilight and saw a rabbit grabbed up by a great big bird, a hawk, it may have been, or an owl. There were feathers on the ground. There was blood everywhere. I stood watching, in my one good dress that was blue as my father's eyes, and I thought I did not want to be the rabbit or the owl. I wanted to be the sky they had both disappeared into. I wanted to never give up.

Being old is not what you think it is. You feel the same. You are the same. The woman beside you is the girl she once was. Remember that. Remember me.

LILLIE LULKIN
1903–1987

RICHARD SHELTON

The world swirls around us when we are young. But as time passes, our memories select certain larger-than-life events and personalities, such as Richard Shelton's iceman. At the time, the iceman might have been a common sight, but the shaved ice he made available to the sweaty kids playing baseball back then serves as Shelton's metaphor for the sweetness of a distant past. Shelton says he begins writing both his essays and poems in the same way: with a simple lyrical line, before building scenes, re-creating dialogue, and narrating related stories.

THE ICEMAN

Sometimes I long for a simpler era, before television, when milk came in bottles and we all knew who the monsters were. In those days the iceman came through the back door carrying a block of ice in ice tongs like huge and delicate calipers, beautifully symmetrical; and he put the block of ice in the top compartment of the handsome brown wooden icebox; and then he went out again with his wondrous ice tongs over his shoulder, usually whistling. He was a magic man, the most magical of all the men we knew.

He came in response to a little square card our mother placed in the corner of the window. The card was divided into triangles and each triangle was a different color and represented a different size block of ice. The position of the card in the window—which color was up—determined how much ice the iceman would leave. No matter how many bad things we did, and we did very many bad things ranging from petty theft to tampering with the plumbing, we never changed the position of that card. Once a mother placed it with a certain color up, it remained. To move it would have been to break faith with the iceman, and we could not do that.

He drove an old green truck and it listed to the left so that the bed wasn't level and the water from the melting ice drained out on the left side, leaving a strange, dribbly little trail of wet sand down the alley. For those who didn't know about the iceman, the trail was inexplicable, as if an angel had flown down the alley at great speed, leaving no tracks and peeing as it went. We wondered about things like that. Did angels pee? Did they . . . but we didn't even dare think about that.

Grown-ups walked down the sidewalks along the streets, but the alleys were our world, where we lived and planned and plotted and played ball and where the iceman was king. The alleys ran straight as could be all the way through town for miles and miles, clear across the valley, and they were all covered with golden sand. Just outside the wooden back fences were trashcans of all shapes and sizes whose lids made perfect shields when we had chinaberry battles or dueled with our homemade swords. (We pronounced the word exactly as it was spelled.) We drew fish or large circles in the sand for our marble games and made little mounds of wet sand, using spit, to elevate the marble we were aiming at. Sometimes a prized agate taw would change hands when its desperate owner had no more marbles to risk, and while the winner swaggered off up the alley with the prize in his Bull Durham marble bag, the loser would head toward home with a tight throat and blinking eyes, but we never cried in front of one another. It would have been unthinkable.

Boise was known as "the city of trees," and not only because its name, in the original form, had been the French word for forest. Every yard had maples or catalpas, walnut or cherry trees. The streets were lined with Dutch elms and the river was lined with cottonwoods and willows. The whole town was hidden beneath a rustling green canopy, and very few buildings, like the State Capitol, were tall enough to emerge above it. But the alleys were free of trees. In the summer, shimmering waves of heat rose from the sand in the alleys as if from the Sahara, reminding the citizens of Boise that their green, shady paradise existed on the edge of a formidable desert.

And down those shimmering golden alleys on the hottest day of summer came the iceman in his old green truck that tilted a little to the left. In the truck were enormous blocks of ice covered with burlap bags, and he sculpted these blocks of ice with his magical tools into smaller blocks with perfectly straight edges and square corners, just the right size block for any particular icebox. One of his tools was a gadget—I don't know what it was called— like a comb with widely spaced, very sharp teeth and a handle, and with it he could shave ice.

The only way to really understand the meaning of shaved ice is to have been playing ball for several hours in July in a hot alley when the iceman arrives in his truck and stops and you feel the dark coolness coming out of the back of his truck and he thrusts into your grimy outstretched paw a handful of the coldest shaved ice ever invented and you put as much of it as you can into your mouth, so cold it makes your teeth ache, and the rest you put on top of your head under your cap and let the cold water trickle down your back and face as the ice melts, until your whole body is shivering with chill and delight. That's the only way to really understand the meaning of shaved ice.

The ice man also let us scramble onto the tailgate of his truck to retrieve any small chunks or shards of ice that he had chipped off while he was turning a few large blocks of ice into many small blocks of ice. These we would suck until there was just enough left to make a very satisfying crunch as we chewed them up. Then he would let us ride on the back of his truck for a ways up the alley, until he had made a couple more stops. The iceman never charged us for any of these valuable services because he knew we had no money, and anyway the idea had never occurred to him. Gods do not think in such terms.

We sat on the tailgate with our legs dangling as the truck lumbered down the alley, leaving behind it the strange, dribbly little trail of wet sand, and we felt the coolness at our backs, a coolness that smelled of ice and the frozen north we had seen in movies and of wet burlap, and we smelled the exhaust from the old truck and the smell of the iceman as he swung another block of ice onto his bronze and sweaty back. We sucked on our shards of ice and looked down the alley as if we were looking into the future, and it was the same for as far as we could see.

We had no notion that we were living at the end of an era—it was 1938 or 1939 or 1940—or that dreadful things were happening far away that would soon affect our lives directly. We had only the vaguest idea of Europe and thought that Japan was a little island next to China and all its people were tiny, like small children, and spoke Pidgin English. Whatever interest we had in orientals centered around what somebody's older brother had told us about the configuration of the oriental female's genitalia, an amazing thing actually, that our informant had sworn was true, and we believed him.

I can see you now, child that I was, perched on the rear end of the iceman's green truck, dangling your white and rapidly sun-burning bare legs from the tailgate. You are not a very promising looking specimen, skinny and bucktoothed, your head and every-thing about you seeming too small for your huge mass of curls stiff as coiled wire and exactly the color of a carrot. Your ears stick out like car doors, your skin is so fair that it is almost translucent, and your face is covered with great splotchy freckles. Your eyes are an arresting shade of blue, but they have dark circles beneath them.

You are not beautiful, my little friend, and because of that I am not beautiful either, nor have I ever been. I see you looking down the long alley, trying to see above the glare of the sand what the future holds for you, what you will become, what I am. At the same time I seem to be looking back more and more steadily, try-ing to see you at the other end of the alley, trying to see what I was.

And so I will strike a bargain with you, my funny looking friend, a simple bargain but not as simple as it sounds, and one we will both have to live with from here on out. If you can face the future, your own future as only I can reveal it to you, I will try, fi-nally, to face the past, my own past, as only you know it. Surely if I can bear to see what I was, you can bear to see what you have be-come. You must have developed a sense of irony, a sense of humor by now. Otherwise, where did mine come from? And courage? I know you are convinced you lack it, but nobody expects it of a child so young, except the child himself, and no one but you is convinced you lack it. But dark circles under such bright eyes. What does that mean?

You are smiling. So it is agreed. Jump down from that old green truck and take my hand. Let's walk down the alley toward home, and the iceman will go on as he always does into some future nei-ther of us can share, although we will stop many times and look back toward his fading image.

DANIEL STOLAR

The images of past and present—the basketball, the two mothers, the children come and gone, and the father who connects them—form a haunting and compelling presence in this bare narrative. Daniel Stolar shares the ghostly aura of his adolescence, to which he clings while confronting the confusion and hopelessness of a future he refuses to accept, yet cannot quite avoid.

MY HOME COURT

There is a basketball rim and backboard fastened to the old carport in the backyard of my house. I say *my* out of habit and stubborn nostalgia, but it is no longer my house. It is the house where I grew up, where I learned to play basketball, where my mother was sick for nearly ten years. But my mom is dead seven years now, and my father is remarried to a woman named Suzanne. The house is Suzanne's now. Since graduating from college, I return home several times a year on vacations and occasionally when I'm not sure of my next destination. Sure, my father still owns the elegant and simple red-brick home, but my father is not a man who notices the color of the carpet or sofa covering, or the arrangement of photos on the fridge. He is happy if the house is not breaking down in some way that requires his immediate attention.

The concrete basketball court dips down at its back right corner and a tree overhangs there, so that a jump shot from there is more like something from miniature golf than basketball. The top left of the backboard is soft and forgiving, my favorite target. The space itself is barely fifteen by fifteen feet of concrete, bounded on two sides by high wooden walls and on a third by a short wrought-iron fence. The one-on-one games I played there were inevitably bruising. I have beaten people on that court who I couldn't touch anywhere else. To make a driving layup, you must know where and how to hit the wooden slab with your body; you must absorb the impact with elbow, hip and knee. There are things I know.

My mother was sick for ten years. For all but a few weeks of those ten years she carried on like nothing was wrong. And we did the same. At the same time, it seemed a matter of course to me. There was always some reason not to tell anybody the most recent bad news: she was campaigning for alderman, she was graduating from law school, she was taking a job at a new firm. Now I know that my parents would have invented reasons not to talk about her illness regardless of the circumstances, that it was the silence itself they needed. To keep the cancer under wraps was, in some feeble way, to keep it under control. Even in the house we discussed it rarely, maintaining instead the high-achieving routine of two professional parents, two precocious kids, as if, once voiced, word of her cancer would ravish our household with the same deadly abandon as the malignant cells themselves. At times, it seemed, we talked about everything *but* her disease. Yet there was undoubtedly a code that permeated the pall: my sister and I wouldn't dare leave dishes in the sink, not because our mom worked hard and deserved better, but because our mom had *cancer.*

None of this is to say that there weren't good times in our house: an April Fools' Day tradition of shaving cream and gags, animated dinner together five nights of the week, surprise parties with long scathing poems set to the tune of Paul Revere—my mother's specialty. But no amount of hijinks or hilarity could extinguish that one unspoken thing that lurked in the corners of our home—under the stairs, in the kitchen pantry—and in the space between my words: my mother was dying. Over the years, our silence became like my mother's wigs and scarves—one of the trappings of her cancer.

When I couldn't talk, I played ball. I was in fifth grade when she first had a mastectomy. I went out back and shot baskets. When she yelled at me after chemo, I pounded the indoor-outdoor basketball against the cement. I threw it off the two wooden walls. In seventh grade when the cancer came back in her spine. . . . In ninth and eleventh grades when they found it in her lungs. . . . Even my junior year of college, home from school for her funeral. . . . I shot set-shots and turnarounds, layups and fancy reverses. I dribbled and passed and rebounded. I can still feel the soles of my bare feet scraping the rough asphalt: dribble, stop, jump, shoot—my body stretching upward, my entire being pointed through my bent wrist at the rim. Sometimes my mom would sit in a lounge chair and talk to me while I shot, but most of the time I was by myself. And soon, I wasn't worrying about my mom, I was just shooting baskets. To this day, I am at best a mediocre basketball player, but the mere sound of the bouncing ball quiets me. Dribbling, passing to myself off the wall, shooting, I felt the anger flow out of my hands into the dry, dusty basketball. It was my mattress-padded wall.

My mother liked to say that other than her children's education, this house was the only good investment she and my father ever made. She took credit for talking him into buying it during a time when nobody wanted to live in the inner city. She would later serve eight years on the St. Louis city council, an ornery, educated Jewish woman in a world of cigar smoke and stupidity (simple illiteracy if I am to believe her telling), working to redevelop our neighborhood. Now our inner-city enclave is the trendiest neighborhood in the city. My dad and Suzanne shower after aerobics at Plaza Fitness and walk to one of the nearby sidewalk cafes for dinner. (Just last year, a full six years after my mother's death, my sister and I were having lunch in one of those cafes when the owner came to our table after staring at us from across the restaurant. "Man, you must be Mary Stolar's kids. Your mom and me had a couple of knockdown drag-outs. Let me buy you lunch.")

After my father married Suzanne, the house changed in increments. Home for Christmas—a new kitchen, whiter, sleeker, shinier than the one before. Gone was the enormous wood table that had always felt like the very center of our house, the table where my mother held court with her back against the stove in the winter, and the grime in the parallel cracks seemed like the physical residue of the stories that floated over it. The new table was narrow and clean, formica. At spring break, the family pictures in the study were missing, the garden my mother had wrestled with for three stubborn springs, torn up. By summer, the den was all new. Trying, I told Suzanne I thought the new den looked great. Airy, I said. She said thanks, and wasn't it dreadful how dark and depressing the old den had been. Who, I have wondered repeatedly since then, did she think had decorated that dark, depressing den?

Suzanne and my father ride the bike path and go to art museum openings and the symphony. They listen to NPR in the mornings, and eat seafood or skinless white meat at night. She has my father putting on his prim tennis whites to do step aerobics in the winter. In the grand scheme of things, this cannot be a bad thing, I think to myself from two thousand miles away. She speaks French and Spanish and has two kids almost the same ages as my sister and myself, both of them graduates of top colleges. When she travels, she wears dangling airplanes in her ears. When she cooks, she flies around the kitchen like an unbalanced Cuisinart.

With the exception of an ill-fated Christmas trip to Puerta Vallarta thirteen months after my mother's death, we have made little pretense of joining the two families into a Brady Bunch fantasy of one big family ever after. They open their Christmas presents in the new downstairs den as my sister and I come and go, sticking our heads in politely, asking if Santa was good this year. We do not invite them to our Chanukah parties. Her kids have brand-new centrally heated rooms on the third floor, a place that was all dusty storage before, and my sister and I have the same rooms we have always had, connected by a bathroom where the ancient toilet is still flushed by my mother's jury-rigged screwdriver. During the ninety percent of the year the doors to those rooms are closed as my father and Suzanne move about in the rest of the eighty-year-old house.

More recently than I would like to admit I stood in the doorway to the new upstairs study after three months of living in this house and had a full-fledged temper tantrum. I had just left medical school on one coast; I had not yet entered an MFA creative writing program on the other; and for the confusing time in between, I stayed at home. I cannot remember now the specifics of the argument—the particular incident that sparked it. But I know exactly what the argument was about: my father felt that I was taking advantage of my presence in the house, overstaying my welcome—disturbing the routine; I felt that I no longer had a home.

My father is an attorney, the most thorough man I have ever met, and he simply cannot be out-argued. But he can be out-yelled. Red-faced and hoarse, I flung the door shut and stormed out of the house. But first I made sure that I was heard. I was being excised from this home just as surely as the memory of my mother, I yelled at the top of my lungs. I knew I was not welcome there. Even my baby pictures had been taken down. Suzanne and my father sat at the bridge table, papers spread in front of them, shell-shocked, while I yelled. I can still see Suzanne's face as she stared blankly ahead, unable to look up at her ranting, adult stepchild.

No sooner did I have a new address than I received a letter

from my father: thirteen professionally typed, single-spaced pages detailing the guidelines for my future visits home. He poignantly noted the irony of my tirade taking place as he and Suzanne pored over the month's bills for the house where I had eaten and slept, come and gone, turned on and off the lights and TV, no questions asked, for the past three months.

Even as I held those thirteen angry, flawless pages in my hand, I was not surprised at my dad's attempt to legislate peace for his new family. For ten years, the routine had been sacred above all else in our house, the predictability of the daily cycles of school and work our source of stability in the face of the chaos of my mother's cells. I will never forget the sight of my father's chin trembling uncontrollably as my parents sat us down at that old kitchen table for another round of bad news; I know how badly he wants now just to hold it all together. But my understanding has not yet led all the way to forgiveness: this house holds my most vivid memories of my mother, and I can't help but feel that they are being taken away.

So now I go home for limited stays on a peaceful but contingent basis. A new kind of silence has been imposed in my old home: there will be no more temper tantrums. Now I am the potentially malignant presence that threatens the day-to-day. Alone in the house while my father and Suzanne are at work, I roam slowly through the rooms, imagining them as they used to be. I can still see the rust-colored couch against the wall, my grandmother's hand-me-down lamps, the shades where now there are blinds. I tell myself to ignore my adolescent impulse to stake my claim, to shatter again the quiet of these impeccable rooms. Because I know that, once again, even to bring it up is to make it worse.

I stand on the second-floor landing and look over our backyard. The professional landscaping is a mean contrast to the image I have of my mother, knee-deep in mud and mulch. I look at my little basketball court, tucked in the far corner, at the end of the hedge. It is an eyesore to be sure, the backboard nearly as old as I am, streaked brown with water stains. I reach behind the washing machine in the back hall and pick up the old ball, uneven from so little use.

For the first few dribbles I am with my mom. I picture her lounging in the chaise, wrists dangling from the armrests. I hear her making fun of my game. I throw the ball off the back wall, I catch it on return, I spin and shoot a turnaround. The old leather is dry and cracked against my finger tips. I grab the rebound out of the air and shoot again. Soon I am alone. Perfectly alone. Once again, I feel the anger flow out of my hands, into the basketball. I dribble, I weave in and out, I shoot jumpers and driving layups. That is all. Somehow this woman who now possesses the house where I grew up knew not to get rid of this basketball court. I would never mention it to her. And my father would not think to say anything. Eyesore that it surely is, she has let it be, and for this I thank her.

The basketball kicks off the short fence that once guarded my mother's dog-eared geraniums. Automatically I take the two steps to where I know the ball will bounce. I square my shoulders as my hands rise together in front of me, my fingers outstretched in position to receive.

PHILLIP LOPATE

Nothing really happens in Phillip Lopate's memoir about his father, especially when compared to some of the more fast-paced essays in this reader. Yet from the very beginning "The Story of My Father" feels eventful and riveting. The secret? Lopate's effective use of the fiction writer's favorite tool: dialog. Re-created from notes and memory, the talk among Lopate's parents and siblings displays their eccentricities and affectations and comprises a vivid and realistic portrait of them all. Contemplating these conversations, Lopate also sustains an inner monologue that fortifies the dialog with irony and humor—and a touch of the tragic.

THE STORY OF MY FATHER

My mother and father had once taken a magazine quiz: "Do You Know Your Mate?" She had been able to fill out everything about him, from his Social Security number to his mother's maiden name, whereas the opposite was true for him. "He didn't even remember my mother's maiden name! I realized I was living with a stranger, who didn't care at all about me, as long as I fulfilled his creature comforts." What my mother says is true, up to a point. My father is a stranger to everyone. On the other hand, his not knowing her Social Security number does not negate the fact that he was completely attached to her, and would have undergone any amount of humiliation to keep living in her presence.

Ten years ago, when my father was 74 and my mother 68, she divorced him so that she could put him in a nursing home. She was candid about not wanting to spend her remaining years nursing an old man she didn't love, and it was clear that he could no longer take care of himself. Apparently the nursing home's regulations stated that a prospective lodger could have no other recourse before being taken in: hence, the necessity for divorce.

After the divorce went through, there was an interim period when my parents continued to live together, waiting for an opening at the nursing home. During this time, my father was "on probation," as it were, and if he behaved well, it seemed my mother might reverse herself and allow him to stay with her. In the midst of that limbo period, I was in New York for a few weeks (I had taken a regular teaching job in Houston) and called on them. My mother sent us out to breakfast together so that we could talk "man-to-man." Since he is so laconic and apt to drift into withdrawal, I could only smile at my mother's fantasy of a "father-son powwow." We stopped at the corner stand to buy a newspaper; I was tempted to buy two newspapers, in case we ran out of things to say. It was raining as we walked across the street to the coffee shop, a greasy-spoon joint, for breakfast. The breakfast special was $1.55, "Hot Pastrami Omelette." Since he was treating, I had chosen the cheapest place around.

"How's . . ." my father began, then lost his train of thought.

"How's Helen?" I prompted, offering the name of my then-current girlfriend.

"I thought the other one was prettier."

"What other one?" I asked irritably, knowing he meant Kay, a previous flame who had two-timed me, and whose prettiness I did not relish being reminded of at the moment.

"You know, I had a funny dream last night," he changed the subject. "I dreamt I was sick and there were about 10 people in the hospital room who came to see me. One of them was Bernie. Now I know my brother's been dead for years. I don't understand the significance of being there."

"I don't either. What happened in the dream?"

"Nothing. Your sister Leah was in the room, and her friends. That's another thing I couldn't understand. Why wasn't Molly in the dream? Or you and Hal? Your mother would have an interpretation."

"Probably." A long silence fell. "So, you and Mom seem to have made peace with each other."

"You know, your mother and I got divorced."

"I know. Does it feel strange, living together after you're divorced?"

"Yes, it feels strange."

"Did you sign the papers too, or—"

"I signed it," he said. "It was a joint divorce. Because your mother was going to go through with it anyway. One of the reasons for the divorce was to get a better tax break. And now they've changed the law, so it wouldn't have made any difference anyway."

"I thought the divorce was so that they wouldn't take Mother's income if she put you in a nursing home."

"Yes. But I don't want to go into a nursing home. My father, my brother and my sister all went into nursing homes, and I don't have fond memories of them."

I liked the understated way he put it. "What I don't understand is, is it your legal right to stay in the apartment now, or are you there at Mother's sufferance?"

"I think it's the second. Besides, she doesn't want to have me forcibly removed."

"So you're on your best behavior now? And you're getting along?"

"Well. . . . There have been some peculiar things lately."

"Like what?"

"We were at a gathering, and your mother was talking as if I had nothing to do with the way you kids turned out," he said, holding his fork in midair and glancing up at me sideways. "She was saying 'My son does this,' and 'My other son does that,' and 'My daughter is such-and-such.' She was taking all the credit, as if I had no influence on you."

"Well, that's not true. We all feel you had a big influence on us." For better or worse, I added in my mind.

"I'm not saying I was the only influence. But I did have a little."

"Of course. She was just bragging, Pop. Like you do."

Another long silence, in which I watched the flies buzzing around the Miller beer sign.

"What have you been thinking about lately?" I asked.

"Nothing. I've been slightly depressed," he said.

"About what?"

"Nothing special."

"Your health all right?"

"My health is as good as can be expected for a man my age. I'm actually in good physical shape, except I have emphysema. I haven't smoked for years, but I still have emphysema from all the smoking I used to do."

"Are you still on medication?"

"Just vitamin pills."

"That's great!" I said with false, hearty enthusiasm.

"And half an aspirin a day for my heart."

"You get any exercise at all? Do you walk?"

"No, I don't walk much," he shook his head.

"You used to love walking."

"But now I walk so slowly. I used to walk real fast. Now your mother walks faster than I do, and she gets impatient."

"You can take walks alone."

"But I walk so slowly that it bugs me. Put it this way: My halcyon days are over," he said, grinning at his use of the unusual word.

"When were your halcyon days, Pop?" I asked skeptically.

"Before I got my stroke. I thought I was immortal. I was healthy as a horse. I used to work all day and night without stopping. I never even took a sick day. Then I got the stroke and I couldn't get out of bed. I don't know if you could understand unless it happens to you. You try to stand up and you can't. That frightened the hell out of me." Now he's warming up. "And I had this internist. Supposed to be one of the top internists in the city. At least that's what he told me. He prescribed Dilantin and something else. The two medications canceled each other out. Later on someone told me that I could have sued him for malpractice. But someone else said that if he was such a big internist, then I couldn't win. So I didn't sue."

"Just as well."

"He's still practicing. Cut down on his hours, though," he adds with a sly grin.

"But that was over 20 years ago. A long time to get over a fright."

"A lot of people at the Senior Center had strokes. So they understand. That's one good thing about that place. The problem is . . . that the two men I played canasta with, one is sick and the other man . . ." he mumbles.

"I'm sorry, I didn't hear."

"The other man passed on."

"That's too bad. So you have to make new friends."

"It's not easy for me. I'm not the gregarious type."

You could say that again. "Why is that, I wonder?"

"Your mother was the gregarious type, but I wasn't."

"What about when you were younger, before you met Mom?"

A pained look. "I didn't have too many friends."

"Were you shy?"

"Probably I am shy."

"Why is that?"

"I didn't have any confidence in myself."

The truth in a nutshell. Another silence. "Well, you don't have to make friends with the people at the center, you just have to play cards."

"I do. I play rummy. And I find I'm better at rummy than I was at canasta.—Eat slowly. Take your time," he tells me. My French toast is so awful that I am trying to get through it as fast as possible.

"Does the center ever go on outings?" I ask.

"They go to Atlantic City. That's not my style. I don't bother going."

"I was once in Atlantic City," I reminisce, "and I enjoyed it. The ocean, the boardwalk."

"The hotels expect you to gamble. I'm not a gambler."

When he is finished he starts to get up and reaches ever so slowly into his raincoat, which is hanging on the hook behind him, for some money. He finds only a dollar. Puzzled. His hand travels with incredible hesitation across to the other pocket. Nothing in there. A look goes across his face, like a child who has accidentally lost something and expects a beating. He puts his hand in his shirt pocket. Pulls out a $20 bill. Satisfaction. The check comes to $5.60.

"You pay the tip," he says cheerfully.

A week later I asked my mother how Pop was doing. "He fell out of bed again. I didn't help him up either. He's got to learn to do for himself. What if I go on the road again? It's what I learned when I was working with those retarded kids—same principle. You've got to teach them to be independent."

"It's not very nice to compare him to a retarded kid."

"Don't worry," she sighed, "I'll do what's right. Because I don't want to live with guilt. I've lived with guilt before and it's no fun."

But fighting broke out between my parents constantly. Before I left the city, I visited them again. My mother was telling me about her stocks. Considering how poor we had been, and how she is still living in government-subsidized housing, having stocks, even worthless ones, is a status symbol. "This stock went from 50 cents to $4, I didn't sell, and now it's down to a dollar."

"If it reaches $4 again, you'd better sell," I said cautiously.

"What's the difference? It only cost me a few hundred bucks. If I can't afford to risk that much, forget it."

My father interjected, in his phlegmy growl, something about the Mindanao Mother Lode.

She blew up at him. "You'll see, you're not getting a cent of that money! Even if the lawyer did say you were entitled to 50 percent of our property after the divorce. I'll fix your wagon!"

My father shrank into himself. I was shocked at the venom with which she had yelled at him, even after all these years of hearing it. I asked, "What's this about a Mindanao Mother Lode?"

She said, "Aw, I invested a lousy hundred dollars in this oil drilling outfit in the Pacific a few years ago, and never heard a word about it. But from him I never stop hearing it! If he keeps rubbing it in, he's the one who's gonna suffer."

Much as I had wanted to protect him in the moment against her temper, after I left them I realized the passive-aggressive cunning of my father in employing just those words that would set her off. (It was the same quiet ability to insert a dig as when he called my previous girlfriend prettier than my current one. For all his solipsism, he was observant enough when he wanted to be, and had a feel for other people's exposed areas of wounded vanity.)

A few months later, the parental truce was shattered. It seemed the toilet had overflowed while my father was using it, and he didn't clean it up. He had phoned my sister Molly to report the toilet had flooded, and she, not having any time that day to stop by, gave him practical advice: Call the maintenance man. He didn't; instead he sat there for eight hours, "with his arms folded," as Molly put it. My mother came home, saw his turds on the floor, the sight of which pushed her over the limit for good.

It was the two women's interpretation that he was not "out of it" at all, but had contrived to punish his wife by his passivity, because only by provoking her fury could he get the attention he wanted from her. I suspected geriatric debility to be the greater cause and was irked at my mother and sister for showing so little understanding of human frailty. On the other hand, most of the burden for taking care of him had fallen on them, not me. It was easy for me to play the compassionate relation at a distance.

My father called me himself in Houston, a rare event, to say that he would not be living at home anymore. My mother was putting him in an adult home near Far Rockaway. I said maybe it was for the best. He said, "Yes, well, in the sense that we weren't getting along."

Desperate for some optimistic note, I added, "And it will be near the beach. That's nice."

"Well, that part doesn't matter to me. I don't swim."

"Still, it's nice to see the ocean." He did not deign to reply to this inanity. "And maybe you can make friends there," I added.

"I didn't make any friends at the Senior Citizens Club. Although there, the people were walking in off the streets. Maybe here there'll be more people—of substance."

Around the time of the divorce, my family tended to split along gender lines. My brother Hal and I sympathized more with our father's eviction from his home, while the two girls shared my mother's point of view. Molly, a practicing Buddhist who usually preached compassion, surprised me by her adamance. "Why should I feel guilty for not visiting him regularly? He abandoned the family long ago." She had taken to calling him Mr. Ross, because, she explained, if you say Albert Ross quickly, it comes out albatross.

After he was deposited in the home, my mother went around depressed for a while. Hal thought it was guilt; I thought it was being faced with a void. Who would she blame now for her unhappy life? She had never admitted how dependent she might be on him, only the other way around.

My own impulse had been to sympathize more with my father because he seemed the weaker party, and because my mother had cheated on him. As a young man, I had taken her infidelity very personally, as though she had somehow betrayed me. Objectively, I could appreciate that it was absolutely necessary for the young woman she was, lost in a miserable marriage, to reach out to other men. Nowadays it isn't her affairs I hold against her, so much as that, in justifying herself, she felt compelled to demean my father before his children's eyes. I know, I know, I am being unfair in blaming her for not "allowing" us to venerate him more, as though it were ever possible for her to lie about her intensest feelings—to situate him, by some trompe l'oeil of maternal tact, on the patriarchal throne.

I dropped in at my mother's before leaving New York. She was going on about how he got what he deserved. My mother, for all her psychological astuteness, is someone who speaks and acts out of a righteous wound. Her recognition that she may have hurt someone can only proceed from the perception that she was hurt first.

"Supposing there were two other people you were looking at whose marriage was this bad," I said, "wouldn't you be inclined to assume they were both a little at fault?"

"Yeah, I suppose," she said. "But he blew it."

"If he was so terrible, why did you stay with him so long then?"

"I wish I knew. That's the $64,000 question. He had so much promise! What happened to it? He just didn't have the drive. After he retired, I tried to get him to be interested in things, I took him with me to the community college. But he thought he was smarter than everyone else, and if they didn't appreciate that immediately. . . . He dropped out, and I got my degree. To me it was a challenge. To Al, a challenge was already a defeat."

My mother has so much life-force, it's hard to imagine what it must have been like to live with her opposite all those years. Vitality like hers, ever on tap, has been a constant delight for me but not a mystery. The mystery has been my father and his deep reserves of inanition.

After my father was put in the nursing home, the next family crisis occurred when my mother announced she didn't want him at the Passover seder at her house. I was outraged. Then my friend Max, the soul of kindness, said he sympathized with her. She had suffered for years in an unhappy marriage, and now she was divorced. Why should she be hypocritical and welcome him? Why pretend we were an intact family when we weren't? Each of the children would have to learn how to adjust to this new arrangement; each would have to make a separate deal with our father.

I began going out to the Belle Harbor Adult Home in Far Rockaway. It took forever on the subway; you had to catch a spur train over Broad Channel the last couple of stops. Once off the train, you found a calm residential neighborhood, one- or two-family homes with hedges, an old-fashioned New York lower-middle-class feeling, with quite a few senior citizens residences and funeral homes in the vicinity. My father didn't like the area because the nearest newsstand was seven blocks away; he was used to a denser city life.

His half of the room contained a bed, a nighttable, some pictures of the family and, I was both flattered and obscurely ashamed to see, my books. His roommate was deaf, 100 years old, spoke only Yiddish and was paranoid; when I tried to bring the empty chair near his side of the room over to my father's bed so that we could sit together, he barked at me. No words, just guttural attack-dog sounds.

My father, each visit, would fill me in on the deathwatch. "There's a guy here who dropped dead the other day from a coronary. Fell over into his soup. He seemed in OK health, too."

I wanted to make him feel better. So, one day I took it into my head to buy my father a pair of swimming shorts. Since he lived only a block away from the beach, surely there might come a time, even if he didn't swim, when he'd want to warm his legs in the sand. We walked the seven blocks to the retail street, taking over a half-hour to do so. At the shop, my father wouldn't let me get him swimming trunks but insisted on Bermuda shorts. He went into the dressing room to try them on.

"Do they fit, Pop?"

"Yeah, they fit." This was his highest accolade—the acme of enthusiasm, coming from my father.

On the way home I asked, "Do you think you'll wear them?"

"Not very often," he said, honest to a fault.

During this time I kept trying to buy my father gifts. First I bought a television for his room (which he never watched, preferring the common room's), then a half-refrigerator for snacks, because he didn't like the food they served. I was doing this partly to lift his depression, and partly to administer a lesson to my family on the right way to treat him—I did not like all their talk about his being an "albatross" or a "vegetable." The problem was, I kept coming up against my own upset at his lack of appreciation. The man had no talent for accepting gifts.

I needed to see my father as a poor, maligned Père Goriot abandoned in old age, who deserved our love as a matter of course and custom, and to dismiss the others' beefs against him as petty. I wanted to start with him on a clean, tender page. But to do so, I had to hide my own scars and keep my buried angers against him in check. And sometimes I could no longer overlook the meaner side of the man, which Molly insisted was holding together the works.

One weekend, I checked him out of the adult home to spend a few days at the loft I was subletting. In a sense, I was trying out my fantasy of what it would be like to have my father move in with me. I had bought us baseball tickets at Shea Stadium so that we could watch Doc Gooden go for his 20th victory. The morning of our planned outing was drizzly, and Father moped that the game was going to be rained out. Luckily, the weather cleared up long enough for Doc to pitch—and win; but still my father seemed morose. All weekend I had cooked for him, taken him around, arranged dinner at a fancy restaurant, and nothing pleased him: The coffee was too weak, too strong. By the end of the weekend I was completely sympathetic with my mother. Every time he complained about something—say, wanting another radio station on the car radio—I could hear her voice in my thoughts: *Why don't you change it yourself?* Though he didn't know how to drive, he was sure I was going the wrong way, and insisted we ask directions at the gas station. Moreover, he seemed completely uninterested in my life—every few hours asking, "When is Hal coming back from vacation?" Prolonged, continuous exposure to the man was eroding my idealized defense of him, making me see him exactly as the other family members did: infuriatingly passive, selfish, hurtful, uncouth.

Looking back at that weekend, I see now what it might have been like for him. He couldn't give himself over to the pleasures offered, when they were so temporary, and when they came at the humiliating price of my expecting his gratitude. If this was indeed a test—a dry run for some possible future living arrangement—he could not afford to be on best behavior. My father would rather disappoint quickly and get the suspense over with.

The trek out to Far Rockaway was too long, the family members were visiting him less and less, and it was agreed that we should try to find a home for him closer to town. My brother was able to relocate him in an ultra-desirable "adult residence" on the Upper West Side, near Lincoln Center. Once again, he could walk to the corner and buy a newspaper. We could take him out to a variety of restaurants, all within a stone's throw of his building. He could look out the window and see Broadway, Citarella's fish store, Fairview's produce stand. He could get himself a haircut. He began perking up again, making observations. One of his repeated bon mots was: "When it says 'hair salon' instead of barber shop, that means you're paying extra." Another: "When you see a cloth napkin, that means you're paying extra." This was his peasant, streetwise side letting us know: You can't fool me, it's still the same baloney.

The new residence home seemed, at first, a paradise for seniors. There were classical music concerts, daily video screenings, poetry workshops (to which my father brought his half-century-old poems on foolskin stock about his wife's defection)—all in a building that felt more like an apartment house than a prison. Each resident had his own separate "apartment" (a room, really), while enjoying the social life of the common parlors. The pretense was that of dignified, autonomous seniors who just happened to need the additional services of a specialized hotel. The problem in such a place was that you could not falter. If you got too sick, too frail, too out-of-it you were told you didn't belong in their establishment, but in a nursing home, and were summarily kicked out.

After awhile, there was no kidding ourselves: My father was on a slow, inexorable path downward. It was not just that he had cataracts (they could be corrected with surgery), or that he was a loner, acting, by the residence staff's standards, uncommunally. It was that he began to experience "incontinence problems"—in short, wet his pants, making him an undesirable presence in the dining room. The family took a crash course in adult Pampers, rubber diapers, prostate surgery and behavioral modification training.

Incontinence was the precise metaphorical situation to galvanize family arguments about my father's will power. "He's doing it on purpose!" said Molly. "He can hold it in if he wants to."

"I don't think so," I said. Meanwhile, my father went around looking utterly hesitant to travel any distance further than a halfblock from the nearest bathroom.

I remember one particular night I had planned to take him to a screening at Lincoln Center. When I got there he was so sloppily dressed that I decided to forgo the movie and just have dinner with him across the street, at a newly opened Italian restaurant.

We had the usual tepid time of it, neither hostile nor affectionate. The most interesting moment was when Father volunteered this short summary of his marriage: "I felt that I loved your mother more than she loved me." Undoubtedly true, and I realized

I had probably contrived my whole romantic life until then so as not to be caught in the same situation.

He also said, "She always attracted dykes. She must have done something for that to happen."

I told my father that Uncle George had died. There was a silence. He finally said, "I have mixed feelings about him."

"Why?"

"Well, I think he played around with her when she was a kid. And then she was madly in love with him, all during the time when we were first married. I couldn't prove anything, but. . . ."

It seemed to me he was casting about wildly for rivals, to explain why my mother had come to detest him.

When the meal ended, he tried to get up and couldn't seem to rise, so I gave him a hand and walked him to the men's room, one flight down. He had become very unsteady on his feet, especially managing stairs. "Why do they always put the men's room where you have to go up or down a flight?" he said. I waited outside the toilet door for 10 minutes. After awhile I thought maybe he had died in there. "Pop, you all right?" I called out. He grunted something in reply, so I knew he was still among the living. "Can I help?" I asked. "No," came his foggy voice uncertainly. Ten more minutes passed. "Pop, what's going on?" Finally I went inside to have a look. "I had an accident," he said. I noticed the tiled floor was smeared with shit. "I made in my pants. I couldn't get them off in time."

"OK. Let's get outta here." I helped him up the stairs and we left quickly, before the waiters could see the bathroom floor. It was their problem, I thought; I'll never go back to that restaurant anyway.

"I'm sorry," he said, as we crossed the street.

"It's not your fault, Pop. It's old age." I was already thinking ahead to what I would have to do. Get him undressed and into a shower. I was very calm, patient, the way I used to be when I was working with kids. We took the elevator upstairs to his room, and he immediately sat on the bed and took off his pants, smearing the bedspread in the process. I helped him off with his shirt and led him into the bathroom across the hall. Two minutes later, I still hadn't heard the sound of running water.

"Pop, what's the matter?" He was standing outside the shower stall, dry and dirty.

"I can't get my socks off."

"Oh, for crying out loud!" I said, sounding just like my mother. "The socks can get wet. Just get in the shower!"

I pushed him in.

"I can't get the hot water to work," he said. Now his total help-lessness was getting on my nerves. He had turned on the hot water, it would just take a minute to warm up. Didn't he know that, after all these years on the planet? I gave him soap and told him to rinse well and left him there. Back in his room, I threw away his soiled underpants. I stripped the bedspread and bunched it on the floor, hoping his attendant would deal with it tomorrow. And I turned on the Mets game, so that he would have something to watch when he returned.

He came back. One of his legs was still covered with shit. I cleaned it off as best I could with water and toilet paper. Wiping off my father's ass wasn't what I'd expected from the evening, but—all in the nature of reality. I tried to tell myself it was good for my spiritual development. As soon as he was lying down com-fortably, however, I said goodbye. I could have stayed longer, but I didn't. He could have said thank you but he didn't. He made his usual "OK" grunt. As I fled the building onto Amsterdam Avenue, a junkie was vomiting against the side of my car. What a night!

There was some hope that a prostate operation might improve the incontinence situation. In any event, he had to have one. After it was done, I received a call from the hospital to pick up my father. Molly was also there to help, but she seemed in a foul mood.

"How about if I go down to pay for his TV and phone," I said, "and meanwhile you can see that he gets ready."

"I've got to speak to you," said Molly. Taking me outside the room by the arm, she told me in a fierce whisper: "Look, I didn't get any sleep last night because I have a splitting headache and a cold, and I absolutely don't want to have to dress that old man and touch his body and see his old balls, I can't handle it today."

I was surprised to hear my sister sounding so squeamish, since she is a professional masseuse; but as usual, I admired her bluntness. "Fine, I'll take care of it." I went back into the hospital room and found an elderly German-Jewish woman in a white hospital coat, who told me she was the social worker. I started to help my father on with his underwear when she told me: "Don't! He has to do it for himself." She then explained to me that the Amsterdam Residence Home had told her they refused to accept responsibility for him unless he could dress himself and walk. The hospital, for their part, refused to keep him there any longer because "this is not a nursing home" and his operation was over and he'd had a few days' rest. So she would have to determine for herself whether he was capable of dressing himself. If not, the family would have to hire an attendant eight hours a day to take care of him in the residence home.

Molly lost her temper with the woman and yelled: "Why did they tell me yesterday that he could go? Which is it supposed to be, go or stay? Why don't you make up your frigging minds?!" She was carrying on like a street tough, and the social worker, who had probably seen it all (maybe even the camps), was undaunted.

I took Molly aside and told her, "She can't say which it is to be until she ascertains whether Father can take minimal care of himself."

"Oh, fine! And he's going to play helpless, because he wants to stay here, where they do everything for him."

The woman kept repeating what her responsibilities in the current situation were. Finally I said to her, as calmly as I could, "Look, we're all pretty bright here, we understand what you're saying."

She blinked her eyes and left the room.

I turned to Father and said under my breath: "Pop! Try very hard. Don't give up. It's important that you show her you can dress yourself. Otherwise they won't let you out. So give it your all."

"All right, I'll try," he said. And proceeded to do just that, dressing himself slowly, manfully, with dignity.

Not to be dissuaded by the evidence, Molly started hectoring him from the hallway. "What's the matter, you like it here, so you don't want to try to get out?"

"Sure. I'm crazy about the place," he answered sarcastically. "Show me someone who don't mind staying in a hospital and I'll show you a schmuck."

"You think if you just give up, everyone will wait on you hand and foot—right?" retorted Molly.

"Leave me alone! Stop giving me the business."

I caught my sister winking at me: This was her version of reverse psychology. I realized that the social worker, now nowhere in sight, might not believe he had dressed himself, so I hurried to fetch her. When I spotted her, I explained my errand, adding: "One thing you have to understand: My father has always been the kind of man who becomes more dependent when there are people around to do for him. But he was like that at 30."

She nodded, with an appearance of understanding. I was trying to establish rapport with her. The stakes were high; we could never afford a full-time attendant. And where would he go, if they kicked him out of his residence home?

The social worker returned just in time to see Molly buttoning my father's pants! Molly said, "That's the only thing he couldn't do for himself." But he still didn't have his shoes on. The three of us watched as Father, with agonizing slowness, tried to get his foot into the Velcro-strap sneakers that Hal had bought him. I tried to smooth the way by explaining: "He always has trouble putting his shoes on. Even before the operation."

"I wasn't told that," sniffed the social worker.

"The attendant at the home does it for him every morning," Molly said. Fortunately he got his shoes on by himself, for once, and now the test was his walking ability. He started down the hallway past the nurses' station, the social worker walking alongside to monitor his progress.

"Maybe he needs a cane," she said. "Why does he take such small steps?"

"He always walks like that."

As he approached the nurses' desk he quipped: "She's too old for me. Get me a younger one." The nurses cracked up. They all seemed to like him. (I'm fascinated by the fact that many people do take to my father right away.)

"Your dad has a great sense of humor," a nurse said.

"He's a riot," said the other.

"Goodbye, Mr. Lopate. You don't want to stay here with all these sick people, do you?"

He waved to his fan club. We bid adieu to the social worker, who reluctantly agreed that he was ambulatory.

An Academy Award performance. Molly and I got him quickly into a taxi before he could collapse.

. . .

Shortly after that, the inevitable happened. He fell down one morning, and in consequence was kicked out of the Amsterdam Residence (whose hoity-toity airs I had come to despise) and sent to his present nursing home. This is no doubt the Last Stop. There is nothing he can do here that will disqualify him from the right to sit in the common room with the television on.

Recently, during a period when he had been feeling too despondent to eat, I visited him there, and wheeled him out to nearby Fort Tryon Park. He noticed a magnificent elm overlooking the Hudson River. "That's a beautiful tree," he said.

"You see, Pop? It's not so bad being alive. Which would you prefer—tell me honestly: to be dead or alive?"

"Alive, of course." He was annoyed to be asked such a childish question.

For the next few minutes, his senescent-poetic mind spliced the word "tree" into different sentences. "They don't brag so much about the trees. Especially since they had that . . . Holocaust."

Later, I tell his social worker that, from my observation, my father likes to be placed in front of ongoing scenes of daily life. Especially activities involving youth: teen-agers playing basketball, tots splashing through the fountain, pretty girls walking by.

She says skeptically: "You caught him at a good moment. We took him to the park, there were plenty of children around and he dozed through it all, no interest whatsoever. You know what he wants? He wants you."

I hang my head guiltily.

"But in today's way of life . . ." she adds, that vague, exonerating statement.

I ask myself: Would it be possible to take him in? Where would we put him? The basement? The baby's room? A shed on the roof? We could manage, somehow, couldn't we? In the midst of this deliberation, I know that I will never do it. I take consolation from what a scientist friend tells me: "Societies choose differently what to do with old people. The Eskimos choose the ice floe, we choose the nursing home."

· · ·

How much does my father understand? Has his mind become per-manently loosed from its logical moorings—like that comment about trees and the Holocaust? At other times, he seems to make perfect sense. During the staff meeting, I had tried to explain the reasons for his depression, adding, "He's also taken a lot of abuse from his family."

My father picked his head up and said, clearly, "I was responsi-ble for the discord."

A final word on failure. The gifted Midwestern writer, Bill Holm, once wrote an essay called "The Music of Failure," in which he tried both to argue against the hollow American obses-sion with success, and to redeem failure, to find beauty in it. In ef-fect, Holm was attempting to invert commonplace values, and turn failure into a victory, or at least show how it could be better, more human than its opposite. Intriguing as the essay was, I fin-ished it with a sigh, thinking: But there is such a thing as failure. There are failed lives, which no amount of rhetorical jiujitsu can reclaim as triumphs.

Maybe my father's insistence that he is a failure does not signal the obsessions of senility, but grows out of a long, enforced, reluc-tant meditation at the end of his life, which has obliged him to take responsibility for some of his very real errors. In that sense, there is hope for all of us. I would like to give him the benefit of the doubt.

ENID BARON

Enid Baron is a mature woman when her mother reveals, in a spontaneous conversation over morning coffee, the details of her immigration to America from Russia, a ten-year-old girl traveling by wagon, train, and boat, alone. But this revelation is only the beginning. As Baron sips coffee and listens, her mother reveals her dream of becoming a playwright, a secret desire that led to a mysterious encounter with the famed movie mogul Louis B. Mayer.

MY MOTHER AND LOUIS B. MAYER

There are times when a woman will reveal certain facts about herself to her daughter, and times when she will not, and there are facts she will reveal at certain times and facts she will not reveal at any time at all. It is a complicated business, this knowing if and when, and most women err on the side of not telling. It seems safer that way.

The year is 1980, and my mother and I are sitting over a second cup of coffee in the kitchen of her Florida condominium, both of us still in our nightgowns, over which we are wearing light, flowery robes. My stepfather has left the breakfast table to closet himself in front of his customary TV programs in the room where I stay during my infrequent visits.

Sleep never comes easily to me in that room. Unfurled, the sofabed sprawls cheek to jowl with the stationary card table and its matching chairs piled high with sofa cushions. At my feet rests the liquor cabinet with its display of scotch and bourbon and murky-looking liqueurs whose levels never appear to wane. "Schicker is a goy," my mother says. Translation: Only non-Jews *drink!*

The shriek of ambulances, police sirens and car brakes nine floors below infiltrates my sleep, despite the room's hermetically sealed atmosphere, and I awaken disoriented and shaky, like a survivor of a car crash.

My stepfather's driving has become unreliable. He sits like a pygmy at the steering wheel of his archaic, boat-sized Chrysler. Positioning it between the lines that mark his private parking space unnerves him, even with his recently implanted lens. My mother sits at his side, her hands balled in her lap, a first mate going down with her captain. Save yourself, I want to scream. Grab a life raft. Jump!

What it is that we have been talking about that has prompted my mother, finally, to speak out I no longer remember. But suddenly she, who has withheld from me all but the most rudimentary information about her early life, begins to reveal herself, beginning with her passage to America.

All I have ever been given to know about the immigration of my mother's family was that they lived "somewhere in Russia" and that my grandfather was the first to leave, at the turn of the century, accompanied by his widowed mother. Two years later he sent for the two oldest children, my ten-year-old mother and her twelve-year-old brother. It was two more years before my grandmother arrived with the five remaining children. A last child was born in America.

Today's tale takes place in a village on the outskirts of Vilna, where a wagon has arrived to transport the two children to a city where they will board a train for a faraway harbor from which ships sail to America. As my mother describes that morning, I imagine the impatient driver lifting the small girl into the wooden cart, as my obstreperous grandmother stands below with an infant in her arms, shouting last-minute instructions to her children. I hear the horses' hooves stamp on the hard-packed ground, and their breath steams in the chill air.

The trainride was endless, my mother says. When I ask the name of the city from which they sailed, she says she doesn't know, never knew, its name. Some neighbors who were booked on the same passage were commissioned to keep an eye on them, but they abdicated once on board. Seizing the opportunity for adventure, my twelve-year-old uncle attached himself to a group of vagabond boys, leaving my mother to look after herself.

Did no one come to her rescue, I ask, flooded with pity for the small girl abandoned on the enormous ship. She passed her days on deck alone, she explains, wishing to avoid the squalor of steerage, the odors of unwashed bodies, the filth, the indigestible food. Even when the sea became choppy, she refused to go below. She came close to falling overboard one day; a passenger standing nearby pulled her back from the rail.

A benefactor, I think with relief. Wishful thinking! What business had a girl her age to be on deck in such foul weather, the man had fumed. Where were her parents? Ashamed to confess to him that she was crossing without mother or father, deserted even by her brother, she made no reply. I stare at her. Where had she gotten that kind of courage at such a tender age? Or that kind of shame?

When at last they reached Ellis Island, she searched the faces of the waiting throng for her father, hoping to be rescued from the strangers who barked orders to stand here or go there and the doctors' probing hands. But he failed to materialize, and the children were directed to a cavernous room, assigned to a wooden bench, and told to wait. Wait they had, all that day, and all the next day, until finally she stopped believing that he would ever come for them. When an old man with a long beard appeared on the third day, she did not recognize him at first. Two years is a long time, she says, wistfully.

In Chicago, her brother adapted easily to the streets, the noise, and the commerce and soon found himself work as a butcher's assistant. The neighborhood settlement house with its kindly social workers became her refuge, and she pledged to herself that she would learn to speak as they did, practicing the strange-sounding words over and over, twisting her tongue around the unfamiliar syllables.

Her grandmother had had a gentle, affectionate nature, and for the next two years, life within their small flat was peaceful. But my grandmother's arrival, with the remaining children, marked the end of tranquility. Now there were ten mouths to feed instead of four. Was my grandfather able to support them, I ask. A shadow passes across my mother's face as she lifts the teaspoon next to her coffee mug and stares into its bowl.

To make ends meet, she says, her mother took in recently arrived "landsmen" from the old country, cooking for them and providing them with beds, one of which had been my mother's. She slept in the living room on two chairs pushed together, she says through closed lips, as if re-experiencing the resentment toward her mother for foisting lodgers on them. Still, there was never enough coal in winter, she says. They were always freezing.

I recall my grandfather as an old man sitting in a high-backed chair like a throne, wearing a tall black skullcap, smiling, crazily serene. He was a tzaddik, my mother had always said. A holy man. Revered. A man no one could ever blame.

She tells of having been selected by the settlement house for a two-week homestay with a wealthy suburban family. There, her eyes were opened to a world that until then had existed for her only in the never-never land of movies—a world in which there was a separate fork for salad and another one for meat, table napkins of soft linen, and gleaming white bathtubs one could bathe in daily, with an abundance of hot water. The entire time she was terrified that she would pronounce a word improperly and reveal what a "greenhorn" she was.

On her return to the tenement with its unsavory smells, the children's bickering in Yiddish, the unmatched crockery, in the crowded kitchen where they ate hurriedly, in shifts, she vowed to remain in school, regardless of family pressure to quit and find work. Education would be her way out of a way of life that she had come to regard as loathsome. When, on completing high school, she received a scholarship to Northwestern's journalism school, she hadn't even bothered to tell her parents. There was only one kind of scholarship they understood: the study of holy texts—and that was not accessible to women.

Why had she never told me about that scholarship? She stirs her coffee. It was the winter of the great flu epidemic, she says. People were dropping like flies. She was working as a secretary, traveling to Northwestern every night on the streetcar, when she too came down with it.

"I was sick for weeks," she says. "I missed so many classes I couldn't catch up."

"You should have made them let you repeat the semester!" I want to cry. "Demanded another chance!"

But the expression on her face stops me. Who am I to take her to task, I who pitied myself in college for having to work twenty hours a week? Had it not been for the money she sent me during those years when she took a job in order to supplement my father's diminished earnings, I would not have been able to go away to school.

"I want to show you something," she says, getting up from the table. I follow her into the bedroom. "Can you get that down?" she asks, pointing to a cardboard box on a high shelf in her closet.

When I hand the box to her, she sits on the bed, removes the lid, and rummages in a jumble of letters and photographs until she comes up with a sheaf of yellowing typewriter paper. It's a play she wrote before she was married, she says, handing it to me. On the title page, in characters that might have been typed on the ancient Underwood of my childhood, I read, "The Island." Underneath, I recognize my mother's maiden name.

I cradle the sheaf like a rare parchment from an extinct culture, a relic of inestimable worth. For that is what it is: an artifact of the woman my mother had once been, neither wife nor mother, a completely autonomous person with a voice and mind of her own. I think of the photograph one of my aunts unearthed recently, my mother in her early twenties. I hardly know her, a beauty with huge dark eyes, a tender mouth, and a small nose that is slightly squashed at the tip, as if pressed against a window too long, looking in on something unreachable.

This very manuscript was read by none other than Louis B. Mayer, of Metro-Goldwyn-Mayer studios, she announces. The words jolt me as if they were charged with electricity. I search her face for a clue to how to interpret them. Although she has a tendency to omit facts, I have rarely known her to fabricate them. But what else could this be but a fabrication? A fantasy? A dream? A hallucination?

"You're kidding," I say, grasping at what would seem the most plausible answer.

"Would I make up a thing like that?" she asks me, with a hurt expression. "I sent it to the MGM studio when I was visiting my uncle Jack in Los Angeles. You can imagine how thrilled I was when Mr. Mayer's secretary called to say he wanted to meet me."

She proceeds to describe the dress she wore the day of their meeting, a pink tulle, with self-covered buttons down the back. She had sewn it herself, of course; in those days she made all her own clothes. She even splurged and had shoes dyed to match. Mr. Mayer sent his limousine to drive her to the studio!

She pauses.

"Yes, go on, go on!" I say.

"There's nothing more to tell," she says. A blank expression has replaced the animation in her face.

"Nothing to tell?" I cry. "That's ridiculous. What happened? What did he say? What did you say?"

"It wasn't meant to be," she says, shrugging her shoulders.

"But . . . but," I stutter, although I know all too well what it means when she shrugs her shoulders like this. No amount of arguing is going to budge her.

The man who has been my mother's husband since my father died and who now sits in the den watching a game show is someone with whom I choose my words carefully, because we disagree about everything, especially matters of race. From his real-estate investments in neighborhoods now turned "colored," he has bought my mother diamonds, and they have sailed to Europe on the *Queen Elizabeth,* "first class."

She doesn't love him. He tells obscene jokes in front of their friends. He monitors the way she cuts the grapefruit rinds for the disposer. She would never have married him, I like to think, had my father provided for her. Despite his continued efforts to be a successful dentist, his lack of aptitude had stood in his way, and he had never managed to put anything away. She calls me long-distance several times each month and sobs that she wants to leave my stepfather, but she's too frightened to live alone.

When she dies several years later, the first thing I look for among her effects is the box with the play. When I open it, the sheaf of yellowed pages confirms that I did not imagine the story, as I sometimes thought I might have, especially after telling unbelieving friends.

The story opens with Una on a steamer, fleeing a forced marriage to a man she does not love. When the steamer hits an iceberg, Una finds herself shipwrecked on an island. Overcome by fear, starving, she wanders the island until she collapses. When she revives, she finds herself being cared for by Peter, the island's sole inhabitant.

Rescuer and mentor, Peter trains Una to assist him in his plant studies. In time, Una falls in love with him. However, he gives no indication that he returns her affections. Then one day a violent storm erupts on the island, destroying everything in its wake and separating Una and Peter. It is only when he thinks he has lost her that Peter realizes he loves Una. Una finds her way back to him and the two of them declare their love for each other.

Biographies in recent years have exposed Louis B. Mayer's voracious sexual appetite for women. What must have happened to my mother when his office door was closed would have happened to dozens, perhaps even hundreds, of girls. My mother would not have known this, of course. And even if she had, it would not have alleviated her shame.

And so, despite the startling and uncharacteristic nature of secrets revealed to me by my mother on a certain morning in Florida, there remained a threshold I was not allowed to cross.

She is trying not to slide on the leather upholstery of Louis B. Mayer's limousine as the chauffeur turns into the studio lot. Like a lost child, she follows him down a walkway to a sprawling white structure and through the door into a reception room with a vast, circular desk.

"Yes?" asks the secretary.

"She's supposed to see Mr. Mayer," says the chauffeur, nodding his head in my mother's direction.

"I'll let him know you're here, Miss," says the secretary, with an odd smile. "Please have a seat."

"Thank you," says my mother, sinking gracefully into a chair.

She is thinking about what she is going to say about which stars she has in mind for Una and Peter, and whether she will be allowed to be on the set when they shoot, when the secretary interrupts her.

"You can go in now," she says. "It's down that corridor. The door at the end of the hall."

In her pink tulle dress and her dream of becoming a famous screenwriter, she enters the office of Louis B. Mayer like the proverbial lamb marching blindly to the slaughter. Casting couch? She's never heard of it. What she knows about Hollywood is as meager as her knowledge of America when she arrived at Ellis Island. But even if she had known about the womanizing for which Louis B. Mayer is notorious, it would not have occurred to her that he would try to seduce her. Anyone can see she's not that kind of girl! Besides, she has written a play!

When he approaches her, her naiveté seems disingenuous to him, a feigned innocence. "Come on, girlie," he says. "If you're nice to me, I'll be nice to you."

When she resists his advances, he becomes impatient. A flapper like her must know her way around, he thinks. Again, she rebuffs him. Losing interest, he rings for the secretary to show her out. What about her play, she asks? It's not right for him, he says, pushing her manuscript to the edge of the desk. Why doesn't she try another studio?

*Clutching her manuscript, she hails a taxi and gives the driver her
uncle's address. At the edge of the seat, she holds the manuscript on her lap
with trembling hands. She doesn't cry, though. (In a family like hers, no one
comes if you cry.) When she returns to her uncle's, she considers tearing up
the play, but she can't bear to part with it.*

Back in Chicago, she hangs the pink dress at the back of a closet
and hides the play in a bureau drawer. Not long afterward she
meets my father at a neighborhood dance. In accentless English, he
tells her that he is in his last year of dental school. They dance together all night. He is a good dancer, easy to follow, and she lets
him walk her home. The next weekend, they go to the movies.

"You're prettier than her," he whispers, during a closeup of
Norma Talmadge or Enis Markey or whoever is playing the female
lead.

My mother flashes him a winsome smile. But what good has
being pretty done her, she thinks? Or being smart, for that matter?
There's only one thing that counts, and she hasn't got it.

"You've got to have luck in this world," she asserts, time and
again, while I am growing up. It's the one fact she feels impelled to
reveal to me.

REBECCA MCCLANAHAN

The twisting irony in Rebecca McClanahan's compelling narrative about marriage in the military (her parents' and her own) is at first subtle, but slowly and steadily engulfing. Her sense of pacing is impeccable: from her marriage to an antiwar activist, to her husband's eventual acceptance of the military, to the deterioration of his personality, and their eventual divorce. Each time the reader seems to understand the direction of the narrative, McClanahan triggers a crisis that sharpens the edge of her story and increases interest. Simultaneously, the military milieu is unique and informative.

DEPENDENT

In one of my earliest memories, my mother is standing on an unpacked crate beneath the ceiling of a quonset hut. Barefoot, she balances like a circus performer, testing her weight gingerly as she leans toward the curved wall, trying to hang a picture of waves. This is the only image in my head that hints at any desperation my mother might have felt in her long career as a military wife. If hers was a war against rootlessness and loneliness, she fought it privately, in small physical skirmishes. She made a home from whatever was given. If the kitchen in our new quarters had a window, she'd size it up as we walked through the empty rooms. The next morning, I'd wake to find she'd stitched and hung yellow curtains, creating an illusion of sunlight that tinted the linoleum and bounced off the toaster she'd polished with her sleeve.

My father was like her in this way—he did what he could to shield us from the difficulties of military life. Since he was a Marine, we could not accompany him on overseas assignments, some of which lasted fifteen months. And since he was an officer, we were able to stay in one place longer than the families of enlisted men. Except for a few months in temporary quarters—the quonset hut, an apartment building, the officers' guest suite—we lived in sturdy houses within driving distance of the base. As we approached the gate, the uniformed guard glanced at the sticker on the windshield of our station wagon, clicked his heels together, and saluted. We children saluted back. If our father was present, he'd reprimand us, reminding us that a military salute was not to be taken lightly.

Once out of our father's sight, we took it lightly, as we took lightly everything related to the military. Cushioned from hardships, we saw the base as one privilege after another—free swimming, dime movies, twenty-five-cent bowling and miniature golf, discount toys at the PX, cheap groceries (unlike our neighbors with their civilian pints of ice cream, we never had less than three gallons in our freezer). The only privilege we did not welcome was free medical care, which seemed to encourage our mother to splurge on tetanus shots and throat cultures.

I was vaguely aware that our sense of privilege stemmed from the fact that our father was an officer, and occasionally I caught glimpses of what my life would have been like had my father been, say, a corporal instead of a major (and later, a lieutenant colonel). On our way to the base swimming pool, I counted the stucco duplexes surrounded by dirt yards where khakis and diapers flapped on makeshift lines. Children's faces were plugged to the front window, hostages along with their carless mothers, while we whipped by in our blue station wagon, creating dust swirls that must have settled minutes later on their wet laundry.

Turn another page in the story, take the next bend in the road, and it was time to leave again—the luggage carrier packed to the gills, the U-Haul trailing. Yet no matter how many times we moved, how many friends and towns we left behind, there was always a passel of warm bodies to fill the station wagon and the empty new house. We were our own portable town: my siblings were my constant allies. Of course we fought (the veins in my brother's forehead pulsing as he lunged toward me), but when the dust settled and the blood cooled, peace was always restored. The more heated the battle, the more dramatic the truce that followed. We knew better than to turn on each other permanently, for soon we'd be moving to a new town where strangers waited at the bottom of the U-Haul ramp. In the long run, we were all we had, our assurance we would never be alone.

And we never felt homeless, for in the distance was our grandparents' farm where we returned every summer—to the same featherbeds, the haymow with the rotting floorboards, the attic crammed with our outgrown clothing, the same worn path to the creek. We were hybrids—half Marine, half farmer—and whenever we grew tired of packing and unpacking, whenever our necks began to ache from watching the jet stream behind our father's plane, we knew the farm would be there. Old as dirt, the saying goes. The land would be waiting for us. I was born a Marine brat and spent my childhood in service, but until my twenty-first year, my life had been lined with escape hatches. Except for one brief remembrance—Mother hanging a picture of waves—nothing prepared me for my stint as a military wife.

I'd been married less than a year, and everything that could have gone wrong, had. Pete's parents had divorced, and his father had been hospitalized with severe bleeding ulcers. When Pete quit two consecutive jobs because he refused to take orders from supervisors, I doubled up on my hours at the printing shop and continued full-time studies at the university. A brilliant linguist, Pete had been studying for a degree in German, but at the height of the Vietnam war, his student deferment was cancelled. A few weeks later he received his draft lottery number. It was a low number, which almost guaranteed that he would be drafted. And almost all draftees were sent to the front lines. If he joined the army, rather than wait to be drafted, he might avoid an infantry assignment. Then again, he might not. I tried to comfort him, but with each step I took toward him, he took two steps away. Being a wife, I'd come to believe, was not something I was good at. Pete's fingernails were chewed to the quick, and the tic on the side of his face had intensified, the spasms more frequent than ever. The draft was breathing outside our door, and we were holed up behind it. I felt helpless, under siege from without and within.

Then, just as the draft was about to break down the door, Pete uncovered a window. Following a tip from a fellow German student, he took a qualifying exam and won a coveted slot at the army's language institute four hundred miles up the California coast. The timing, it seemed, could not have been better. It would take Pete two months to finish basic training and three more months to complete the introductory language course. Then he'd send for me. In the meantime, if I moved in with my parents, I could quit my job at the print shop and finish my literature degree.

I told myself that this turn of events would also be good for Pete—he could escape Vietnam while being paid to study languages.

My father had never been fond of Pete, but as soon as he joined the army, my father's feelings seemed to soften. For one brief moment I saw my husband and father joining forces, as if their arms were linked, rocking me between them as in a child's game. The day Pete left for boot camp, I stored our belongings and moved back to my parents' home—my father had recently retired from the Marines. My older brother and sister had left for marriage and college long before, and my teenage siblings, having claimed the empty bedrooms for their own, were not about to relinquish their privacy. I moved in with my youngest sister, Lana, who had recently turned nine. Several times over the first few weeks, I looked up from the book I was studying to see a little girl standing beside Lana in the doorway, staring at me silently. Each time it was a different little girl. Later I learned that Lana was charging her friends a quarter to see the bride who was now her roommate. She'd told them that my husband had been killed in the war, and did they want to see the veil?

Every night as I climbed into our shared double bed, I felt relief. Lana's body, small as it was, was a great comfort. Surrounded by stuffed animals and nursery rhyme wallpaper, I was rocked backward into another time, sleeping longer and deeper than I'd slept since I'd left my parents' home. And waking to the clatter and bang of breakfast, my mother working in the kitchen, was a pleasure so exquisite I couldn't imagine why I'd ever left. These feelings worried me. I had a husband. Shouldn't I be missing him more?

I wondered if my mother had ever felt this way. When my father was overseas, she stayed busy every daylight hour; I never saw her cry. But on nights when insomnia claimed her, I'd wake to the sounds of table legs scraping across the wooden floor, casters squeaking as the sofa was rolled to one spot, then another, the electric mixer whirring, the rat-a-tat-tat of the Singer accelerating to unsafe speeds. Then the pause. The quiet. The click of the presser-foot being lifted and, in the space between seams, fragments of a top-ten song from the radio. I'd lie in the dark, wondering if they were playing American songs where my father was—in Japan or Korea or Hawaii or Vietnam. For years I counted the distances between my parents in time zones I traced in the Rand McNally atlas. Their lives, it seemed, ran smoothly on separate, parallel tracks. The moment my father returned, the tracks converged, the double seam healed, and only the white strip on his arm, the place where his Japanese watch had lain, recorded the lost time.

Reunited, their bodies made a spoon curve on the sofa—my mother in a pink housedress with covered snaps, my father behind her with his hand cupped over her waist. I thought all married people acted that way. It did not occur to me until many years later that their union was not typical, that it lacked the quality of dailiness that dulls the shine on marriages where partners eat and work together and sleep beside each other every night. The Marine Corps built a wall of time and distance, a wall my parents were forced to scale again and again in order to reach one another. Perhaps that's why their marriage wore so well, and why they had so many children. My aunt tells of the day, forty years ago, when my mother announced she was pregnant again. The child would be her fifth. The fourth, a baby girl, was nursing at my mother's breast. My aunt's reaction to the news was "Not again!" My mother simply shrugged her shoulders and laughed: "I can't help it. I'm always so happy to see him."

Weeks grew to months. I began to miss what previously had annoyed me—the sputter of Pete's motorcycle in the driveway, the damp fossil his feet left on the bathroom rug. I missed his rough freckled hands and his smell, an odd mixture of motorcycle oil, cigarettes, and English Leather. Surprised by the force of my longing, I wondered if Pete was missing me too. Maybe the army was what we'd needed all along.

The day Pete called to say our apartment was ready, I rented a U-Haul van. My father loaded the furniture; in the cab I piled clothes, boxes of books, my grandmother's Wedding Ring quilt, my framed diploma in English literature, and my mother's portable Singer. Early the next morning I was on my way, driving the first leg of the four-hundred-mile journey up the California coastline. On the radio Roberta Flack sang "The First Time Ever I Saw Your Face." Sun glinted off the waves. With each tick of the odometer, the difficulties of the past year receded like the images in my rearview mirror. How many times through how many years had my mother made a journey like this to her husband, who waited for her in their new quarters hundreds of miles away. Suspended on the road between my parents and my husband, with the ocean to my left and the sun overhead, I felt hopeful. Things were going to be better. We were making a fresh start in a new place.

But the man who met me at the base welcome station was not the man I had married. His eyes were gray, not green. He was thinner. He had poked an extra hole in his belt to cinch the trousers around his waist, and the fabric puckered above his buttocks and thighs. When I ran to hug him, my legs weak from the ten-hour drive, his kiss was hurried and dry. He smelled of beer and an unfamiliar brand of cigarettes. The tic was alive on his cheek. When we got to our quarters, we made love on a pallet spread on the living-room floor, but the lovemaking was as hurried as his kiss had been, and as dry.

Military dependents is what they were called, the wives and children living beside us, below us, and on top of us, in apartments identical to our own. Theirs was another world, one I'd never seen from the inside, the underground world of the enlisted. The officers' wives I'd known throughout childhood had been anything but dependent. With their husbands gone for months, sometimes years at a time, these women not only shopped, cooked, cleaned, and sewed, but balanced checkbooks, mowed lawns, made house and car repairs, and negotiated all necessary public affairs. If their responsibilities were doubled, so were their freedoms. They came and went as they pleased, subservient only to their own needs and the needs of their children. When my father was overseas, our household ran on a different clock. We stayed up later, slept later, played more games, ate more child-friendly foods—beanie weenies, macaroni and cheese, fish sticks, Frito loaf, and my favorite, a dish I named Train Wreck, a Sunday night treat in which the week's leftovers collided in one large iron skillet, topped with Tabasco sauce and sopped up with white Wonder bread.

And over it all, my mother presided. I never doubted her authority or her ability to keep us safe and happy. She moved easily through the days and nights with a grace I associated with *her* mother. Poor farmers are another breed of independent women. Partnered by necessity, they worked as equals beside their husbands in field, garden, and pasture. My grandmother, trained in self-sufficiency, not only managed the indoor chores expected of farm wives—stoking kitchen fires, frying chickens, making sausage; she also chopped the wood that made those fires possible, wielded saw and hammer to build the chicken coop, and repaired the fence that encircled the hogs waiting to be slaughtered.

This was my heritage, a legacy of independence passed from grandmother to mother to daughter. But there were no pastures on this army base, no squads of officers' wives gathering at the pool or golf course. Instead, I was surrounded by young wives trapped without cars, without jobs, with two or three preschool children crammed into a two-bedroom apartment, their only escape Wednesday night bingo or a rerun at the base theater. Or morning classes in the damp windowless basement they called the Craft House, painting ceramic Santas, Virgin Marys, pumpkins, and elves, while their children scuffled on a rug at the child care center, over-seen by women with bad teeth who stared at the television bolted high to the wall.

Despite what my I.D. card proclaimed, my laminated face and name stamped with the word "dependent," I was determined never to become one of those quietly nervous women I saw in the laun-dromat of the apartment complex. I renewed my prescription for birth control pills, hung my diploma over the kitchen sink, and set about camouflaging the apartment. I covered the khaki walls with daisy contact paper. My grandmother's quilt went over the couch. I painted a Seven Sisters constellation on the bathroom ceiling and strung a mobile of kites and balloons over the dinette table. At the windows I hung colored beads that rattled when an occasional civilian breeze found its way through the maze of concrete hall-ways that led to our third floor unit.

The language institute position might have been a plum, an assign-ment draftees would have killed for, but it was still the army. Pri-vates like my husband still stood inspection, still pulled K.P. and all-night guard duty, a task made all the more demeaning by the fact that they were issued shovels instead of rifles. It was a pretend war, the enlistees were constantly reminded, but to Pete it might as well have been Vietnam. Each order given, each exam, was an enemy rustling in the bushes. In sleep he thrashed at the covers. When I reached to calm him, his chest was beaded with sweat.

Late one night I woke to an empty bed. I called his name and searched the apartment, and when I looked out the window I saw him slouched inside a phone booth across the street, his boots pressed against the glass. He had left the door open to darken the booth, but the streetlight silhouetted his lean body. One hand held the phone against his cheek; the other hand caressed the cord, running lightly up and down its uncoiled length. Suddenly what had encased him, the exoskeleton of phone booth and bone, of boots and jacket, fell away, and what had been invisible to me came into microscopic focus. It wriggled on the slide—blood and tissue, muscle, the soft inner membranes—a secret life pulsing on its own. I knew that he was talking to a woman.

I ran a bath and soaked until my fingertips were shriveled. Only four more months, I told myself. Then the Chinese course will be over and we'll leave for the next base, but this time I'll be with him from the first day on. And I'll be pregnant—that way, he can't leave. Until then I'll wait it out. You can survive anything for four months. I climbed out of the tub, powdered and creamed my body, combed the tangles from my hair and sat by the space heater until my hair was silky, spilling over my folded knees like the Oriental woman in the painting my father brought back from overseas the summer I turned twelve.

An hour later, perhaps two, Pete climbed into bed. When I asked where he'd been, he turned his face to the window. I never asked again, not when he began disappearing for hours at a time, not when he stayed out all night. I put the unpacking on hold and attended to him, resolving to be a better wife. I would cook more of his favorite foods, steam his khakis with a cleaner pleat. This thing I was living was my life.

Even when I missed the second period, the possibility still didn't register. I'd been sleeping fitfully, troubled by a low-grade nausea that weakened my appetite. As a result, I'd lost several pounds, yet my body felt strangely heavier. My breasts had begun to swell, and there was a strange metallic taste in my moth. One night I woke with a tightness in my belly, a wrenching, as if something were twisting me from the inside, a vise clamping down.

Pete stirred but did not wake as I left the bed. At the bathroom door I flicked on the light, and the fluorescent tube above the sink flickered, went black, buzzed, and flickered again, coloring the room in a bluish wash. The toilet seat was cold. The vise gripped me again. I concentrated on the veins in my thighs, tracing the intricate network, and when the vise came again, I closed my eyes and pushed the pain out my mouth, in rapid, nearly silent animal pants.

When I finally stood and looked down, what I saw was the size of a man's outspread hand. I watched it floating, a viscous crimson island, watched the edges peel away into strands that thinned and separated, marbling the water with pink streams, leaving only a thick dark center. Then I lifted off. My bloodied nightgown billowed, and I rose toward the ceiling, where my mother and grandmother were waiting. *What took you so long?* read the cartoon bubbles over their heads. Long fingers reached out to me, caressing the sleeves of my gown. We hung there suspended, looking down at the scene below, where a woman's hand was reaching for the chrome handle. I heard the flush and saw the water swirling in ribbons of red and pink and black, a child's pinwheel spinning dizzy circles.

A few weeks before the scheduled move, my mother arrived to help out. Boxes were stacked in the living room. The walls were bare once again. "Looks like you've got everything under control," she said brightly, but I could tell she had sensed trouble. As the hours passed she kept checking the clock; she never asked where Pete was. "You look thin," was all she said. "Are you eating enough?" She spent the evening at the Singer, finishing a maternity dress for my sister, whose second child was due in a few months. I lay on the bed, comforted by the whir of the machine, the drumming regularity of the needle. It was a rhythm as old as my first memory of her, lulling me into a safe place. I sat up on the bed.

"He's having an affair. I know who she is. He's there right now."

My mother's lips, pressed together to secure a family of straight pins, opened, and then pins scattered to the floor. I told her everything—about the dark-haired neighbor, about walking in on her and Pete in the laundromat. I told her that the woman's husband was overseas, that I suspected it had been going on even before I'd arrived, and that now every evening when I went outside Pete was on the playground with her sons, pushing them on the swings or throwing baseballs he'd bought at the PX. I said I couldn't wait another minute, that I was going to the woman's apartment to confront him, to ask him to come home.

My mother raised her hand as if hailing an invisible cab. Her index finger was cocked. Then slowly her hand drifted down. Her eyes brimmed for an instant, cleared. "Do what you need to do," is all she said.

I knew the words she was holding back. *She* would not have gone. Years before I'd overheard her comforting a neighbor. Women were always coming to my mother for help pinning up a hem or doctoring a fevered child, and Mrs. Owens came by often, her face tight and red, the seams in her stockings a little skewed. I was used to Mrs. Owens's outbursts, but I'd never seen her like this. She was crying fitfully and loud, the way I thought only children cried, those sobs that lift your shoulders and deepen your voice.

"What. Would. You. Do," Mrs. Owens cried, each syllable punctuated by a jerky intake of breath.

My mother's voice was even and calm. "I've never had cause to doubt him. I would swear by it."

"But. What. If. He. Did." It's the kind of question you ask when you're desperate. What you want is for the other person to tell you it's okay, to pat your hand and say everything will be all right. My mother gave the truth, and I could tell by her tone that she meant it. I could also tell that she had considered the question more than once and the decision had been reached long before this moment. Her words flowed like water.

"I'd walk out the door and never look back. The more I loved him, the faster I'd walk."

"But. What. About money? Where would you go?"

"I'd live in a shack before I'd take a penny of his money."

"But. The children."

"We'd manage."

I sat on the bed and looked across the room at my mother. Her brown eyes, lit with anger and pain, held no answers. In desperation I reached back in memory, past my mother's eyes, past her fierce pride, searching for another way to finish this, a way that would better suit me.

What I saw was my grandmother cutting off the dying dog's leg to save him. *Whatever it takes, you do.* Then I saw her decades before I was born, standing at the back door of the farmhouse with two children at her side and a baby, my mother, asleep in her arms. Suitcases are stacked beside her and she is facing my grandfather. Her words are like bullets. "Look at that woman again, and we're gone."

I don't know how long she stood there before he gave his answer. Knowing my grandmother, not long. My grandfather must have played his part well, for she never took that first step through the door, into the garage and the waiting car. The scene freezes in that moment—the suitcases, my grandmother's silent stare, my mother waking in her arms as if from a bad dream, releasing a strong hoarse cry.

The marriage ended at the runway of a California airport where I boarded a plane to Columbia, South Carolina, my brother's city. After I'd confronted Pete with my knowledge of the other woman, we'd attempted a half-hearted reconciliation, but it soon became clear that he was not going to end the affair. "And even if I did," he said one night during dinner, "I can't promise that it wouldn't happen again." I looked across the table at him, and the years stretched out before me. I knew I couldn't live that way. I packed my bags that night.

Once in South Carolina, I underwent the initiation rites common to newly separated women. I wept, lost weight, cut my hair, found a minimum-wage job, bought a used car, rented a studio apartment. Fort Jackson was a few miles away, and over the next few months I often found myself cruising its perimeter. My half of our furniture was delivered to me courtesy of the United States Army. Officially I was still a dependent and would be for another year, the grace period the army had extended to me. Desperately close to the poverty line—I now qualified for food stamps—I told myself I could use the services. I needed groceries, I was past due for a medical exam, and my first troublesome wisdom tooth was starting to push through.

When the long-distance divorce decree arrived in the mail, I contested nothing. With one signature, I swept away the previous three years, agreeing to no fault on either side. Only one remnant of the marriage remained—my military I.D. card, which I found, to my surprise, I did not wish to relinquish. It had taken months to mourn the marriage, the man, and the almost-child. But my tour of duty was not over. Something yet remained, a loss that ambushed me one winter afternoon as I was driving past the base. This time, my car turned, headed toward the front gate, and stopped. I pulled the I.D. card from my wallet and held it out to the guard. With a snappy salute, he motioned me forward. It might have been any of a dozen bases I'd known—Fort Ord, Fort Belvoir, Fort Meade, Quantico, El Toro, Corpus Christi—bases named for generals, chiefs, bulls, the bodies of lesser and greater gods. Bases so familiar I could have driven their streets in my dreams—and I had, many times since I'd left California. I'd also been dreaming my future, in dreams that took place outside the gates of the military and prefigured the circumstances of my new life—a new husband and a home on a civilian street, a marriage secure though childless, the death of my grandmother and the farm.

Once inside the gates of Fort Jackson, it felt as natural as breathing, this tour past the barracks, the commissary, and the PX, past the swimming pool and tennis courts with their tall fences, the officers' quarters and the quonset huts. My gums were aching, my swollen jaw pulsing with pain. I passed the clinic once, twice, then circled back to the parking lot. I stopped my car and sat for a few minutes, staring at the entrance and watching the parade of soldiers and dependents. A woman emerged, holding the hand of a little girl who was rubbing her upper arm (a vaccination, I suspected) and sporting an imitation medal on her shirt, some army doctor's award for courage in battle. I'd earned the right, I thought. Even the army thought so—that's what the grace period was for. I got out of the car and walked toward the clinic, tonguing the swollen gum where the tip of the wisdom tooth had pushed through the surface. No question about it, the tooth would have to go.

LEE GUTKIND

The creative nonfiction genre permits—even encourages—the writer's voice, point of view, and involvement. But essays don't require a writer's active presence and, in fact, can be weakened by it. The unique quality of this essay is that the writer has recognized and embraced a character with a story and then established himself as a willing listener, waiting for the story to be told. From beginning to end, the reader hears the protagonist's voice—but visualizes the action through the subtle filter of the writer's perceptions and interpretations.

TEETH

After breakfast, her husband looked up from across the table and announced that he was taking her into town to have all her teeth pulled out. It took a while for the meaning of his words to penetrate. Even when he said he was getting her a new set of teeth, she stared at him blankly. The memory of that morning nearly six months ago pained her even now.

"My teeth ain't perfect, but they never give me or my husband no trouble," she said, rolling her eyes and shaking her head back and forth slowly. "And suddenly, there he wanted to go and pull them all out. I've never been so surprised in all my life."

She was sitting on a stoop in front of the tarpaper-covered cabin in which she and her husband lived, petting their old coon dog, curled in a grimy heap at her feet, and watching the tractor-trailer trucks go by. Each time a truck went up the road, she would wave and smile. The truckers would invariably wave back, as they roared by, bellowing smoke.

She told me that her loneliness was sometimes awful. It wasn't the mountains—she had lived here all her life and wasn't interested in anywhere else—but the fact that there was no one around to talk to. The gloomy shadow that fell across her face blatantly telegraphed her desperation. Each time I visited, she went on and on, could hardly stop herself from talking.

She was a river of fat. Her body bulged and rippled in every direction, and her eyes, tucked into her pasty skin, looked like raisins pressed into cookie dough. Her hair was dirty gray, tangled and woolly, but you could tell her face had once been pretty. When she showed me her picture as an infant, I remarked that she looked like the Ivory Snow baby. Blushing, she covered her mouth and turned away. That was how we had first got on the subject of her teeth.

One day in town her husband was approached by the new dentist, a handsome young man in a white shirt and a blue and red striped tie, who explained that his house needed a new roof. Would he be interested in installing it in return for money or services?

Her husband was a short, wiry old man of seventy-two, who resembled a chicken hawk, with a hooked nose and arms that bowed out like furled wings. He hunched forward when he walked, as if he were about to take off flying. He told the dentist he would think on it for a while.

That evening, after supper, he stooped down and peered into her mouth, testing each of her teeth with his thumb and forefinger to see how well they were rooted. "Smile," he told her. "Laugh." She followed his instructions to the letter, as was her habit. Over the next few days, he watched her every chance he got. It was early autumn when he finally went back into town to make the deal. She never knew anything about it.

The woman explained that she and her husband had very little use for cash, bartering for almost everything they needed. They traded vegetables, cultivated on their tiny patch of land, for fruit— corn for peaches, tomatoes for apples, pickles for pears, beets for pretty bluefire plums. He chopped wood in return for mason jars. Periodically, he repaired a car for a guy who owned a dry goods store in town in exchange for clothes for both of them. By bartering instead of buying and selling, they hardly paid Uncle Sam a penny's worth of taxes.

Last summer, he raised a barn for some city folks, recently retired near here, in return for an engine from a '64 Buick and a side of beef. The engine went into a pickup truck they had gotten for a hundred and fifty dozen eggs. Paid out over a period of three months, the eggs came from their chicken coops out back. The pickup was then swapped to the owner of a local filling station for credit for two hundred gallons of gas, plus an assortment of parts and tools. Meanwhile, she boiled up the beef on the old black cast-iron stove that had belonged to his grandfather, and canned and stored most of it in the cold-cellar cave under the house. She cut the remainder of the beef in strips and hung them like wet socks above the stove, smoking and shriveling them down to jerky. From the spring to the fall, her husband went fishing each evening after dinner. When he collected a big batch of trout, she stewed them in the pressure cooker until the whole fish, bones and all, was white and meaty like tuna. This was what they would eat next winter and the winters thereafter. Their cave was stocked with years of stuff.

Her husband never talked about his work and what was owed to him in the way of goods and services, and she never asked. Despite her significant contribution, the actual swapping wasn't her business. Years ago, her daddy had told her in no uncertain terms exactly what she needed to know to get herself through life. He was a man much like her husband, didn't owe anyone and never wasted anything. No words in conversation, unless some specific point was to be made. Otherwise, silence was golden.

One night, however, her father came outside and squeezed down on the stoop beside her. They lived in an old house along the side of the road, about the same size as the one in which she and her husband lived now. But her father only rented it for fifty dollars a month. Neither her father nor his father before him had ever owned a piece of property straight out.

At the time, she didn't know that the old man was dying from cancer. Her mother had also died from cancer, and she had had to quit school in the sixth grade to take care of the rest of the kids and keep house. Recently, her two older brothers had joined the army, while the younger kids were sent to foster homes. Now, she and her father were home alone. She was fifteen at the time.

They sat side by side as the night grew colder. The moon shimmered in the glittering dish of sky, but the air felt like rain. Suddenly, she remembers, he cleared his throat. The sound of his voice made her feel uncomfortable, similar to how she felt trying on a new pair of boots.

"What else is there in life?" He said this as if in summation after a long conversation that she had somehow missed. Then, he paused. She would never forget his face as they sat there. His hard, sharp features seemed to disintegrate in the darkness. The glitter reflecting from the moonlight faded from the blue of his eyes.

"You work to eat, you eat to live, you live to work." He sighed. "That's all there are to it."

The next morning, the man who was soon to become her husband made himself known. Miraculously, all the details had been worked out between him and her father in advance, without her having the slightest idea of what was happening. The following afternoon, the man came and took her away. Two weeks later, her father died.

She cleared her throat and motioned toward the house. "We came right here to these two acres and moved into an old shed out back. It ain't there no more. Tore it down to salvage the wood for this place. First we made sure we had good water, then we started building. From start to finish it took two years to get all set up. The winters were awful, but the summers weren't too bad."

All this happened some thirty years ago. Her husband had been married once before. His first wife had died or left him, she wasn't sure, and his children, who she never met, were all grown up and living somewhere in another part of the state. Once in a great while, there was a letter, which he would read carefully, his lips moving, then stuff into his pocket, shaking his head and muttering. He would go on, muttering and cursing, shaking his head, for days at a time, without so much as an explanation.

Her own brothers and sisters all lived near here, but they hardly ever stopped by or invited her to visit. Like almost everyone else, they were more than a little afraid of her somber, silent husband.

Once again, she paused to wave at a trucker, barreling up the narrow two-lane highway. Their shack had been built unusually close to the asphalt. Even from up in the sleeping loft inside, you could hear the cinders and feel the wind when the trucks rumbled by.

She said she was so shocked and angry when she found out about the deal her husband had made with the new dentist that she started screaming and yelling. "I had never acted that way before, but I just couldn't help myself. All of a sudden, I went crazy. My husband didn't know what to do."

He had turned away, glaring in silence out the window. It was still early. The sun was just beginning its ascent up the hill toward them. His eyes narrowed. Time passed as he started down the road. His brows, thick and hairy, cast a shadow, like umbrellas over his eyelids. When the sunlight reached up as far as their house, he got up and finished dressing. He bit off a plug of tobacco, stuffed it under his cheek, put on his old grimy baseball cap, climbed into his pickup, and turned it over. When he saw his wife come out onto the porch, he threw the truck into reverse, backed up, and leaned out the window. He wanted to have his say one more time. "We shook hands on a new set of teeth. It's owed to me."

She turned and walked back into the house without a word. He peeled out onto the asphalt, his tires spitting gravel.

In no time, her best clothes were out of the drawer and piled on the bed. She found an old suitcase, and she cleaned it inside and out carefully, before laying her clothes in it. The last time she had been on any sort of trip was when her husband had come to take her from her daddy. They didn't have a suitcase then. All her possessions, including her mother's big black roasting pan, fit easily into a medium-sized cardboard box. Her father had carried the box down to the road, and they had waited together until the man who was to become her husband arrived. The whole thing—packing, waiting, and driving away—had taken about ten minutes. It went by in a blur, one moment stacked up on top of another.

Thinking back, she realized that her life had ended right about then. She had been isolated with this man who hardly talked to her and whom she hardly knew, a man who had refused to discuss his past for over thirty years. At least with her father there was evidence of some roots and another life somewhere behind the one he had been living. But this man's world was bleak, both behind and beyond. He offered little more than a nod or a grunt for sustenance each day. Her father's words, uttered with such sadness and resignation on that damp, dark night so many centuries ago, came back to her now. You work to eat, you eat to live, you live to work. That's all there are to it.

All right. She had lived her life in accordance with her father's wishes, had never asked for anything from anyone, never shirked her responsibilities or wasted a breath. She had always done whatever her husband had told her to do—and more. But giving up a part of her own body simply for the sake of a business deal was too much. It was going too far. A person has a God-given right to own certain things, especially when they were born with it.

The last thing she did before leaving was to go out to the pumphouse and peer into the mirror. The image she saw glaring back at her was awful. She was too old, too fat, and too dirty. But, if anything, her face had held up best of all. There was still a spark, a hint of the beauty that might have been.

Her daddy, who never had more than a dollar in his pocket at any one time, had always bragged that the Good Lord had made him rich by blessing him with a daughter with a million-dollar smile. Even now, she could hear the distant echo of his praise. She wasn't going to let that damn bastard she married squash the memory by pulling out her teeth.

She looked up at me. The shroud that had fallen over her face as she told her story momentarily lifted. "Used to be my husband would leave me alone from early morning until supper. But now, things is different. He's liable to ride by anytime, just to check and see if I'm still here. Sometimes I hide out behind the chicken coops and wait for him. When the house looks empty, he'll stop to see where I am. He always pretends he's come back for tools or materials, but I know I got him worried. It serves him right."

She dug her fingers into her scalp and shook her head vehemently, scratching simultaneously, before continuing. "I left the house that morning, hitchhiked into town, and bought a ticket for Davenport, Iowa. Davenport was the only city in Iowa I could think of. My daddy traveled all over the country when he was younger. He told me you could drive for half a day in any one direction in Iowa and not see anything else but a green carpet of corn, just bending and stretching in the distance."

She pushed her big blubbery legs out into the grass, near where the old coon dog was lying. Once in a while, the dog would thrash around and thump its tail against the ground. A couple of times it pushed itself up and crawled over on top of us. The woman had on brown double-knit slacks worn through at the knees. Her blouse was white with alternating pink and blue pastel stripes, although the colors were graying from repeated washings. This was the outfit she wore as she climbed aboard the bus and headed toward Davenport. Her clothes looked a lot better back then, she said.

It took nearly three hours to get to Pittsburgh, where they stopped and idled in the depot for about forty-five minutes. She did not get off the bus. They stopped twice on the highway in Ohio and once more in Indiana, but she remained in her seat, guarding her suitcase.

"I tell you, I've never done so much thinking in my entire life as I did on that bus, looking through the window, reading the neon signs, and watching the headlights from the cars. Most of the people around me were sleeping, and none of them were too friendly. Not that I tried to do much talking. To tell the truth, I was scared half to death."

She wasn't actually thinking, she explained, as much as she was dreaming—with her eyes open. Her window was like an imaginary

TV screen, and she could see the images of her past reflected before her. She saw her father carrying the cardboard box down to the side of the road. As the cancer took its toll, he had shriveled up like an old root. Then she saw the man who was to be her husband pull up. He put the cardboard box into the bed of the truck, opened up the passenger door, and helped her inside.

"I remember looking right into his face as he done this, the first time I had ever looked him full in the face. And then, as I sat in the darkness on that bus, I pictured how he looked earlier that morning when he leaned across the table and told me he was going to take away my teeth. And you know what? He was the same. Those thirty years we had spent together had bloated me like a balloon and wrecked up my face but, except for a little more gray in his whiskers, that bastard ain't changed one bit."

She paused, shook her head, chuckled, then shook her head again and again. It wasn't easy to suddenly accept the reality of what had happened. The shiny sadness of her life was reflected in her eyes.

I looked away, down behind the tarpaper shack toward the outhouse across the field. It had a three-hole bench. There were four or five old cars dumped into a gully behind the outhouse, and an abandoned, windowless school bus teetered on the edge.

"I never made it to Davenport," she said, after a while. "But I got all the way to Chicago. You ever been to the bus station in Chicago? More people there than I ever seen, all in one place. Half of them don't speak English, and none of them was white. The moment I got off that bus, seeing them all colored and hearing all that foreign commotion, I was completely confused. I was hungry, but didn't want to spend any money. I also wanted to clean up a little, but with all them people, I was afraid to make a decision."

After a while, she found herself a bench back in the corner, out of the way, and sat down to try to think things out. She still had her ticket to Davenport, but she didn't particularly want to go there any more. She didn't want to go anywhere, as a matter of fact. She wasn't willing to move one inch from where she was. She must have dozed off, for the next thing she remembered was feeling a hand on her shoulder, shaking her gently. Someone was saying her name. No one would know her name in Chicago, so maybe she really was back home, about to emerge from a terrible dream.

But when she finally opened her eyes, an elderly man with

horn-rimmed glasses and a tiny, pinched nose introduced himself as a representative of the Traveler's Aid Society, whatever that was. The man's voice was soft and reassuring. As he talked, he picked up her bag, wrapped his arm around her ample shoulders, helped her up, and led her across the bus station.

When her husband had discovered her missing, the man explained, he had contacted their minister, who somehow traced her to Pittsburgh and then to Chicago. There was also a Traveler's Aid representative waiting at the Davenport bus station, just in case she had made it that far.

They were moving at a brisk pace, passing the ticket counters and neatly wending their way through the milling crowd. She felt like a piece of livestock. "Where are you taking me?"

"There's a bus to Pittsburgh leaving in about ten minutes. Your husband already wired the money." He smiled and continued to talk to her in his quiet and reassuring manner, as they pushed through a big set of swinging doors and headed on down a broad cement runway toward a long line of idling buses. Drivers in neatly pressed gray uniforms stood by the doors of their respective vehicles puffing cigarettes and punching tickets, as she and the man hurried by.

"But I already have a ticket to Davenport, Iowa."

"You can cash it in when you get back home . . ." He paused, while continuing to lead her down along the row of buses. "Of course, I can't force you to do anything you don't want to do." He shrugged and smiled apologetically. "I can't even help you make up your mind."

By this time, they were approaching the bus to Pittsburgh. She felt his hand on her back, urging her gently toward the bus. He handed a ticket and her suitcase to the driver.

She hesitated, momentarily resisting the pressure on her back. She tried desperately to think things out, but her mind was blank, as was her future.

With nothing better to do, she walked up the steps, dropped into a seat by the window, and closed her eyes. She did not allow herself to open her eyes until hours later, when the bus pulled into Pittsburgh. She was so confused and embarrassed, she had completely forgotten to say goodbye to the man with the horn-rimmed glasses who had helped her.

Now she looked up at me, smiling and winking. "My husband

came to meet me." The thought evidently amused her, for she shook her head back and forth, chuckling. "On the way home, we talked things over, got everything out in the open for the very first time. I told him how lonely I was, how it wasn't fair the way he constantly mistreated me. I said that I should be consulted in his decisions about how we spend our money. I told him that I didn't have enough clothes, that I wanted to go into town more often, and that, because he was such a damn hermit, I didn't have no friends or family." She nodded emphatically. "I let him have it with both barrels. He had never allowed no one to talk to him that way before in his entire life."

I stood up. More than two hours had passed since we had started talking. The sky was clouding over. In this part of western Pennsylvania, rain erupts suddenly, swallowing the hillsides and ravaging the roads. Besides, I was getting cold, sitting so long on that stoop. And my pants were filthy; the old coon dog had tracked mud all over them. I walked briskly back to my motorcycle.

"He tries to be nice," she said, as she followed along behind me. "But you really can't change him. You couldn't ever change my daddy, either," she added. "When you come right down to it, they was both dark and silent men."

I nodded, pulled on my helmet and kicked down on the starter. The machine cranked to life as I straddled the seat. From past experience, I knew I couldn't wait for the right moment to leave. Otherwise, I'd be waiting forever. I had to depart even while she was still in the act of talking.

She planted her foot in my path and grabbed my arm. "You know, he drove by two or three times while we was sitting here talking. He'll want to know who you are and everything was said. Hell," she said, smiling and winking, and finally stepping out of the way so that I could pull out. "I ain't telling him nothing. It serves him right."

The woman prepared herself extra special for her husband's homecoming that evening.

She went into the pumphouse and sponged herself down from head to toe, ran a brush through her hair a hundred times, and scrubbed the grime from her fingers until the half-moons of her nails were white. Back in the house, in the loft where they slept, she got out the nice green cotton jumper dress with the pretty yellow and white floral design and laid it out on the quilt. He had bought her the dress the day she came home. She had only taken it out of the box once, the following Sunday when they went to church.

After preparing dinner and setting the table nice and neat, she went back upstairs and put on the dress. Then she dusted herself with some fancy-smelling powder she had ordered through a magazine and gotten in the mail. She was just about ready, when his truck crackled outside on the gravel. He walked into the house. She could hear him move about downstairs, looking into the big pot on the cast-iron stove, sniffing what was for dinner. But not until he walked across the room and started up the ladder toward the loft, did she reach into the water glass on the nightstand beside their bed. Only then did she put in her new teeth.

DEBORAH TANNEN

The tone of Deborah Tannen's profile of her father, Eli, captures the innocence and anxiety of youth and the mystery and morass of memory without feigning immaturity. The reader actually senses two Tannen voices simultaneously: the adult looking back and reflecting on her past and the child experiencing and responding to the same vivid memories. Tannen focuses on six incidents—stories and scenes—that together establish a foundation for her essay and her transition from being cared for by her father to becoming, inevitably, the caretaker.

DADDY YOUNG AND OLD

INCHING

"You loved your grandmother so much," my mother says, talking of her own mother, who lived with us until she died. "When you were little, you'd walk along and hold her hand. Mimi would run ahead, but you always stayed with her. You had such patience."

This praise I hear as an indictment, because I know how wrong she is. I was not patient. I held my grandmother's hand and inched along beside her because I didn't know how to escape the expectation that I would. I resented being the chosen one. Like a pony tethered to a post, I envied Mimi, my middle sister, two years older, who was not thus bound.

I have always felt I hid a terrible secret: I loved my grandmother, but not as much, or as completely, as the little girl in my mother's stories. I did love things about her. I loved to look through the old pictures she kept in a shoe box in the room that was hers in our big old house. One by one, I'd pull out small discolored photographs of people and ask her who they were. And I loved to comb her long thin hair, not entirely gray even when she was in her eighties. Then it was her turn to be patient, and I think she really was. But I also harbored nuggets of resentment; being leashed to her pace while she walked was one.

It is years since I've thought of those slow walks along the uneven squares of Brooklyn pavement, stony corners of pebblespecked concrete sidewalk jutting out. I think of them now because I find myself inching along beside an old person again. But this time I do feel patient—not only because I am older and slower myself, no longer burning with the fever of a child's energy, but because this time I am truly burning with the fever of love. The person I am walking slowly beside is my father.

DADDY

My childhood, in my mind, is an endless train of days spent with my mother, missing my father. My mother is a continuous arc; my father is a series of snapshots that I take with me wherever I go.

In one, I am walking along the Brooklyn street of my childhood holding my father's hand. When my father holds my hand, he has to slow his pace to my little girl's steps. I love the hard rough skin of his huge calloused hand, a big safe house around my fragile little one.

My father rides the subway home from work in Manhattan to the Cortelyou Road station in Brooklyn, then walks the twenty minutes from the station to our house. On the lucky days when he comes home while it is still light, Mimi and I wait for him to appear at the end of the street. When we see his tall thin shape taking form, we run to him. He lifts us up, one by one, and holds us in his arms, then sets us down and walks the last half block with us—a little girl fastened to the end of each arm.

If he arrives home before we go to bed, Daddy tucks us in. When my blanket is a jumble, he stands at the end of my bed, takes the blanket by its corners, spreads it between the enormous expanse of his outstretched arms, and gives it a great shake, making it fly in the air above the bed and come to rest over me, smooth and comforting. As Mimi and I lie in our beds, he tells us stories he made up himself, in which we are the heroes who save the town from dragons. Our favorites are "stories with actions." In telling one of these, he moves around our beds, acting the story out, rushing, at key points, toward our mock-scared, upturned, laughing faces.

But most nights he comes home late after working overtime as a cutter in the garment district, then putting in more hours at what

I know as his "being active" in the Brownsville–East New York
Liberal Party. I beg in vain to be allowed to wait up so I can see
him before I go to sleep.

My sister Naomi is not in these pictures. Eight years older than
I, she must have been in her own world of friends.

DADDY AT HOME AND AWAY

My father leaves the house before anyone else wakes
up in the morning. He sometimes eats breakfast in the candy store
on Coney Island Avenue, around the corner from our house. This
is the same store that I walk to when I want to buy whatever it is
the neighborhood kids crave that season—hula hoops or yo-yos or
slinky balloons—or, if Mimi or I have an upset stomach, the pure
Coke syrup that amazingly is considered medicine. When I go into
the store during the flat daytime hours, I look with awe at the
round counter stools, upholstered in red leather with silver chrome
encircling their sides, because I know that my father sat on one of
them, eating fried eggs and bacon while my family slept. That he
wakes up so early seems to me heroic; that he has breakfast at the
candy store seems exotic and adds to the magic of the store.

The strongest presence that I feel in the house is my father's absence. It clings to his places and possessions. One is his dresser: he
has built dividers into the top drawer so his socks are lined up in
compact little lumps sorted by color. Another is his desk, which he
built himself. It has row on row of little compartments just the
right size for what they hold: four wide shelves for different kinds
of paper, tiny compartments for paper clips and rubber bands, vertical dividers for the small slips of scratch paper he makes by cutting up sheets of outdated stationery. The cellar is where he builds
these things. His tools line the walls, hanging from nails. One wall
is covered with narrow shelves on which baby food jars hold nails
and screws, sorted by size.

My favorite object in the house is an old black typewriter with
yellowing keys rimmed in tarnished silver. I spend hours typing
letters to my father, telling him what happened to me during the
day and laying out my grievances against my mother. I can't have
any grievances against him, because he isn't there.

. . .

My father is home, working in the cellar. I sit on the steps and watch. He asks why I don't go outside and play, but playing is dull beside the excitement of being with him. Times I am allowed to enter his world stand out like sentences highlighted in yellow. I love helping him stuff envelopes for political mailings (line up the flaps with blue exposed and swipe a wet sponge over six at a time) or going from house to house distributing political leaflets.

My father is working at his desk. I enter the room and stand beside him. He hasn't heard me come in, and he doesn't notice that I am standing there. Without thinking, I do something to get his attention: I squirt him in the face with my water gun. He erupts, roaring like a frightened tiger and shaking suddenly with a great shudder of fright. Terrified, I dart out of the room, down the stairs, and onto the first landing of the staircase, where I crouch, waiting to run down the rest of the way if he is angry at me. He appears at the top of the stairs, looming like a tower, and laughs, his laugh opening like his arms, inviting me to run against his chest and into his huge hug. With his arms and his hug and his laugh reassuring, he apologizes for scaring me.

I have a splinter in my finger, and I want my father to take it out. If I give my finger over to my mother, she will jab at it with a straight pin; it will hurt, and I don't trust her to get the whole splinter out. When my father takes out a splinter, he elaborately sets up an operating table: lays out alcohol, matches, pin, tweezers, and a razor blade. He holds the point of the pin to a burning match, then sterilizes both the pin and the razor blade with alcohol. Then he turns to the operation. Methodically, he shaves off thin layers of skin with the blade, so carefully that it is painless. The razor blade—redolent of masculine ritual—is a dangerous instrument that only he can be trusted to wield. When he exposes the splinter, he loosens it with the pin, then lifts it out with the tweezers. It never hurts. I insist on leaving the splinter in place until he gets home.

TRANSFORMATION

Our lives change when I am in junior high school.

My father is leaving for work at what seems a languorous hour: 8:30 A.M. Wearing a suit, he is standing at his dresser, transferring to designated pockets the items he emptied onto the top right corner of his dresser the night before. He is going to the office where he practices law.

My father has a law degree and a master's degree in law. But he graduated from law school in 1930, when there was no work for lawyers. In 1958, twenty-eight years after graduating from law school, he is finally rewarded for the years of evenings and weekends spent working for the Liberal Party. He has been appointed Assistant Counsel to the Workmen's Compensation Board. But after only six months, Nelson Rockefeller, a Republican, is elected governor, and my father loses his job. This time, however, he doesn't go back to the factory. He begins practicing workmen's compensation law.

And I begin going to high school in Manhattan. Now I too take the long walk to the subway station. But I still don't see my father in the morning. Now I'm the one who leaves the house before he or anyone else wakes up.

When my father goes to work in an office, the calluses that formed on his palms over the years of handling the cutting machine and giant shears gradually wear off, and his hands turn soft. I miss the calluses that made his hands rough and hard.

My father is standing at the door. We are in the apartment he and my mother moved to after I went away to college. I am home during a break. He is asking where his nail file is. Careless and chaotic, I am always losing things. When I want something, I know I can find it among his possessions. This time I have taken his nail file, which is always lying at the outer edge of the second shelf in his desk, to the right. It is a dependable metal file, slightly bent because he has had it all my life. Finding it gone, he knows I am the culprit. He stands and confronts me, not in anger, but in quiet exasperation, and although he does not reprimand me, but simply asks where his nail file is, I feel found out. I do not remember where I left it. Standing there, not angry, he looms over me like an implacable judgment.

My father's orderliness is a foundation I can count on, and his height is a bulwark against chaos. When I was a little girl, he seemed, at 6 feet, to be as tall as the Empire State Building. Because of this, very tall men fill me with awe, making the backs of my thighs tingle as if I were standing at a precipice.

MY FATHER AT A REMOVE

I have been asked to write a piece for the theater. Because I have published a book about the conversational styles of women and men, I am certain they expect an amusing dialogue that dramatizes misunderstandings typical of couples. I have been staring at the computer screen for days, writing and deleting sentences.

At the same time, I write a poem about a trip my husband and I made with my parents—a trip to Warsaw, where my father was born and lived until he was twelve. Standing on the street where he played as a child, my father described the world he grew up in. The outlines of his childhood that I had always known took on life. (His father died when he was six, but his mother had thrown her husband out when my father was two, so he never knew his father.) I send the poem to a friend to whom I also complain that my attempts to write a play are leading nowhere. He comments that the poem sounds like the beginning of a play. The next day I start writing a play based on our trip to Warsaw. It juxtaposes my father's memories of his childhood in Poland with my memories of my childhood with him.

I read the play to my parents. I am sitting on the couch in the living room of their apartment in Westchester, and my mother sits beside me on the couch. My father sits on an upholstered chair at the far end of the couch. When I finish reading the play, my mother, weeping, throws her arms around me, telling me how wonderful the play, and I, are. My father begins speaking about something else. I am stunned. I have written a play about his life, and he doesn't seem to care. The next day he writes me a letter telling me how moved he was, and explaining that he changed the subject because he didn't want to show his emotion. He also makes a comment that captures the point of the play: "I had no father," he says, "but I didn't miss him. You had a father, but you missed him."

THE TELEPHONE

From the time I left my parents' house for college, when I called home it was my mother I spoke to. After we'd spoken for a long time, she'd say, "Your father wants to talk to you."

I'd feel a little leap of excitement, almost as if a boy I had a crush on finally called. My father would get on the phone and say, almost at once, "Well, it was nice talking to you." "Wait," I'd say, with a panic-like sense that something I really wanted was slipping away. "You haven't talked to me yet." "We'll talk when we see each other," he'd say. "There's no point in making the phone company rich." He'd gotten on the phone just to get me off.

When I call home now it is not much changed. If my father answers, he quickly says, "I'll tell Mother you're on the phone. She'll be so happy to hear from you." He calls to her and she picks up an extension. It's not long before I realize I haven't heard his voice for a while. "Where's Daddy?" I ask. "He hung up," she says. My father isn't interested in the things my mother and I talk about: what relatives and friends are up to, what they said.

If my mother answers the phone, she and I talk for a long time. I finally say I have to go because I am tired or have something I must do, but then I add, "Can I say hello to Daddy?" "Do you have time?" she asks. "I thought you were tired." "I am," I say, but I just want to say hello." One time she makes a joke: "Well, I don't know. If you're nice, maybe you can."

There is one situation in which my father will talk on the phone: if I call when my mother is not home, and I ask him about his past. I delight in these conversations, but my mother doesn't. She accuses him: "You only want to talk about people who are dead."

When I hear my father's voice on the phone, that rush of excitement is still there. I feel a lightness in the air, a giddiness. He is always cheerful and funny. My mother's aging has been nearly invisible: at eighty-five she does not move like an old person, and she has developed her very first ache: a sore shoulder. My father has suffered pain his whole life, from dental work, from a perforated ulcer, from arthritis, from surgery as recently as last year. He has trouble getting up and trouble walking. But he never lets on if he is in pain. When he was immobilized with excruciating and relentless pain from sciatica running the entire length of his left leg, from hip to toe, I asked, "How are you doing?" He answered, "Wonderful! The whole right side of my body doesn't hurt at all!"

To write another play about my father, I decide to interview my family about their perceptions of him. I ask my oldest sister, Naomi, what she remembers about Daddy when she was a child.

"He used to toss ideas back and forth to me the way other fathers play ball," Naomi says. "He used to have debates with me where he would pick an issue and take the hard-to-defend side that he obviously didn't believe in. For example, we once discussed slavery, and he took the side that slavery was good so I could take the other position, the right one. I never felt put down. You know, some fathers, when they play competitive games with their kids, they like to win. But I never thought it was competitive. It was fun. He was teaching me to think and to argue."

When my father tossed ideas like baseballs back and forth with Naomi, I must have been a baby, or not yet born. Yet I hear her as if I were deliberately left out, cheated. I recall having political discussions with him when I was older, but it was over dinner, with others present. And I recall that I loved to have him give me words to spell. But I have in mind only one specific occasion when he did this, as we were walking along Coney Island Avenue. I was accompanying him on an errand, so my presence was an afterthought, not the main point.

I can't imagine my father having time to sit and talk to me when I was little. Is this simply because I was the youngest of three? He couldn't be alone with one of three as he was when there was only one. But this can't be the whole story. Naomi was born during the Depression. During those years he either worked for the WPA—which wasn't full time—or held jobs with normal hours, which gave him evenings and weekends at home. When I was conceived, the family was living in Providence, Rhode Island, where my father had a civil service job. But my mother wasn't happy living in Rhode Island and wanted to be nearer her family when the baby came, so they moved back to New York City. As a stopgap measure, my father returned to working in a factory while he entered politics in the hope of receiving a political appointment to a position for which his law degrees qualified him. The thirteen years that it took for this to happen were the first thirteen years of my life. Perhaps his absence was my punishment for setting those years in motion with my birth.

Naomi says, "My earliest memories are of his being nurturing, maybe because I heard about it. I'm astounded at how much child care he did. Because he worked all day! He would come home from work at the end of the day and wash my diapers. He knew it was twelve diapers. Every night he'd come home and wash the twelve diapers. And he used to iron my little dresses. He remembers that he knew how to iron the puffed sleeves.

"My earliest memory," Naomi continues, "is living in Bensonhurst. I guess I was about four. I hurt myself. I fell, skinned my knee or my arm, and I remember a side door to a building, maybe to our apartment, and Daddy brought me inside through that door and bandaged it for me."

My memory of splinters shrinks to a paltry shadow beside Naomi's accounts of his ministries. He was so present in her young life, in searing contrast to his absence in mine, that listening to her causes almost physical pain.

DADDY'S CHILDREN

I ask my father what he remembers of our childhoods. He says, "I only remember little incidents. One is when Naomi had chicken pox. She must have been a year and a half? Two years? And the doctor warned us, 'If you scratch, you're left with scars. So you mustn't scratch.' And she was suffering. She said, 'Itch me, Mommy! Itch me!' And we said, 'No, you mustn't.' And she was such a good girl, she didn't scratch. Now they have cream. I put on cortisone, and it stops the itch. It's amazing. Every time I have an itch and I put on the cortisone and it stops the itch, I think of Naomi."

I ask, "Do you think it was different when Mimi and I had chicken pox?" His answer is straightforward: "I don't remember." The explanation is self-evident, but I say it anyway: "Maybe by the time we had it, you weren't around so much." He concedes the obvious: "I was too busy." But he adds, "I was earning better. And it's a good thing."

I ask for more memories, and one after another, he gives me Naomi. "She must have been five or six. She was playing with these older girls, and there were a few stairs in the back, and I gathered a big pile of hay, and the bigger kids started jumping—not with the feet down but with the tushy down. And Naomi followed them, and one jump, she missed it, and she hit with her tushy on the concrete. And I got terribly scared—she could have fractured her spine. I brought her into the house. And she was all right. But I was more careful after that."

Naomi's triumph cannot be challenged. She is the native citizen of my father's memory. I am the resident alien.

DADDY OUT OF REACH

Here is another bit of evidence my mother often provides of how much I loved her mother: my grandmother's death when I was seven was one of the great traumas of my childhood. She is right that I was horrified by my grandmother's death. I can see myself back then in the Brooklyn street outside our house, standing beside my father's black Buick with its three chrome notches on the side fender, stunned that children were still thoughtlessly playing after such a dreadful thing had happened. But, as I recall the dread I felt, it wasn't the loss of my grandmother that shook me. It was the fact of death: that I could go blithely off to school in the morning, unsuspecting, and return to find a person gone—vanished, poof, never again to be seen on the earth. If it could happen to my grandmother, then it could also happen to the person I really loved: my father.

I had a fear that I knew was trivial but was terrifying nonetheless. When my teacher told us to look up something in the encyclopedia, I often asked my father instead. He knew everything. If he died, I thought, I'd have to look things up in books, like everyone else. The prospect left me desolate.

Years ago I had this dream: I'm at my own birthday party. My father is there, but he's suspended about two feet off the ground, with his head near the ceiling. I don't know what he's doing up there; he doesn't seem to be doing anything, just floating in his own world. I can't reach him, and he doesn't hear me or see me. I desperately try to make contact with him, but he's stuck up there and I can't get him to come down.

Around the same time, I had a dream about Bob, the man I was seeing then: a tall thin man with prematurely gray hair. He was riding a horse, and something terrible had happened to him. Finally, the horse, with him on it, was led back to the stable. Bob's leg had been hurt, and he was dazed. As they took him down from the horse, I rushed over, trying to help. But he couldn't see me, and he couldn't hear anything I was saying. I was desperate to make sure he was okay, but he was oblivious of me.

INCHING

I am visiting my parents in Florida, relieved to be away from the chaos of my own office, where every surface is covered with papers and nothing is where it should be. This small, sun-filled apartment was never home to me, and the furnishings are not the ones I grew up with, yet the order my father has created in these scaled-down rooms makes me feel like I have come home. His desk is a white laminate surface built in against a wall. He has added plastic trays with tiny compartments into which he has sorted tacks, safety pins, paper clips and rubber bands—all ordered by size. Three dispensers perfectly aligned hold three different types of tape. In his closet, over the shelves, he has hammered in nails on which to hang his hats.

My father is recovering from bypass surgery in his leg. I walk with him on the catwalk that runs along the building to the elevator. How strange, I think, life is to bring things round to this: my father, who never walked up stairs but sent them sailing behind him two at a time, inching along.

I am grateful to time for having slowed him down. My father old has time for me as my father young did not. The skin of his hand is stiff, as it was when I was little, only now the hardness is not from calluses but from age: the skin dried, the muscle between thumb and palm shrunk concave from a pinched nerve. If I am holding his hand, he can't disappear, run away, recede. I feel as if, were I to let go of his hand, he would fall, as he does in my dreams: thudding to the ground. So I hold his hand, hold him in my hand.

ALEC WILKINSON

I selected "Nancy Gahl," a chapter from Alec Wilkinson's book, *A Violent Act,* because of the empathy with which he approached his subject and the way in which he was able to perceive the frightening shock of experience through the eyes of a living victim. In writing this chapter, which initially appeared in *The New Yorker,* Wilkinson told me, he made a conscious decision "to use the simplest language. The emotional weight of the material seemed sufficient to hold a reader's attention, and I didn't feel that the effects I hoped to achieve would support any self-consciousness on the part of the writer." The ending is forever memorable because of the surprising and offhanded intimacy of the final detail.

NANCY GAHL

The Indianapolis policemen who arrived at Mike's house in response to the report of a shooting did not immediately learn the name of the man who lay on the sidewalk. They were required to wait for the coroner before they could touch the corpse. Having knelt beside him and found his wallet and badge, one of them called Tom's office, and Tom's boss and another probation officer came to the house. By the time they arrived, Tom's body had been taken to the morgue. The two men looked briefly through the house, and then they drove out to tell Nancy.

Nancy had called her husband at his office around nine-thirty. She wanted to hear his voice. All she learned from her call was that he was not at his desk. Had she happened to turn on the radio she might have heard of the murder that morning of a probation officer whose name the announcer was pronouncing "Tommy Galt," instead of Tom E. Gahl.

Nancy was on the telephone in the kitchen with a friend when she heard the knock on her door. It was about eleven. She was by herself in the house. She put the phone down on the counter and went to answer the door. When she saw who was waiting and their somber expressions, she said the first thing that came to her mind.

"Is he dead?"

Tom's boss said, "Let us in," and once they were inside she said again, "Is he dead?" and he said, "Yes."

She found her way back to the kitchen and sat down. Tom's boss saw the phone off the hook and picked it up and explained what had happened and then hung up. One of the men asked Nancy if she didn't think it would be a good idea to call her parents. She said, "Yeah, that's a good idea," and she did it and sat back down. Then one of the men asked if she shouldn't call Tom's parents, and she said, "Yeah, that's a good idea," and she did and sat down again. She felt as if her mind and her body had simply closed down. Then her stomach began to churn, "as if it were rebelling against what the mind was saying," she later recalled, and she felt that she had to go into the bathroom. And there, of course, was the towel Tom had dried himself with that morning after jogging. It was where he had hung it, it was still damp, and its presence seemed more than her mind could take in. How could what they were saying be true, she thought, if his towel is still here?

Her pastor arrived. So did the chaplain who worked for the police department. He apologized for not having delivered word of Tom's death; he said he was held up by other responsibilities. Nancy was happier to have learned from someone she knew. She told the chaplain she wanted to see Tom in the morgue, and he discouraged her. She pressed him, but he continued to say he didn't think it would be a good idea. In frustration she turned to her pastor and asked why they wouldn't let her see him, and then something just clicked in her mind, and she said, "Was he shot in the head?" and the pastor said, "Yes."

Nicholas, four, arrived home on the school bus. Then Nancy and Nicholas and the pastor went to Christopher's school. Nancy was known to the people who worked at the school as a parent who often volunteered, and when she asked in the office to see Christopher, the woman she spoke to asked if something was wrong.

"I said that Tom had just been shot and killed, and the woman started shaking," she recalls.

Christopher was on the playground. The tone of voice of the teacher who sent him to the office made him wonder if he had done something wrong. Then he began to worry that something had happened to his mother; he thought maybe she had been in a car accident. When he got to the office and she knelt down and told him, he didn't cry. He clenched his fists, and then he said, "Daddy?" Then he said it again. The effect of the shock was to produce in him a kind of exalted state. He said that when he died he was going to tell his father everything that had happened in his life, and what kind of person he had been, and what he had accomplished.

That afternoon a reporter from the paper came to Nancy's door. Nancy wondered why the paper was interested in her family's story—that is, against all that had gone on, her own feelings and the events of her day seemed inconsequential—but she sat in the living room and talked to the woman. When the afternoon's edition arrived, "I saw the headline," she says, "and I saw some of the details, and I knew it was about us, but I didn't really know how to take it in."

Christopher found himself shooting baskets through the hoop his father put up for him, first at a height his small frame could manage, then at the one the rules called for. A neighbor's boy, home early from school, passed by and said, "What are you doing here? You're playing hookey," and Christopher said, "My father was shot and killed this morning."

Throughout the day friends and relatives arrived—Nancy's father, her mother-in-law, a brother from California, neighbors who came to express their sorrow. Before her family got there her pastor did what he could to shield her, but finally she said that she needed to be alone with her children. Her pastor asked if she was sure and she said that she was. Then everyone left and Nancy and Christopher and Nicholas sat upstairs on her bed and held each other and tried to understand what had happened to them.

When she went to bed that night she put her face to the pillow and found the scent of her husband. She thought of how they would embrace in the darkness before sleep. She thought of all the plans she and Tom had for raising the boys and for growing old together, and she felt a terrible sadness. It seemed to her that her mind was like an engine racing, as if the pain had a will and momentum of its own. She kept returning in her imagination to the place where Tom died and trying to figure out how it had happened. What did Jackson say? Did he say anything? Did Tom have any warning? She would run through every aspect of it she could think of and when she finished, she would start all over again, with some variation. Did Tom know he was going to die? Did he run? Was Jackson chasing him? Had he stalked him? Then: Did Jackson know Tom was coming? Did he know he would kill him? *When* had he decided to kill him? Was he going to kill someone else and had Tom only appeared at the wrong moment?

Now and then during the night she thought she could hear Christopher sighing in his bed in his room down the hall. She thought of going to him, then held back, thinking, He's asleep, don't disturb him. Later he told her that he heard her, and thought of coming in, but decided she was probably asleep and that he shouldn't wake her.

At five she got up and went downstairs and turned on the television. And saw Tom's body on the sidewalk, covered by a sheet.

Around six, she went back up to bed, and found Tom's shorts and the T-shirt he'd worn to go running. She picked them up and held them to her face, thinking, How can this be, I can still smell him here, he can't be gone. The deep, heaving tears she wept woke her brother, who came in and sat next to her on the bed and put his arm around her and cried too.

She went downstairs again around eight and called the office of the lawyer who handled Tom's and her affairs. No one answered, so she called him at home. His wife said cheerfully, "Oh, hi, Nancy," and Nancy asked to speak to her husband. When he came on, he said, "What's up?" Nancy said, "I guess you haven't read the papers or heard the news." He said, "No, what's happened?" and she said, "Tom was shot and killed." The long silence that followed was broken finally by his saying, "Oh, Nancy, I didn't know." She explained that she was calling because she was uncertain about what happened with her money, whether it was tied up, and whether she faced some additional difficulty, and he told her he would take care of all of it for her.

Then the phone rang and it was her doctor, asking if she was all right, and saying he would phone in a prescription to help her rest.

That afternoon she opened her door to a policeman who placed in her hands Tom's wallet and his wedding ring—each in a plastic bag with a case number written on it—and his briefcase with the same number written on the side in chalk.

The house was full of people. Tom's brother from D.C. arrived. Friends brought food. Others appeared simply because they felt the need to be there with Nancy and the boys. Most didn't really know what to say—Nancy would open the door and they'd fall into her arms—but it meant a great deal to her that they came. Nevertheless, there were moments when she felt overwhelmed and needed to be alone. She kept feeling that if she could just get outside and away from the activity of the house she could take stock of her thoughts and place them in order. She didn't want the people who'd come to see her to feel she had turned her back on them, and she thought of going upstairs to her bedroom, but the bedroom was too lonely a place for her now, so she opened the front door to step out, and there was one of her friends from church with cleaning buckets in her hands. "I just had to come and see you," the woman said. "I don't know what to say, but I had to be here. Do you mind if I wash your windows?"

Nancy decided to have Tom buried in Valparaiso, in northern Indiana, where he had grown up. As a resting place, it struck her as safe, whereas Indianapolis did not. A difficulty arose over when he could be buried. The coroner had called for an autopsy, but there was the question of when he could find time to perform it. A friend of the family who had influence with the coroner called his office, and the autopsy was scheduled for Tuesday morning. The coroner would release the body that afternoon; the burial could take place on Wednesday.

A man at the funeral home called when Tom's body arrived, and said it would be several hours before they could make the body presentable. Nancy didn't know what was left of Tom that she would recognize, but she knew she needed to see some part of him. "I don't care if it's even just the hand," she told them. "I need to see something."

The man called around four and told her she should bring them the clothes she wanted Tom to be buried in. She said there was no need for clothes, because no one would see him in his casket. With her father and Tom's mother, her brother, and the boys, she went to see him. Her pastor met them at the funeral home and said he had already been in and that Tom didn't look too bad, and that was the first time Nancy realized his head was still there.

Tom lay on a table at the far end of a dimly lit room, covered to his neck by a pale-blue shroud. His head rested on a pillow and was turned slightly to his right. Viewed from the side that was unharmed, he looked like himself, but from straight on his features were altered by his skin's being stretched toward his wounds to conceal them. Around the edge of that side of his forehead Nancy saw small cuts and scrapes from where his head struck the pavement. He wasn't wearing his glasses—the police had them—and the funeral home had parted his hair on the wrong side, but as she stood there, the thought was borne in on her, It's Tom, it really is Tom. She walked around him. She leaned over and stroked his hair and Christopher did so too. She held Nicholas up to look at him. Then she leaned over to touch her nose to his and that was when she discovered he no longer smelled like her husband.

Seeing Tom's body gave Nancy and the boys a peculiar sense of relief. Christopher said, "I feel better now." Tom had been torn from them and was now in some way returned, and perhaps it was the shock of their grief and suffering that protected them, but in some obscure way it made all of them feel eased of a burden.

After they had taken in the sight of the shroud and his face and his oddly parted hair, the pastor called them together in a corner of the room and led them in a prayer. Then Nancy took her last look at her husband. She stayed by his side for what she recalls as only a moment. She wishes now she had seen more of his body. She wishes she had touched his hand. What stopped her was an awareness of all the other people in the room. Not until later did it occur to her that she might have asked for a moment alone. Instead, she felt that everyone was there to support her, and a request that they leave her might strike them as thoughtless. She worried also that they might think her wish to be alone with his body was morbid. And she didn't want to keep them waiting.

The salesman from the funeral home took Nancy to the room where they kept their caskets. In a voice lowered almost to a whisper he told her that any money she saved on a coffin could be put toward the future of the boys.

The sleep she managed that night came with the help of a sedative.

"Wednesday morning the hearse came by the house to pick us up," Nancy says. "We had three cars making the trip. We drove the two and a half hours to Valparaiso, and since the hearse driver was from Indianapolis and didn't know the way to the cemetery, our car led them at the end. I just wanted to have the family at the burial, to say goodbye. I hadn't had the hour or the place of the ceremony published in the paper, but when we turned into the cemetery there were about two hundred people—people who'd known Tom growing up, relatives, and friends who found out about the service and came all the way from Indianapolis. We drove up and they were all peering in the windows, looking at me, and their faces were just ashen. We got out and people came up saying how sorry they were. I could see the faces of people I knew on the fringes of the crowd, but a lot of the people I just didn't even recognize. Finally everyone walked away to the gravesite. The service went by so quickly, it was over in no time. Pastor gave a beautiful sermon, and then you threw a few handfuls of dirt on the grave. Then I was alone with Tom in his casket, and I don't even remember what went through my mind. Honey, I love you. Goodbye."

Nancy and the boys spent Wednesday night in Valparaiso and left for home Thursday morning around eight. She stopped at a McDonald's restaurant along the way where she and Tom always let the boys run, and sat there in a storm of memories. When she got home she saw the pastor and told him she was having a really hard time and he took her into his office and they cried together.

Friday a service was held for Tom in a church downtown. Hundreds attended. Many were forced to wait outside or in a room where a speaker was wired to broadcast the service. From the front pew, Nancy and Nicholas and Christopher heard the pastor tell the mourners, "What shall we say to this horrendous crime that took Tom from us? Where was God when Tom needed him?"

Nancy stood for three hours in the receiving line, time after time recovering her composure, only to see someone approach from the corner of her eye who would cause her to weep all over again.

On Monday she woke and watched the hands of the clock approach five after eight and then pass. With Christopher and her father and her brother, she went downtown to clean out Tom's office. On the day that he was killed the door was closed, and his office left more or less as it had been. The files of his cases had been removed, and the pages of his notebook that dealt with the business of the department were gone, but his calendar still hung on the wall with his appointments noted and the paydays marked off, and the pictures of his family still met the eyes of anyone sitting in his chair. He might almost have been expected at any moment, except for the wreath on the door.

They took the pictures down from the walls and emptied the drawers of his desk. Nancy's father lost her mother, to cancer, when she was only forty-seven. So it was natural that it was toward him Nancy turned to ask, "How long will it hurt this way?"

That afternoon they left Christopher off at school, during the noon recess, just exactly where he'd been called from a week before. He hadn't wanted to ride the bus that morning and have everyone lapse into silence when he climbed aboard. Nancy watched while his friends came over and took him in. Some time later he told her he believed that the first period of their mourning was easier for him than for her, because he had his friends to distract him, whereas she had just to sit home by herself and be sad.

Everyone stayed as long as they could. The second Friday night was Nancy's first alone with the boys. Around nine a hard rain started to fall. She went to bed and by midnight she was back downstairs trying to stop the rush of water flooding underneath the patio door. The room had flooded a few weeks before and she had just had the furniture repaired and the rug shampooed. The towels she held to the bottom of the door made no difference in the flood, and before long she was leaning against the door and crying, knowing Tom would have dug a trench to deflect the water, or swept it away from the door, or figured some way to defeat it. She felt as if a new journey had begun and she hadn't asked for it, or wanted it, and she couldn't have felt more alone. Finally she just gave up and went to bed.

In the middle of the night, Christopher rose to go to the bathroom. He walked to the door of his room and looked down the hall and sensed in its shadows something forbidding that he'd never been aware of before. He returned to his bed, and that was the first time he recalls ever feeling afraid of the dark.

. . .

Nancy had been aware that the police were searching for Jackson in Missouri and that he hadn't been found. She kept the television on. Occasionally she saw the image of his mother, asking Mike to surrender, or his brother Jimmy surrounded by reporters, so she knew that Jackson had family, but much more than that she didn't take in. She was too involved in what was happening to her and the boys to think at any length about Jackson. After a few days she began to feel that an account of the search would be a document the boys and she might someday want, so she started to clip articles from the paper and record the news from her television. The image of Jackson that appeared most frequently behind the shoulders of television anchors and at the heads of columns of newspaper type was taken in prison in 1985, when his particular obsession with grooming had been subdued by some other passion. Christopher and Nicholas found this version of him terrifying. "His hair was wild, his eyes were wild, he didn't look human," says Nancy. "He looked more like an animal to me."

A couple of weeks after the murder an agent from the F.B.I. came to ask her some questions. Most of what she told him he already knew—what time Tom left the house, his concern about the visit, his brief acquaintance with Jackson, his wish that Nancy not worry. When the agent asked if there was anything else, she said, "I think if Tom knew Jackson was dangerous he wouldn't have gone."

A fund was created to receive donations toward the boys' education. Contributions arrived from classrooms, from children and their parents, from neighbors, from people who had known Tom as a child or in college or through the church or at work, from people who didn't care to identify themselves, and from probation offices all around the country. Nancy never had days when she felt like staying in bed with the curtains drawn, but she lost interest in eating. What with donations to the fund and cards and letters of sympathy, there were thousands of pieces of mail to answer. She prepared a letter of reply for strangers, who wouldn't be acquainted with her handwriting, and her friends copied out versions. Writing, "Thank you very much for your generous contribution . . . ," they sometimes completed as many as eighty letters in a day.

Friends gave her books on grieving but she had no time to read them. Struggling to arrive at some understanding of what happened, she made herself become accustomed to saying that Tom was murdered; he had not passed on, it had not been a natural way to die.

She endeavored to hold herself together for Christopher and Nicholas. She did not mind letting them see her cry—often there were moments when they all cried together—and she saw no point in pretending to strengths she didn't have, but she told her boys that they were going to make it, that she knew how to write checks, she would get them through. She told Christopher that he didn't have to occupy the place in the household his father had held; she had lived on her own before she was married. If she could do nothing else, she felt that the preservation of their sense of family and whatever portion of their childhoods remained was something she must guarantee.

Without knowing exactly what happened to Tom there seemed to Nancy no way that she could put his murder behind her. The accounts in the paper and on television were insufficiently complete. One afternoon a few weeks after the killing an agent from the F.B.I. sat at the table in the kitchen, and by the time he left she felt she knew most of what mattered. She could close her eyes and imagine her husband with his arm at his side walking backwards and pleading with Jackson not to shoot again, and she could see Jackson bearing down on him with the shotgun. She has a scrapbook with a picture from the newspaper of Tom on the street and from the say he is lying she reconstructed how he fell. "I studied that for so long," she says. "It was all I had."

A few weeks after Tom died, Nancy had an intuition that he had left some message of farewell. She took all his clothes out of his dresser and removed the paper at the bottom of the drawers. She turned out all the pockets of his trousers and coats. She combed his shelves and the corners of his closets. And found nothing. About a month and a half after his murder, she discovered a camera that had in it a roll of pictures taken before Tom died. What she hoped was to find in it something that would ease the pain she felt over losing him, some gesture, some sign of love. To the part of her mind that gave rise to this feeling it did not seem impossible that Tom might have anticipated his end and made some effort to make it less painful. When the roll was developed, it turned out that the pictures were mainly of the boys. In the corner of one was Tom's foot.

PERMISSIONS